Trading Technology

TRADING TECHNOLOGY

Europe and Japan
in the Middle East

Thomas L. Ilgen
and
T. J. Pempel

PRAEGER

New York
Westport, Connecticut
London

Library of Congress Cataloging-in-Publication Data

Ilgen, Thomas L.
  Trading technology.

  Bibliography: p.
  Includes index.
  1. Technology transfer — Near East. 2. Technology
transfer — Europe. 3. Technology transfer — Japan.
4. Near East — Commerce. 5. Competition, International.
I. Pempel, T. J., 1942–   . II. Title.
HC415.15.I45 1986   338.94'06   86-21197
ISBN 0-275-92483-1 (alk. paper)

Library of Congress Catalog Card Number: 86-21197
ISBN: 0-275-92483-1

First published in 1987

Praeger Publishers, 521 Fifth Avenue, New York, NY 10175
A division of Greenwood Press, Inc.

Printed in the United States of America

The paper used in this book complies with the Permanent
Paper Standard issued by the National Information Standards
Organization (Z39.48-1984).

10 9 8 7 6 5 4 3 2 1

To our sons:
    Jonathan and Colin
    Aaron and Sean

CONTENTS

Preface ix

1 Technology Transfer and the International Political
    Economy 1

2 Trade and Technology Transfer: The Major Trends 26

3 Britain: Trading Technology in the Postcolonial Era 50

4 France: Technology Trade, Politics, and the State 72

5 West Germany: Technology, Industrial Development,
    and the Denial of Politics 97

6 Japan: Marketing Technology Unencumbered by History 122

7 The European Community and the Euro-Arab Dialogue 143

8 Conclusions 159

Notes 177

Select Bibliography 191

Index 197

About the Authors 205

PREFACE

The quadrupling of oil prices in 1973-1974 sent shock waves through international politics and world markets that scholars and policymakers are still seeking to explain and to understand. One ramification of the transfer of wealth from oil-consuming to oil-producing countries, particularly those in the Middle East, was that the latter group was able to purchase new technologies from international suppliers in an effort to advance their economic development. Oil revenues underwrote the introduction of modern telecommunications systems, nuclear power, and computer facilities; they financed the construction of new airports, ports, and medical centers; and they launched new industries such as oil refining and petrochemicals. In turn, many in the West sought to take advantage of the new Middle Eastern wealth by expanding their technology sales, by investments, and by trade.

As we move toward the end of the 1980s, much of the enthusiasm for technology imports in the Middle East has been dampened by the collapse of petroleum prices and the shrinking revenue base. Nevertheless, the experience of active technology exchange in the region during the 1970s tells us much about the dynamics of technology transfer when pursued during a time of great benefit for both recipients and suppliers. This book seeks to identify the lessons of this extraordinary period of international trade in technology. Both the volume of that trade and the rapidity with which transactions were concluded provide ample material for study. By chronicling the dynamics of this trade our hope is to offer insights for both industrial suppliers and third world importers.

Much of the research for this volume was undertaken as part of a large project organized by the Office of Technology Assessment (OTA). Our contribution to that project was to examine and evaluate the national policies of major suppliers of technologies to the Middle East. In the early stages of this research, Ilgen examined the efforts of Britain, France, West Germany, and the European Community; Pempel treated Japan, Taiwan, and South Korea. In 1984 OTA published a report based on this work and the work of others titled "Technology Transfer to the Middle East" which is cited at various points in this book.

The OTA study was designed as a tool to help American policymakers improve US commercial performance in lucrative technology markets abroad. Following its publication, we concluded that our research on the policies of technology suppliers offered broader analytical insights into the dynamics of technology transfer, what we have called the generic process of technology transfer. It also permitted us to link scholarly understanding about the unique national features of foreign economic policies to the particular characteristics of technology trade. This book, therefore, expands the work conducted for OTA and places it in a framework that we hope will yield greater analytical payoffs.

We benefited from the help and guidance of many during this project. Martha Caldwell Harris, the director of the OTA project, was superb in her role and provided invaluable advice and counsel both during and after the OTA study. We benefited also from comments provided by others on the OTA staff as well as from those who contributed to the project as outside consultants. We also wish to thank all of those public and private sector officials that we interviewed in each of the four countries and at the European Community (EC) who were generous with their time and knowledge and provided us with information unavailable elsewhere.

Carolyn Rhodes-Jones, Miranda Schreurs, and Shoko Tanaka served ably as research assistants at various stages of the project and compiled much of the trade data that is presented in Chapter 2. Christopher Allen provided research assistance with the Chapter on Germany. We also benefited from students and colleagues at the institutions at which we have taught over the past few years—Ilgen at Brandeis University and Pitzer College in Claremont; Pempel at Cornell University. In particular we wish to thank Peter Katzenstein who read the material in an early form and encouraged us to develop it through what has proven to be a most rewarding and congenial collaboration.

We have dedicated the book to our four sons whose literacy in technology will soon surpass our own and whose lives will increasingly be shaped by the decisions we make today about technological change and exchange.

1

TECHNOLOGY TRANSFER AND THE INTERNATIONAL POLITICAL ECONOMY

Technology trade and transfer have become some of the most vigorously debated issues in international affairs. Among the major industralized countries, global competition for markets and shifting patterns of foreign direct investment have focused attention at home on the need to foster innovation and technological change. This is particularly true in the United States. There the loss of economic hegemony that prevailed for nearly three decades following World War II, combined with the major slowdown of the world economy in the 1970s, has led to extensive discussion centered on strategies to recapture economic well-being. In this context, technological leadership is often seen as an essential component in reestablishing a nation's position in the international division of labor.[1]

Control over the diffusion of new technologies to other countries has also received considerable attention, an issue that has long been of concern to students of East–West politics. The efforts of the Soviet Union, virtually all Eastern European countries, and China to import sophisticated western technology to compensate for failures in their own economic modernization programs opened the door to a flurry of economic exchange. For a time, these appeared to offer great hope for cooperation and reduced tensions between East and West. Growing Eastern bloc difficulties in financing such imports plus renewed suspicions, particularly in Washington, that western technology was assisting a Soviet military buildup, have refocused the political debate on the wisdom of such sales and, ironically, on their contribution to heightened East–West political tensions.

In the competitive environment of international trade, questions have also been raised about the wisdom of earlier technology transfers from the United States to Western Europe and Japan, suggesting that such flows were responsible for creating trading competitors that grabbed larger and larger shares of U.S. markets in the 1970s and 1980s. And as the economies of the so-called newly industrializing countries (NICs) show the capacity to absorb sophisticated know-how and compete successfully with the advanced economies, comparable questions about the wisdom of technology transfer are posed in a broader context.

Issues of technology trade and transfer have also been uppermost in the minds of third world leaders and others seeking viable pathways to economic modernization and development.[2] The import of technology has long been viewed as a possible shortcut for late modernizers, but its negative ramifications have often been said to outweigh the advantages.[3] These include either dependence on the provider of technology (often a multinational firm), or the political, social, and economic distortions that technologies bring to rapidly modernizing societies. However, a growing number of developing countries, particularly in East Asia, have successfully introduced Western industrial technologies into their economies and have subsequently penetrated western markets with competitively priced goods of comparable quality. Their success has prompted leaders in many other countries to rethink their positions on the role of technology in development.[4] Moreover, successfully assertive positions vis-à-vis foreign multinationals have increased the confidence of many of these countries that technology can be made to serve the needs of host countries as well as the interests of the resident firm.[5]

As the international economy has become more integrated and interdependent over the past four decades, the questions of who produces what for whom have increasingly been shaped and defined not only by each country's technological capabilities, but also by the political and economic infrastructure employed to take advantage of those capabilities. In part, the growing importance of continuosly sustaining and enhancing technological progress derives from the rapid diffusion of scientific knowledge and technological developments in an interdependent economy. Analysts of the multinational firm have stressed the rapidity by which such firms, through the establishment of production facilities abroad, transfer knowledge and skills developed in the home country to foreign settings. Raymond Vernon's analysis of the product cycle stresses the advantages of technological leadership as vitally important to large firms anxious to maintain their competitive edge. At the same time it shows that the benefits of individual innovations are diminished as they are ever more quickly emulated by foreign competitors.[6] Robert Gilpin argued that this diffusion of know-how through the multinational firm has had certain negative consequences for the U.S. economy and U.S. political power over the past two decades, just as it undermined the British international position in an earlier era.[7]

The diffusion of technology is not only the result of foreign direct investment by multinationals. It also grows out of the vigorous trade competition among the countries participating in the liberal postwar trading system. The trading regime put in place under U.S. direction after the war, and regional experiments such as the European Economic Community, fostered postwar recovery and enticed a number of industrialized countries (most notably, West Germany and Japan) to embark upon domestic economic strategies that gave great prominence to exports in an environment of free trade. Vigorous export competition among these advanced industrialized states has included intense competition for technology sales to prospective importers, often including an attractive range of products, equipment, and services. In the 1950s and 1960s, much of the trade in technology goods and services was among the industrialized countries themselves. By the early 1970s this had leveled off. Finally, the recession in the latter part of the decade, as well as growing demand from Eastern bloc countries and the third world, turned the attention of these exporters to sales in new areas.[8] The newly rich oil exporting countries in the Middle East were a logical target. Not only were these OPEC states flush with the capital to facilitate import financing, but their imports helped the industrialized states to cover their own mounting costs for imported oil.

In sum, the internationalization of the large firm and the intense commercial competition among industrialized countries to maintain or enlarge their market shares, both integral features of what we have come to call economic interdependence, have ensured that most technologies will not for long be the province of single firms or countries. And because technology has become so accessible, it now occupies a key role in determining shifting comparative advantages among national economies and in shaping a dynamic international division of labor. In this limited sense, it is perhaps appropriate to speak of a technological imperative acting on the international economy, influencing in important ways the choices that leaders of individual firms and public officials make about the patterns of economic activity they will pursue.[9] In some respects, this imperative has always been operative, as individual firms and national economies scrambled to take advantage of opportunities offered by potentially lucrative innovations. Indeed, the economic history of individual industries since the industrial revolution is a testimony to the repeated efforts to exploit one major new technological breakthrough after another—in textiles, steel, chemicals, electronics, and automobiles.[10] Yet, exploitation of or adaptation to technological change was simpler at a time when it was easier to maintain control over new knowledge during the sometimes lengthy stages of product development and when the number of international competitors was relatively small. Reasonably effective patent laws and licensing agreements permitted the innovator to enjoy the fruits of his or her labor for quite some time, while the small number of industrialized countries engaged in manufacturing limited one's potential rivals to a handful. Today, proprietary knowledge is ever more difficult to protect, patent rights are frequently ignored by some countries, and there is increasing pressure to sell technical knowledge before one's competitors sell similar information to the same eager customers. Moreover, the list of potential competitors is lengthy, and many of them enjoy special advantages such as cheap labor, government subsidies, and a less regulated domestic economy. One must be nimble to secure the advantages of innovation before they pass to others.

The picture that emerges is one in which both the generation of new knowledge and access to the best available technology are viewed by both exporters and importers as key ingredients to future economic wealth and welfare. This conventional wisdom emerges at a time when critical choices about where to sink research and development funds or which technologies to import and mimic require the shrewdest judgment and most careful planning. Unwise decisions or ineffective measures for reaching stated objectives can be extremely costly in today's fast-moving and unforgiving market. In other words, technology acts and will continue to act as a crucial independent variable shaping the interdependent international economy of the coming decade. Yet its consequences for individual firms or countries are far from clear. Therefore, the strategies that countries adopt to advance or adapt to technological change are likely to bear directly on their future economic performance.

This book addresses an important dimension of the challenges and opportunities presented by technology for the international economy. It focuses on the role of technology in the relationship between advanced industrialized countries and rapidly developing economies in the third world. It proceeds from the logic elaborated above that (1) industrialized countries increasingly view their most important assets in international trade to be the sale of high-technology or high-value-added goods and services, and that (2) vital and growing markets for such exports are to be found in the more prosperous third world countries. Almost all of the developed countries have given attention to industrial policies that mix public- and private-sector initiatives as a means of ensuring their share of what they hope will be extremely lucrative technology trade opportunities. In a less predictable market, those who develop strategies to harness their own domestic production capacities to the dynamics of technological change are expected to perform best.[11]

The book is also informed by the growing attractiveness of the "East Asian model," and the ability of some third world countries to facilitate the transfer of readily available technology from North to South, adapt that technology to their own economies, and generate good quality, competitively priced products that find their way into western markets.[12]

East Asian successes have given more credibility to what John Ruggie has called an "associative" strategy of development. Rather than withdrawing from the international marketplace or redefining the rules of the international trade regime, as some advocates of a new international economic order would do, many developing economies have instead devised ways to beat the industrialized countries at their own game.[13] As David Yoffie has shown, some of these strategies have permitted developing countries such as South Korea and Hong Kong, who began with very modest industrial technologies, to upgrade those technologies and at the same time continue to sell their more sophisticated goods in western markets.[14]

In short, this is a book about the process of transferring technology, from advanced industrialized societies seeking to maximize their returns from technology sales, to societies in the throes of development that are eager to use technology as a vehicle to modernization. Technology transfers from North to South, it is important to note, imply potential costs as well as benefits for both parties. By encouraging the indiscriminate diffusion of technology to countries that aspire to become future competitors, developed countries may nudge themselves out of niches in the international marketplace they have worked hard to establish.[15] The short-term benefits of increased trade and licensing revenues may obscure the long-term damage done to industrial competitiveness. Similarly, the wholesale importation of technologies ill-suited to the capabilities, resources, and needs of developing countries may create more economic problems than they alleviate, while also generating political and social disruptions that prove to be serious drags on development.[16] With these pitfalls in mind, we do believe that technology exchange can offer significant benefits to both suppliers and recipients to the extent that the process of transfer is well understood and strategies are carefully crafted by both parties. Technology transfer need not be a zero-sum game, but can provide substantial rewards to all participants. It is our contention that a careful elaboration and understanding of the workings of technology exchange (what we will call the generic process of technology transfer) is useful in identifying mutual benefits and in giving guidance to both suppliers and recipients in devising export or import strategies. We elaborate this generic process below and then focus our attention in the rest of the volume on its consequences for supplier country policies.

TECHNOLOGY AND TECHNOLOGY TRANSFER

Thus far we have used the term *technology* very loosely; it is important to define the concept more precisely. When the terms *science* and *technology* are used together, the former is generally defined as the pursuit of truth or knowledge, while the latter refers to the application of that knowledge for some social purpose. Similarly, the paired concepts, research and development, refer to the discovery of new information and its translation into some useful product or service. Our concerns here, then, are with science applied to a wide range of projects or problems.

Root defines technology as "the body of knowledge that is applicable to the production of goods and the creation of new goods."[17] Jones terms it "the way in which resources are converted into commodities."[18] Aiming for even greater breadth, we will define technology as any scientific knowledge that can be put to some socially useful purpose. Those who have examined the concept also often speak of "embodiment" as an integral feature.[19] Technology does not stand alone or apart as we often think of scientific knowledge. Rather, it is embodied in products, processes, or individuals. H. G. Johnson classifies technology according to how it is embodied.[20] Knowledge that is contained in hardware (plants, machinery, and products) he calls "physical capital." Technology found in intangible assets such as production processes, information manuals, patents, and designs, he calls "knowledge capital." That found in people, in their labor skills, their management techniques, and their general experience and know-how, he calls "human capital." Embodiment forces us to think broadly about technology, to push beyond the notion of technology as hardware and to include the intangible aspects often indispensable to the proper utilization of that physical capital. It is these intangible dimensions of technology that are frequently key to a successful transfer from one society to another.

By thinking of physical, knowledge, and human technologies and by defining the concept of technology broadly as scientific knowledge put to social purposes, it follows that all societies are technological societies to some degree. All employ knowledge, based on their own empirical experiences or those of their ancestors, to achieve individual or common purposes. Societies become more technological as their reservoir of scientific knowledge deepens and the uses to which it is put expand.[21] Modern technological societies are those that have laid great stress on the acquisition of scientific knowledge and the application of that knowledge to society's problems and opportunities.

Our broad view of the nature of technology has consequences for our treatment of what is normally called "technology transfer." We seek to understand better the process by which technology can be passed or transferred from one society to another, more particularly from a modern technological society to one where the application of scientific knowledge is not as deeply rooted or as far advanced, or both. Too often, those who have talked or written about technology transfer have focused only on the sale or export of hardware, how to put the accouterments of industrialized societies in the hands of modernizers. A broader view leads to the recognition that transfer of technology from one society to another is a much more complicated process, its acceptance among the recipients requiring careful thought and planning. Most importantly, the flow of technological hardware must be accompanied by the transfer of technical expertise and know-how to the indigenous population. Achieving the embodiment of technology in those who will make use of it must be an integral part of any successful process of transfer. An understanding of this process should be welcomed by supplier countries, since it will better enable them to sell their wares in ways that will satisfy their customers. The understanding should also be useful to receiving countries that are attracted by the hardware, but frequently overlook the challenges of acquiring the requisite human skills and individual knowledge needed to ensure that technology "takes" in an unfamiliar environment.

THE GENERIC PROCESS OF TECHNOLOGY TRANSFER

Thus far, we have claimed that technology is an important factor in shaping the international division of labor among national economies. Its importance has grown as the world economy has become more interdependent, because integral to interdependence has been the rapid growth of multinational firms and fierce trade competition among leading industrialized states. These developments all foster the rapid diffusion of technology, which in turn constantly redefines the international division of labor. Further, knowing that advanced industrialized societies are competing to sell technology abroad and that rapidly growing developing countries are eager to use technology as a short-cut to modernization suggests that a carefully orchestrated program of technology trade and transfer could well provide benefits that significantly outweigh the costs for both North and South.[22] To be successful such a program must fully appreciate the complexities of the concept that we are calling "technology," and the difficulties and challenges inherent in its transfer from one society to another.

Our position is not that every country should or must employ imported technology in its efforts to promote development. Indeed, economic conditions or political circumstances in some countries may argue strongly against a strategy of vigorous technology imports. The financing of such imports poses serious problems for some countries, while agricultural economies with abundant labor supplies may not be in a position to benefit much from industrial infusions at their current levels of development. Moreover, certain political leaders may be interested in technology for personal gain rather than for its contributions to broader national objectives. This poses the risk that decisions about what to import may distort rather than enhance economic development. Many students of dependency have been critical of technology transfer for the disruptive links allegedly created between domestic political elites and multinational firms.[23] Following such experiences, some groups may be opposed in principle to technology imports and prefer a strategy of self-reliance or dissociation in the technology sphere.[24] However, if properly managed, under many circumstances technology transfer can be a useful vehicle for industrialization and modernization in the third world. We would go further and claim that the more countries discover and demonstrate the advantages of technology transfer, the more other countries will attempt to employ the process for their own purposes, shaping and tailoring it to their particular needs.

To identify the possibilities for mutual benefit, it is useful to speak of a generic process of technology transfer, a process that maps the technological needs of recipient societies, identifies potential technology providers, indicates various forms that transfer might take, and outlines a chronology for technological acquisition. The process not only gives some flavor of the planning and decision-making required of recipient societies (if technology imports are to serve desired purposes and facilitate development objectives), but it also pinpoints profitable opportunities for technology exporters.

Technology Needs

Following from the conceptual distinctions discussed above, technology imports can be divided roughly into three kinds: physical or tangible capital assets (plants and factories, tools and machinery), scientific or technical knowledge that facilitates the productive use of the physical assets, and the skills and know-how necessary for productive workers and managers.

One normally associates technology transfer with the import of plants and equipment. A multinational firm decides to open a subsidiary in a foreign setting and builds a new plant to manufacture a range of products, filling the factory with state-of-the-art machinery that the host country is unable to provide domestically. In the early stages of development, imports of these large-scale "packages" of hardware are common; infrastructural needs are met and new industries are introduced, or major changes in the agricultrual sector are undertaken. With time, imports are likely to become smaller and more specialized as domestic suppliers increasingly substitute for foreign providers.

To complement such physical capital, importing countries must give attention to the acquisition of knowledge required to employ such resources productively. For example, the import of plant and equipment to produce steel must be accompanied not only by a thorough under-standing of modern methods and processes for making steel; plant owners must be able to ensure quality control and know-how to adapt the pro-cess and product to customer specifications or to particular requirements of local conditions. Stories abound of countries that have imported new and sophisticated facilities, only to be disappointed by poor performance records and rapid deterioration of the facilities due to inadequate main-tenance and repair. The knowledge required to master the physical hard-ware may be purchased separately through licensing or as part of the larger package, or it may be passed on by broad–based scientific and tech-nical cooperation agreements between supplier and recipient countries or supported by international agencies or institutions. But it is unques-tionably essential to successful transfers.

Finally, importing countries must invest in human capital. A grow-ing pool of skilled workers (to operate new equipment) and trained managers (to ensure that new processes run smoothly) is indispensable to the effective absorption of new technologies. Training may be under-taken in institutes and educational facilities in the supplier country, or on-the-job instruction may be negotiated as part of a larger technology purchase. Expanding the base of human capital may also require the training abroad of scientists, technicians, and engineers who are crucial for the adaptation of foreign technologies to local circumstances and for the initiation of indigenous research and development capabilities that offer the hope of greater technological independence.[25]

Each of these needs depends importantly on the other two if tech-nology transfer is to be successful. Capital-rich countries such as those in the Middle East have frequently found that shiny new facilities are of little use if managers and skilled laborers are in short supply. Indeed, the need to bring in foreigners to make such facilities operational has even increased local resentment of modern ways in traditional countries like Iran and Saudi Arabia. In contrast, India has invested heavily in human capital over the years, only to see this resource underutilized because of the country's unwillingness or inability to finance complementary im-ports of plant and equipment.

Actors in the Process of Technology Transfer

Perhaps the first, albeit obvious, point to make is that technology trans-fer will involve actors from two typically very different sides, that of the exporter of technology and that of the importer. Naturally, in certain cir-cumstances this particular division will be less salient than others. It is not unusual, for example, for the potential buyer and the potential seller of a technology to be allied with one another against advocates of alternative technologies. Similarly, an exporting or importing government may find itself at odds with private-sector actors within its own borders.

In this context, some have argued that the diffusion of technology should be in the hands of international institutions and development agencies mandated to promote industrialization and modernization in third world countries. Institutions such as the World Bank have for a long time focused on project-specific lending to facilitate access to technology on terms affordable to recipient countries. Such international and regional institutions have also sponsored international scientific conferences and technical cooperation agreements in an effort to make new knowledge available to those seldom involved in its development. The work of such agencies should not be minimized, but resources for such undertakings are limited, and seldom is the knowledge diffused at the cutting edge of industrial development. Possibly an even greater hurdle faced by international agencies is that of competing private and national governmental interests in transferring technologies. As different groups and governments compete to transfer technologies in ways that will benefit their own interests, the likelihood that much important technology transfer could be placed in the hands of a neutral international agency is proportionately reduced.

A broad cross section of actors in the private sector have been attracted to technology trade. Large multinational firms have introduced technology through strategies of direct foreign investment, although often on terms not readily accepted in receiving countries. Large firms have also entered into short-term agreements to build public works projects or new industrial facilities. Firms, both large and small, have also become suppliers of everything from the simplest building materials to the most sophisticated machinery, from industrial process technology to worker and management training. Finally, firms of development advisors, scientists, engineers, and other experts have built flourishing consulting businesses with developing countries looking for independent and objective assistance in reaching difficult development decisions. Naturally, not all of these private agencies share common perspectives on the goals, processes, or benefits of technology transfer generally or of specific technologies.

The governments of technology-exporting countries have also become active in the promotion and regulation of technology trade. Where opportunities for trade seem promising, governments have frequently sought to facilitate such deals with a variety of incentives aimed at reducing the costs to the importer and minimizing the risks for the exporter. Where technology trade has been viewed as potentially dangerous to the competitiveness of domestic industries, or when governments have given priority to competing political objectives, public officials have considered measures to slow the outflow. As with private agencies, different governments often hold widely varying perspectives on how best to accomplish various technology transfers.

The governments and firms in importing countries have also sought to shape and control the pattern of technology imports. Unlike in the past, very few governments throw open the doors and permit foreign firms to make their own private deals. Governments increasingly participate in or direct decisions about what technology to import and on what terms.[26] Such government leaders have been frequent and effective negotiators of contracts involving technology trade, demanding conditions and terms that address not only hardware requirements, but knowledge and human skills as well.

The Forms of Technology Transfer

Technology may enter a country in a variety of forms, some more readily absorbed and usable than others. Transfer may be facilitated by scientific and technical cooperation agreements on a government-to-government basis. A recent Organization for Economic Cooperation and Development (OECD) study classified such bilateral agreements as passive or active.[27] Passive agreements have an indirect effect on technology flows and include conventions designed to avoid double taxation or to promote or protect private investment, treaties to permit the establishment of business in each other's economies, and procedures for arbitrating economic disputes. The French and the Germans have concluded agreements to promote investment and to avoid double taxation with a large number of developing countries.[28] Active cooperation agreements may take many forms; the OECD report identifies five types: technical consultation, operational aid (providing assistance in managerial tasks), training aid, assistance with the supply of plant and equipment, and aid designated for specific projects (energy development, nuclear power, etc.).[29] Among the most common are general economic cooperation agreements and scientific and technical cooperation agreements. The former are more numerous; Germany maintains such agreements with 42 countries, France with 40, and Japan with 25. France has concluded the largest number of scientific and technical cooperation agreements (43), while Germany (11) has limited its attention to the larger and more rapidly growing developing countries. Among the transfer agreements directed to specific industry technologies, most have been concluded in nuclear energy. Germany has six such agreements, France and the United States, twelve.

The enthusiasm for such cooperation agreements grew rapidly after 1965, and most of them were initiated between 1965 and 1975. It is difficult to judge how helpful they are in promoting technology transfer, but clearly they provide a framework for scientific and technical activities that should facilitate public or private technology flows. One conclusion of the OECD study was that the advantage a country gained by being one of the first to conclude an agreement with a particular developing country is often eroded by the developing country's negotiation of similar agreements with a large number of supplier countries.[30] The consequence has been to produce agreements very similar to one another, in effect, pushing toward a multilateral agreement on the terms and conditions of technological assistance.[31] Most countries have insisted on maintaining the bilateral format, but the net effect is a convergence in arrangements.

Such bilateral arrangements are usually intended to develop an indigenous pool of scientists and technicians whose expertise may then be directed to an assortment of tasks. As noted above, the training of scientific personnel may also be underwritten by international agencies and regional institutions. The United Nations Educational, Scientific, and Cultural Organization (UNESCO) and the European Community are two institutions that have been prominent in promoting such accords. These agreements build the stock of knowledge and deepen the resources of human capital, and are certainly beneficial as far as they go. Some industrialized countries have viewed these bilateral accords, which are often augmented with foreign aid, as vehicles for establishing close scientific and commercial relations with the third world, aimed at yielding significant future technology sales for the exporting country. Familiarity with a particular supplier country's equipment and processes often becomes a persuasive factor in purchasing particular exports in the future. Close personal relations between scientists and technicians in the two countries further steer the importing country to look first to such associates when contemplating specific purchases.

Technology also enters developing countries through foreign direct investment. Its obvious advantage is that it brings technology to capital-poor countries at low initial cost. However, because foreign firms have strong incentives to maintain control over the profitable features of their operations, valuable technologies are not readily diffused or easily absorbed by wider host societies. Foreign direct investment can also create a growing dependence on foreign technologies and discourage the emergence of indigenous capabilities for technological development.[32] While the leadership in some countries has continued to accept such investments with few questions asked (comfortable with the personal benefits they offer or believing that control would do little to shape the behavior of these giant firms), political elites in other countries have sought to redefine the rules affecting foreign investment. India, Mexico,

Brazil, the Andean Pact countries, and Algeria have all insisted on reviewing all technologies introduced by foreign firms. They have also established guidelines and operating procedures to facilitate technology transfer.[33] Foreign direct investment will continue to be an attractive option for both exporters and importers of technology, but where it is permitted, one can anticipate continuing efforts by importing nations to negotiate new arrangements designed to secure a better distribution of benefits.

In some countries, such regulatory safeguards are always viewed as insufficient to protect against the anticipated loss of control to foreign firms; the only acceptable option for these countries is to ban foreign direct investment altogether. In such countries technology transfer has been facilitated by "turnkey" ventures and extensive reliance on licensing. Technology is purchased outright and, in the case of turnkey projects, foreign firms come in to build plants or facilities and install the necessary equipment to make them operational.[34] The providing firm or firms then depart, with management and operation of the facility left in the hands of local personnel. Licensing or the purchase of patented products or processes is a more limited form of tehnology import, but similarly insists on full control by the importer. While they may provide some measure of political autonomy, these routes to technology transfer also have drawbacks. Turnkey projects and licensing can be extremely costly; technological access is therefore closely tied to the ability to pay. These forms also direct primary attention to hardware imports and the construction of new plants and factories. Once the hardware is in place and the supplier has departed, importing countries often cut themselves off from the managerial and training assistance necessary to ensure that plants operate productively. Inadequate attention to maintenance and repair and the unavailability of replacement equipment also diminish the performance records of turnkey projects. Consequently, when turnkey deals are struck, the political advantages of full control for the importer and limited commitments for the supplier are often not balanced against the range of technology needs and the benefits of longer-term economic relationships.

Turnkey agreements were a popular vehicle for expanding economic contacts between Western economies and Eastern bloc countries in the 1960s, when socialist economies were eager to get their hands on western technology but were unwilling to accept a long-term presence of capitalist firms in their economies. Frequently, the agreements proved unsatisfactory to all parties. Modern plant and equipment, when not paired with Western managerial techniques and labor skills, resulted in inefficient use of such new resources and low productivity levels. However, the need to finance these imports with hard currency earnings led to the dumping of new products on world markets, which drew charges of unfair trading practices in the West. Ongoing financing difficulties and mounting debt problems have limited the viability of turnkey plants as vehicles of technology transfer for these socialist economies. One can observe similar problems in the third world.

Two additional forms of technology transfer have emerged as responses to the problems raised by both foreign direct investment and turnkeys. They are the management contract or technology assistance agreement and the joint venture. The management contract grows primarily from the shortcomings of turnkeys and licensing; the joint venture addresses some of the problems raised by foreign direct investment.

In the technology assistance agreement, the importer contracts with the exporter for a range of management and training services. Such service contracts assist domestic managers and workers in operating and maintaining newly purchased capital equipment by focusing on the acquisition of knowledge and human capital. At the same time, they extend the involvement of the supplier firm or firms in the economy of the importing country, often to fixed periods of five, ten, or even fifteen years beyond the completion of the initial project.

A broad range of services can be negotiated, from a provision that technicians supervise the operation of the facility, to spare parts contracts or access to new equipment and machinery, to initial on-the-job training and long-term retraining and refresher course provisions. While many importing countries have become more knowledgeable about what contracts ought to include and have become able negotiators in representing their interests, such agreements may also be prepackaged and offered by international consultants. Such consultants then negotiate special provisions for the importing country with the supplier firm or firms.

The principal advantage of the management agreement for the importing country is that by addressing a fuller range of technology needs, there is a greater likelihood that hardware investments will be used productively and that these new patterns of production will be understood and assimilated by modernizing societies. For politicians and others sensitive to issues of control and dependence, the contract affixes a more reasonable date when foreigners will leave, and control over new processes will be fully in domestic hands. This allows for the development of local talent and native familiarity with the new processes. The principal drawback for the recipient country is cost. To demand more services requires an ability to pay; possibly only capital-rich developing countries will be able to afford the full range of assistance. Some suppliers attracted to the "quick and clean" turnkey approach may find the longer commitments implied by management contracts to be unwelcome. However, for most they represent an opportunity to broaden the range of their earnings-producing goods and services. Moreover, the greater likelihood that technology will be successfully absorbed should create demands for new imports and continuing sales. Effective service contracts should foster good working relations between managers, technicians, and workers in importing and exporting countries. In turn, this should lay the foundation for future economic exchanges.

For capital-poor countries, those unable to afford the inclusive technology agreement and yet unhappy with the terms and loss of control suggested by most foreign direct investment, the joint venture offers a reasonable compromise.[35] Technology imports are provided by foreign firms who anticipate long-term gains from production facilities in foreign settings. At the same time, shared ownership of the enterprise gives local governments or firms an influential role in management and presumably a voice in the manner by which technology is employed and absorbed by local personnel. While the terms of joint ventures can vary widely, some commitment to the common objectives of economic viability would hopefully provide a framework for successful accommodation on issues of technology transfer.

Regrettably, joint ventures frequently generate objections and uncertainties on both sides that have limited their usefulness. Recipient countries fear becoming a junior partner in the undertaking, committed to a project in which the foreign firm dominates by the virtue of its technical know-how and considerable hands-on experience. Among capital-poor countries at the earliest stages of industrialization, this feeling of economic and technical inferiority may be particularly strong. For their part, many multinational firms worry about the political environment in the host country. New political leadership or a changing political climate may result in the nationalization of foreign assets or in the imposition of new business regulations that significantly disadvantage the foreign partners.

As we will discuss later, the use in the Middle East of joint ventures to promote technology transfer may emerge, not as a fallback strategy for capital-poor countries unhappy with direct foreign investment, but rather as a logical extension of relations between large firms and capital-rich developing countries that have successfully employed management contracts. In other words, the good working relationships that are fostered by a fully elaborated process of technology exchange may suggest joint business opportunities of a continuing sort that are not accommodated by fixed-length contracts. Joint ventures suggest a certain equality of position among business partners that is necessary for success. Therefore, joint ventures may be more likely once the process of technology transfer is operating effectively. Exporters and importers are bound together by mutual confidence and trust.

This discussion indicates that technology may enter developing countries by many routes, and that the political and economic circumstances found in each country are likely to have an important bearing on the route chosen. What seems evident, and is certainly not surprising, is that technology transfer is most successfully promoted when developing countries have access to abundant capital and when it is in the hands of political leaders committed to broad development objectives. Such countries are likely to find the technology assistance agreement and the joint venture to be the most promising routes to successful transfer.

The Process of Technology Transfer

Meeting the range of technology needs and employing the most efficient routes of entry require a plan of action and careful management. At least four groups of tasks or projects must be included in a successful process of technology transfer. The sets of tasks follow a chronological sequence, although it is probable that a country will be engaged in all four simultaneously. Our expectation is that as time passes and as technology is successfully transferred, more attention will be directed to the latter steps of the chronological sequence. The four stages are: technological planning and project design, infrastructural projects and transfer, large-scale industrial imports, and small-scale industrial transfers and specialized technology needs. Each stage addresses physical, knowledge, and human capital needs in different mixes and proportions.

The first stage in this generic process is broad-based planning—determining development objectives, identifying the most promising technologies to achieve them, and establishing priorities. Too often technology imports are undertaken on an ad hoc basis, with little sense of larger economic objectives or how a particular import links with other technological investments being undertaken simultaneously. The planning stage ought to be particularly mindful of matching imports with existing national resources and capabilities. As many students of this process have noted, imported technologies must be "appropriate" for national conditions.[36] It makes little sense, to cite the classic case, to import capital-intensive argicultural technology into an economy with abundant and underemployed rural labor. Similarly, one is courting failure by importing technologies for labor-intensive light industry where unemployed workers are in short supply.

Technological planning and evaluation is an ongoing process that should take account of changing national conditions as well as developments in the international marketplace. Even if national resources and capabilities should point to the transfer of technology to launch a particular industry, growing international capacity in that sector and projected demand for its products may argue against such a move. Decisions such as these are always made amid considerable uncertainty. If they are difficult for policymakers and entrepreneurs in industrialized societies armed with abundant resources and the best available information, they are undoubtedly even more perplexing for those in developing states. In different countries, planning of this sort may be undertaken by some centralized government authority or by individual firms or industries in an ad hoc fashion. For countries in the midst of development, state involvement of some sort would seem almost unavoidable. Historically, the most viable model would seem to be one in which government exercises some general guidance to ensure the compatibility and complementarity of individual decisions, while relying heavily on the advice and suggestions of the private sector to assess economic feasibility. Clearly, however, many countries have opted for almost total top-down planning.

Technological planning may also be augmented by the advice available from a growing number of international advisors and consultants. Some of this advice may be provided as a regular service of international institutions and development agencies; other assistance may have to be purchased from experienced individuals and firms who make that their business. While uninitiated customers may have little protection against bad judgment or inappropriate advice, the experienced buyer should discover how to tap reliable expertise. Outside advice may be particularly helpful in identifying appropriate state-of-the-art technology in changing international markets and in predicting future global supply and demand in targeted industries. Put somewhat differently, investments in information and advice contribute to the national store of knowledge capital, critical to making intelligent technological choices. Moreover, the experience in working with such advisors and experts contributes to the development of a local pool of human capital better able to make such choices independently in the future.

Reliance on independent consultants frequently extends well beyond the initial decisions about what technologies to import. Organizations of consulting architects and engineers may regularly be employed to assist in the design of particular projects, in the selection of foreign suppliers, or in the negotiation of implementing agreements or long-term contracts. When such consultants are viewed as staunchly independent purveyors of objective knowledge rather than instruments of particular national economies or selected multinational firms, they become trusted and valuable allies to importing countries. Such independence is encouraged by the large fees attached to such services and by the vigorous competition among these experts in this lucrative business.[37] A reputation as a reliable and independent consultant is valued both by the developing country and by the exporting nation whose trade in services benefits handsomely from these growing sales. A flourishing and competitive market for knowledge, advice, and information provides benefits to both importer and exporter.

For a country in the early years of industrialization and modernization, planning generally calls initially for the completion of large-scale, high-cost infrastructural or public works projects, the second stage of the generic process. Transportation and communication systems, water and power projects, medical facilities, and educational institutions are among the most important. Such undertakings are crucial for the productive use of subsequent technology investments. As such they are frequently financed by government resources. The introduction of new manufacturing establishments makes little sense without road or rail systems, or adequate energy resources.

The technological assistance required for these large-scale ventures can be arranged in a number of ways. A popular method employed in the 1950s and 1960s, when foreign aid was viewed as a useful means of securing political support, was to solicit both Western and Eastern bloc governments for large grants and technical assistance on favorable terms. Supplier governments were often willing to underwrite the economic costs to advance their broader political objectives. Egypt's construction of the Aswan Dam is perhaps the best-known case. The recognition that economic assistance rarely pays the desired political dividends, and the unhappiness of some third world governments, led to diminished levels of foreign aid. This in turn reduced the number of projects underwritten.

Large infrastructural projects may also be sponsored by international agencies such as the World Bank, which in its early days devoted much of its rather meager budget to infrastructural project assistance. However, World Bank lending directs most of its efforts to the poorest of the developing countries. Some infrastructural projects, once completed, are managed as domestic industries (for example, telecommunications and electric power companies). These may attract foreign direct investment, both to underwrite the project and to manage the operation of the company that grows from it. Such operations in developing countries by ITT or NTT are well known.

However, given the growing sensitivity and resistance in many countries to extensive foreign direct investment, the choice of technology provider is today most frequently determined by a call for bids from large private or public international firms and the negotiation of either turnkey or management contracts. The chosen firm organizes and supervises the tasks to be completed, undertaking some of the work itself, but frequently subcontracting with a wide variety of other firms to provide necessary supplies or to take on particular tasks requiring special expertise. Keen competition for such lucrative contracts generally requires that lead firms look far and wide for the most capable low-cost suppliers and subcontractors. In the construction of a new hospital, for example, a U.S. medical services company might be awarded the contract, but a Korean construction firm may build the facility, utilizing German heavy machinery and Japanese construction materials. British and French medical instruments may be used throughout, alongside Dutch medical supplies. Vigorous competition generally assures the importing nation of quality construction at prevailing world market prices.

Success in landing large contracts such as these often means substantial revenues to the principal firms and healthy benefits in national trade. As a result, the government of the exporting country often takes an active role in securing them. Inducements such as flexible financing arrangements and elaborate insurance schemes are frequently employed to persuade the importer to sign on with a national firm. Importing states, in turn, have learned to insist on provisions that transform the turnkey contract into a technology assistance agreement—demanding access to research and development skills, manpower training programs, and provisions for maintenance and repair. In short, there are substantial benefits to be shared in these public works projects by both supplier and recipient. The technology assistance agreement is normally the vehicle through which terms are negotiated and benefits distributed.

A third stage in this process of technology transfer, not always neatly distinguished from infrastructural construction, centers on the introduction of new economic ventures or the modernization of existing ones through projects designed to upgrade industrial or agricultural productivity or capacity. Attention may be directed to capital-intensive industries such as steel, oil refining, petrochemicals, and automobiles, or to light industries such as textiles, footwear, or the processing of agricultural products that mix widely diffused technologies with abundant supplies of low-wage labor.

Initial efforts during this stage generally focus on the acquisition of capital hardware, the construction of a production facility such as a steel mill, an oil refinery, or a factory to manufacture apparel. Such capital investments often take on special political appeal as symbols of movement toward modernization. A second task is to equip such plants with the appropriate machinery and to gain access to the relevant knowledge about industrial processes so as to ensure that the plant operates efficiently. Finally, managers and workers have to be trained to run and maintain these new facilities, to market and distribute new products, and to exercise solid judgment about plans for growth and expansion.

In a fast-paced and uncertain international economy it is no wonder that some countries put these tasks in the hands of experienced multinational firms rather than tackle such ventures themselves. Moreover, it is not surprising that turnkey agreements that provide little more than physical capital frequently result in colossal failures when modern production processes and management assignments are given over to domestic personnel. For those determined to find an alternative to foreign direct investment, the management contract offers guidelines for addressing a spectrum of technology needs sumultaneously, while retaining significant control over these new ventures.

Defining the terms on which new industries and economic sectors are established gives shape and character to the particular process by which technology is introduced to each importing country. This stage of the generic process is critical, because it is during the establishment of new industries and economic sectors that importing countries define the terms on which technology will be acquired, not only for the initial investment but for the future as well. Rules and patterns of relations with outside suppliers, while not impossible to change, set important precedents. Foreign direct investment, turnkey ventures, and technology assistance agreements result in quite different patterns of technology transferred from the exporting country and absorbed into the importing nation. It is our view that the technology assistance agreement has the potential of meeting technology needs most completely and for fostering mutually beneficial arrangements between providers and recipients, arrangements that may result eventually in collaborative research undertakings or commercial joint ventures.

As in the case of lucrative public works projects, governments of supplier countries may design policies to enhance the attractiveness of the industrial technology packages offered by their national firms. Financing and insurance schemes, domestic manpower training programs, institutes of technical education, and government-to-government programs of scientific and technical cooperation all may be used to influence the importing country to look favorably upon particular national suppliers. The general state of political relations between exporting and importing countries may also have an impact on this pattern of technology trade.

The final stage of this generic process, which again overlaps with and is not totally distinct from those that precede it, involves the transfer of more specialized and sophisticated technologies. In some respects, many of the features of the complex management contracts described above respond to this part of the generic process. One way of distinguishing the preceding group of imports is to suggest that during the third phase one introduces whole industries, while in the fourth phase one is concerned with improving and updating processes, upgrading skills, or increasing technological sophistication. During this final stage, indigenous innovation and technological development also begin to appear, as the industry and the economy take on more of the features of a modern technological society.

This specialized technology trade and exchange is similar to that taking place continuously among advanced industrialized states. Firms in such countries generate their own technology, but they are constantly looking to innovations elsewhere to improve their own performance. The brisk business of technology licensing attests to the pace of this diffusion and exchange. Importers are not usually looking for new plants or facilities, but for particular equipment or subtle improvements in production processes. The application of computers to a wide number of industries is a current specialized import that may hold great appeal. To facilitate technology transfer in this final step one needs access to information both large and small regarding specialized suppliers. Absent the large and lucrative contracts of the earlier stages, potential suppliers are unlikely to step forward, thereby requiring more initiative on the part of the importing country to search out potential providers. Governments on both sides might usefully develop ways to put buyers and sellers together. Commercial attachés in foreign embassies, private and quasi-public trade associations, international trade fairs and exhibits, and the use of commercial missions by high-ranking diplomats are all means to improve communications and to increase contacts among parties likely to do business. Importing states are also likely to have ongoing and more specialized training and educational needs. The retraining of workers as capital equipment is updated, and the introduction of new entrepreneurial and marketing wrinkles are crucial if international competitiveness is to be maintained.

These four identifiable parts of the technology transfer process—planning and choosing which technologies to import, pursuit of infrastructural projects, transfer of new heavy and light industries, and specialized process-oriented imports—together make up a very general generic process through which all developing countries are likely to pass, if and when they make the decision to import technology as a vehicle to modernization. As noted, these stages are not necessarily pursued sequentially; indeed, most countries will generally be engaged in some of each at any one point in time. However, our view is that the first and second parts of the process will receive more attention in the early phases of modernization, while more attention will be directed to the latter two once the fruits of modernization become apparent.

We should also stress that there is no guarantee that a process like this will operate smoothly, that appropriate choices will be made, that reliable suppliers will be found, or that domestic populations will easily or readily accept what is brought in from abroad. Perhaps most importantly, there is no assurance that the importing country will be able to finance its technology needs; careful planning and skillfully negotiated contracts will be of little use if adequate funding cannot be found to act on them. It should also be noted that our description of this generic process is only of the roughest, general sort. Importing states may exercise great discretion at all stages, particularly in the routes they follow to secure foreign assistance. This may then result in the character of technology imports (and hence, the character of modernization) taking quite different forms country by country. We are not arguing that all countries could or should pursue modernization through a strategy of technology imports. But should they chose this route, it is clear what tasks lay before them.

To restate, our purposes in outlining this process were two. First, we aimed to give a sense of the complexities involved in transferring technology from society to society. Done properly, technology transfer requires successful planning on both sides, the utilization of hardware appropriate to domestic economic conditions of the importing nation, and careful attention to the introduction of new ways of thinking and working by the indigenous population. Second, we attempted to identify points in the transfer process where common interests could be derived for both importing and exporting countries, such that both might realize significant benefits and therefore have considerable incentive to promote such trade.

This perception of a common interest is critical to what follows in this book. While at one level of abstraction technology transfer may be said to follow a generic process, in the concrete day-to-day dealings between donors and recipients, the hurly-burly of politics, perceptions of self-interest, and the search for economic benefit are always present. As will become clear, different countries have followed rather different strategies in encouraging technology transfers from inside their borders to countries abroad. And each has achieved varying levels of success in different parts of the process. Some countries have relied heavily on governmental direction in encouraging exports of technology; others have relied primarily on the private sector and market mechanisms. Some countries have done extremely well at one stage of the generic process; others have done better at other stages; few countries have been able to secure substantial benefits through all parts of the process.

The remainder of this book focuses on the benefits of technology trade to supplier countries and what such countries might do to position themselves or their firms to profit from these opportunities. Consultancies, landing large infrastructural or industrial construction contracts, the provision of training and other management and maintenance services, and the ability to provide smaller-scale and more specialized technology to more sophisticated importers are among the opportunities we have identified.

While there are many opportunities for technology suppliers, there are also very real costs associated with such transfer, as some have taken pains to point out. Our view is that for most countries the benefits far outweigh the costs, particularly in a competitive market where the refusal of one supplier to export generally only ensures more business for their rival. However, the costs of such transfers are not insignificant, especially for domestic industries and employment, and we will discuss them further in the final chapter.

Finally, although different countries are positioned better for certain tasks than others, we will also argue that we do not find any single "best" strategy for technology transfer viewed from the perspective of the supplier country. Rather, the strategies followed emerge logically from particular domestic political and economic conditions and specific historical relationships with recipient countries. Desirable as it might appear to advocates of some single best model of technology transfer, in fact the legacies of history, the balances of political strengths, and the comparative advantages of economies are impossible to ignore in making any sensible recommendations regarding the transfer of technology. This is a point that will emerge throughout the chapters that follow, but it deserves to be underscored from the outset.

TECHNOLOGY TRADE AND TRANSFER IN THE MIDDLE EAST

The quadrupling of oil prices in the early 1970s, and the immense riches that this brought to oil-exporting countries in the Middle East, set the stage for an explosion in technology trade and transfer over the course of a decade that provides a rare opportunity to observe the dynamics of the process we have attempted to describe. Suddenly flush with vast sums of capital, most Middle East nations (particularly the oil-rich nations such as Algeria, Iran, Iraq, Kuwait, and Saudi Arabia) did not confront the problems of how to finance technology imports. Instead, they focused on planning and designing a rapid inflow of both infrastructural and industrial technology in order to rapidly modernize their societies and economies. It is probably too early to assess the overall consequences of this extraordinary rush for development. Iran is an obvious casualty of the process, while results in countries like Kuwait and Saudi Arabia are still far from clear. Nevertheless, each of these countries stepped up its imports of technology markedly in the 1970s, offering lucrative markets for a number of Western suppliers, who in turn viewed expanded exports as not only a means of offsetting the enormous costs of oil, but also as a vehicle for establishing closer political and economic ties with these countries, and hence creating stability in petroleum supplies.

The experience of the Middle East countries over the past decade provides a good laboratory for examining the consequences of rapid technology transfer. But the uniqueness of the case may limit its applicability for understanding technology transfer in other regions of the third world.[38] Indeed, it could be argued that the abundance of capital with which to purchase technology, the dependence of supplier countries on the Middle East for energy needs, and the relatively small populations and limited labor pools in most of this region's countries, result in a pattern of technology trade and transfer unlikely to be duplicated anywhere else. Put this way, we could hardly disagree. Nevertheless, the unique advantages enjoyed by the oil exporters only serve to outline in sharp relief the opportunities that technology transfer can offer to importing countries in pursuit of development objectives and to exporting countries in the way of expanded trade under the best of conditions. Granted, the opportunities may be more limited elsewhere, but in such circumstances they are often overlooked or ignored altogether. Technology transfer commands our attention in the Middle East; the dynamic relations between suppliers and recipients are clear for all to see.

We are certainly concerned about and interested in the impact of technology imports on these Middle Eastern countries, for if the experience of Iran was repeated several times elsewhere, we might seriously question the wisdom of technology trade and transfer altogether. Still, our concern in the following chapters is with the strategies that technology supplier countries employed to promote exports to the Middle East. We focus on four countries (Britain, France, West Germany, and Japan) that have been particularly active in the region, but which have contrasting historical relations with Middle East countries and which define their economic roles in the region quite differently. Our objectives are to describe and explain the strategy that each country employs to promote transfers to the region. We are particularly interested in understanding the roles played by public and private sectors in each country, and knowing the phases of the transfer process to which their strategies are directed.

To preview, we advance three related propositions. First, we argue along with those who have written on foreign economic policies of advanced industrialized states that technology transfer strategies that countries adopt with respect to the Middle East derive from historically determined patterns of political and economic processes practiced at home, and to a smaller extent from the legacy of foreign policy relations between the country and the Middle East region.[39] Second, unlike much of the industrial policy literature, we find no one strategy practiced by any of these four countries that is clearly superior to another. Indeed, our elaboration of the generic process enables us to identify particular strengths (and weaknesses) of each strategy as it matches up with particular needs of each phase of the process. Third, supplier countries should learn to recognize their country's peculiar strengths in the process of technology trade, and develop ways to capitalize on those strengths rather than devoting time and energy seeking to replicate the strategies of others.

We begin Chapter 2 by tracing the legacy of European and Japanese political and economic involvement in the Middle East, giving some attention to the longer historical sweep of these relations, but focusing principally on relations during the 1970s. We outline changing patterns of trade between the two supplier regions and the Middle East, and draw examples from five technology sectors: civilian aircraft industries, telecommunications, nuclear power, medical services, and petrochemicals. Chapters 3 through 6 treat the three European countries and Japan in turn, attempting to characterize and to explain their experience with technology trade and transfer. Chapter 7 examines the multilateral efforts of the European Community to negotiate with Middle Eastern states individually and collectively through the office of the Arab League. Chapter 8 offers some conclusions about the experience of technology suppliers, particularly as they offer lessons for the United States. The final chapter also attempts to evaluate individual country policies for both the short and long term as they relate to the generic process of technology transfer.

2

TRADE AND TECHNOLOGY TRANSFER: THE MAJOR TRENDS

Trade and technology transfers between the countries of Europe and those of the Middle East can be traced back at least to the era of Alexander the Great. Many of the roots of early Western science and philosophy emerged from the ancient regimes of the Middle East. Western mathematics, astronomy, medicine, and education all owe a large technological debt to the ancient Arab empires. Through subsequent centuries, peaceful trade and travel combined with the turmoil of war and conquest to maintain a rather continuous flow of technologies and ideas between these two important regions. From the nineteenth century through the first half of the twentieth, this interaction took on an increasingly unidirectional character. The industrial revolution had given to the nation-states of Europe, as well as to the United States, vast technological and military advantages over the culturally fragmented, industrially stagnant, and eventually heavily colonized Moslem world. As a result the West essentially "gave" what it wished to the Middle East, which in turn had little alternative but to "take" whatever was available on terms that were rarely of its own choosing.

Chapter 1 pointed out that any successful transfer of technology requires a synergy between needs and capabilities on both sides of the transfer. The transferring party must not only have the technology (capability); it must also have the wherewithal to make it attractive. From the late nineteenth century to the early twentieth century, the West was relatively rich and technologically sophisticated, while the Middle East was relatively poor and technologically backward. The West had the ability to provide and the Middle East had the desire to acquire many Western goods and services. But Western countries rarely saw much reason to make such transfers, while the Middle Eastern nations lacked both a commitment to technological change and the financial resources to import know-how from abroad.

In the twentieth century, national independence was followed by aggressive, governmentally directed programs of industrialization, in an effort to redress some of the imbalance in influence between the two regions. However, as is well known, it was the formation of OPEC in 1960 and the quadrupling of oil prices in 1973 that produced new political and economic influence for the oil-rich Middle East countries and their neighbors. This magnified the already considerable economic dependence of the industrialized countries on the region. For the most part, technological superiority remained with the West, but many Arab countries used their new-found influence to position themselves to acquire desired products and technologies on terms consistent with their own development and modernization plans. Furthermore, oil dependency and the need to cover higher import costs loosened the hold that industrialized suppliers had maintained over sought-after products and technologies. The result was a vigorous market for technology trade. Moreover, the declining technological dominance enjoyed by the United States for more than two decades after World War II and the emerging prowess of suppliers such as West Germany, Japan, France, Italy, and even the so-called NICs ensured a competitive marketplace. For many of these countries, the Middle East offered a vast new market as trade among the OECD countries began to level off. Such competition among suppliers allowed careful Arab purchasers to bargain on favorable terms for the goods and services they imported.

These changes produced a new era between the industrialized countries and the nations of the Middle East in economic exchange generally and in technology transfer in particular. Increased financial strength, combined with a growing desire to utilize Western know-how in an effort to hasten their own development, made many Arab countries able and eager suitors of the West. Potential suppliers, recognizing the commercial potential and economic importance of the Middle East, demonstrated a similar willingness to provide what was desired. In its broadest terms, the situation approached that of mutual need and capability.

Not all Western countries or companies were equally well equipped to meet Middle Eastern demands, however. Britain and France, with longstanding political and diplomatic relationships in the region, used such associations to deepen economic ties. Similarly, the geographical proximity enjoyed by France and Italy facilitated exchanges with neighbors across the Mediterranean. For West Germany and Japan, historical ties ranged from much weaker to nonexistent.

The degree of dependence on Middle East oil also affected the relative eagerness of many industrialized countries to promote technology transfers to the Arab states. At the beginning of the 1970s, Italy, France, and Japan all depended on the region for most of their domestic energy needs, while energy sources were more diversified in the United States, West Germany, and Britain. The former group was more inclined toward technology-for-oil swaps, while the latter three resisted such a linkage.

Nor was every industrialized country equally ready or willing to meet the specialized demands of potential recipients. France, the United States, and to a lesser extent Britain, were far more prepared, both technically and politically, to supply military equipment, for example, than was Japan or West Germany. The Americans enjoyed certain advantages in the delivery of services, while the Japanese could capitalize on their ability to deliver mass-produced consumer durables. The British reputation for objectivity in consulting made national firms ready candidates for preparatory work, even if actual project awards and sales went to the firms of other nations. Washington's and Bonn's sensitive political relationships with Israel usually made them far more charry of establishing close commercial ties with that country's adversaries than was either Japan or Italy.

In sum, while the broader character of relations between the two regions over the past decade or so shows a deepening in many areas (one of which has been a rapid increase in technology transfer), the role played by individual supplier countries has varied, shaped by political circumstances, commercial motivations, and domestic economic strengths and weaknesses. Our purposes in this chapter are first to review the broader trends in trade between industrialized suppliers and the Middle East over the past decade, and then to look at more specialized patterns of technology trade by country and product group. The chapter concludes with a section on other forms of technology transfer. For purposes of comparison, we include data on the four supplier countries treated in Chapters 3 through 6, as well as data on the United States, Italy, and other OECD countries that have active commercial interests in the region.

TRADE

As was noted in Chapter 1, the transfer of technology is difficult to measure. Generally speaking, however, technology transfer is a process that occurs when a recipient attains an improved capability to design products or to operate a production facility or a service system.[1] In this sense, a good deal of trade, particularly that of relatively sophisticated exports, automatically involves technology transfer. At the same time, while the sale of a nuclear reactor, a computerized lathe, a satellite, or a communications network could reasonably be argued to represent a transfer of technology to buyer from seller, one would be much harder pressed to make the case for the sale of every bar of soap, breakfast cereal, or video tape recorder, although even in some such cases the recipient might be exposed to something called a "new technology," or at least to a new way of doing things. Harder still to treat as technology transfer are generic raw materials such as timber, rubber, maize, or bauxite, even when these may be integral to subsequent manufacturing ventures involving new technologies or improved production. In short, not all trade involves technology transfer, although surely a large part does. Given the exigencies of data gathering, however, it makes some sense to attempt a first approximation of technology transfer between the industrialized countries and the Middle East by an examination of trade statistics, even as we recognize that they are at best an inadequate surrogate.

Trade statistics are probably the most striking indicator of the changing relationship between the Middle East and the industrialized world. As can be seen from Table 2.1, in 1970 the Middle East as a region accounted for less than 6 percent of the total export market for each of the major industrial countries. In 1970 total exports from the industrialized countries to the 15 Islamic countries in the Middle East totaled about $5.5 billion of total exports of $224 billion. Quite simply, the preponderance of Western goods went elsewhere, primarily to other western countries.

It would be fair to say that with the exception of a few minor bilateral relationships that remained from a prior colonial period (such as that between France and Algeria or Italy and Libya), the Middle East was not a central focus of Western export or technology transfer efforts.

By 1982 the picture was very different. Total exports had risen from $5.5 billion to $100 billion, an eightfold increase in constant dollars. Moreover, the Middle East took a rapidly growing share of exports from

TABLE 2.1
Exports to the Middle East for the Major Industrial Countries

Country	Exports to Middle East as percentage of country's exports, 1970	Exports to Middle East as percentage of country's exports, 1982
United States	2	8
Japan	3	12
West Germany	2	8
France	6	10
Britain	4	9
Italy	4	15

Source: International Monetary Fund, *Direction of Trade Statistics Yearbook*, 1975 and 1983 volumes.

each of the major industrialized countries, in several cases tripling or quadrupling its share of suppliers' exports. The region, which accounted for only 4 percent of Italian exports in 1970, took 15 percent in 1982, while the share of Japanese products jumped from 3 to 12 percent. In France, where the shift to Arab purchases was slower, the region's share grew from 6 to 10 percent. Indeed, by the early 1980s, many nations of the Middle East purchased more from individual Western suppliers than did a number of other industrialized countries. For example, Saudi Arabia typically ranked as the sixth, seventh, or eighth largest market for U.S. goods. Libya was Italy's eighth largest market in 1982, while Algeria and Saudi Arabia were the ninth and the tenth largest purchasers of French goods, respectively. All three were larger as export markets for Italy and France than were Canada, Japan, or the Scandinavian countries. Saudi Arabia ranked as Japan's fifth or sixth largest market, buying more from Japan than any European country except Germany.

Seven countries in the Middle East account for the bulk of Western exports to the region. Saudi Arabia had by the middle of the 1970s become by far the most important single market for the industrial countries as a group, purchasing some $30 billion worth of goods in 1982 alone. Egypt, Kuwait, and Algeria have been steadily expanding markets. Iran, Iraq, and Libya have all taken large amounts of exports from the industrialized countries, although the revolution in Iran, the war between Iran and Iraq, and the political vicissitudes of Libya have all led to rather wide annual swings in the amounts purchased. Figure 2.1 provides a graphic portrait of the exports from the industrialized West to these seven markets over the period 1974–1984.

Much of the increase in the importance of the Middle East as a market for Western products was obviously in response to the massive increase in the value of Middle Eastern oil imported by the industrialized countries and the desire of the latter to cover petroleum costs by expanded sales to the region. At the time of the oil embargo, the European Community imported some 71 percent of its crude oil from the Arab countries; for Japan the figure was about 80 percent. With the quadrupling of oil prices, products from the Middle East assumed a much larger share of the import portfolios of these industrialized countries. For example, Middle Eastern imports constituted 12 percent of total imports for both Japan and Italy in 1973; by 1981 the figures were 30 percent and 22 percent. To cover these growing costs countries such as Japan and Italy sought most aggressively to expand exports to the region. Where dependence on oil was less, most notably in the United States, Britain, and West Germany, total trade grew more slowly.

While the steady growth in commercial exchange continued without interruption from the early 1970s to the early 1980s, with important con-

FIGURE 2.1.
Western Exports to Selected Middle Eastern Countries, 1974–1984

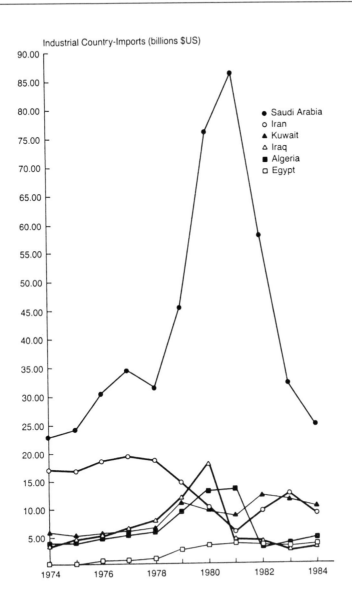

sequences for technology transfer, it is important to note that the soft-ness in world oil markets in the mid-1980s with falling demand and declining prices has, in most cases, altered the trade patterns of the earlier decade. Political instability in the Middle East and the disunity evident among the OPEC members has added further to this new environment. The bargaining positions of most Arab states have eroded, again with im-portant consequences for technology transfer.

The balance between need and ability seems again to have shifted— many countries in the West no longer need the Middle Eastern markets quite as much as they did, while the Middle East has lost some of its col-lective ability to attract Western technologies, products, and services. There is no inevitability therefore to continued technology transfer, even after the process is well under way. Broader political and economic capa-bilities inevitably condition its flow.

Thus, as is evident in Table 2.2, the relative shares of both the im-ports and the exports of the major industrialized countries have fallen in the middle 1980s from the high levels recorded at the turn of the decade. However, in no case have trade totals returned to anything approaching pre-1973 levels. Clearly, the Arab states have remained crucial trading partners for Europe, Japan, and the United States, although the leverage afforded by oil has declined. Nevertheless, the reduced revenues avail-able to Arab states and the ability of oil consumers to meet more of their petroleum needs from non-Arab sources certainly diminish both the abil-ity of Middle East countries to finance technology imports and the will-ingness of supplier countries to provide them.

Although the Middle East clearly grew in importance for the West-

TABLE 2.2

Exports and Imports to Middle East as a Percentage of Total Exports and Imports for Western Nations, 1973 and 1981

Country	Exports			Imports		
	1973	1981	1984	1973	1981	1984
Japan	4	11	8.5	12	30	24.1
France	5	9	8.2	9	18	11.2
West Germany	3	8	6.0	6	9	4.5
Italy	5	17	13.2	12	22	15.5
Britain	4	9	7.4	7	7	2.5
United States	3	8	5.6	2	6	3.1

Note: Middle East includes Saudi Arabia, Iran, Algeria, Egypt, Iraq, Kuwait, Libya, UAE, Syria, Lebanon, Jordan, Qatar, and Oman.

Source: United Nations, *Trade With Industrial Countries;* International Monetary Fund, *Direction of Trade Statistics Yearbook.*

ern suppliers collectively between 1970 and 1982, and although the region clearly gained more rapidly in significance for some countries than for others, there was surprisingly little fluctuation in the overall Middle Eastern share of the exports of the countries examined. France and Japan registered the only significant changes in regional market shares, changes that were mirror images of one another. France saw its share of the regional market fall from 17 percent in 1970 to 9 percent in 1982 while Japan increased its share from 10 percent to 17 percent during the same years. In absolute dollar terms in 1982, the United States claimed the largest share (18 percent), followed closely by Japan (17 percent), West Germany (15 percent), Italy (11 percent), France (9 percent), and Britain (9 percent).[2]

Bilateral Strengths in Trade

Figure 2.1 showed the overall pattern of trade among the major Middle Eastern countries and the West as a whole. Clearly, Saudi Arabia has been the largest importer of goods from the industrialized North. From the early to the mid-1970s, exports to Iran also rose rapidly, falling off sharply following the 1979 revolution. Figures 2.2 through 2.7 provide bilateral export data for the six major industrialized countries.

With the exception of French exports to Algeria (which rank slightly ahead of French exports to Saudi Arabia), Italian sales to Libya, and Iranian and Iraqi purchases from Germany (which occasionally outstrip Saudi purchases), the Saudi kingdom has been the leading Middle Eastern export market for each of the industrialized countries. For the United States, the Saudi share has been two to four times that of Egypt, which ranks second in purchases of U.S. goods. Japan exports four to five times more to the Saudis than to any other Mideast country. All of the industrialized countries have sharply increased their exports to Saudi Arabia over the past decade, reflecting that country's oil riches and its commitment to industrialization through massive imports of new technologies, plants, and products.

While expanding trade with the Saudis has been the most striking feature of commerce for all industrialized countries in the Middle East over the past decade, there have been important developments in other bilateral trading relationships. The U.S. share of Mideast exports was unchanged at 18 percent in 1970 and again in 1984. But between 1974 and 1978 its share jumped to 22 percent, based on expanded trade with Iran, only to tumble to 14 percent after the 1979 revolution. By the mid-1980s, U.S. sales to Egypt had become substantial, and those to Kuwait, Algeria, and Iraq had remained generally at high levels. Conversely, sales to Iran

FIGURE 2.2.
U.S. Exports to Selected Middle Eastern Countries, 1974–1984

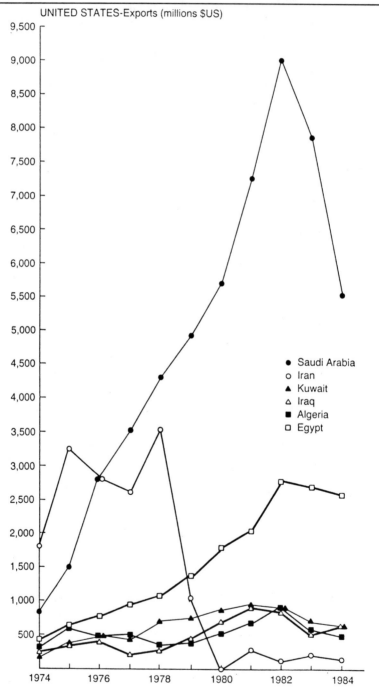

UNITED STATES-Exports (millions $US)

- ● Saudi Arabia
- ○ Iran
- ▲ Kuwait
- △ Iraq
- ■ Algeria
- □ Egypt

and Libya had fallen sharply. It is also worth noting that several countries such as Israel, Jordan, and the UAE regularly made larger purchases from the United States than did countries like Iraq, Algeria, and Kuwait, although these patterns were the reverse for the other industrialized countries.

France has enjoyed a strong position in the Maghreb and Mashreq countries, although its share of the Algerian market has fallen from 55 percent to just over 25 percent today (Fig. 2.3). Declining French influence in Algeria dictated that France would have to diversify its oil supplies. French export attention was directed east to Iraq and Iran, as well as to Saudi Arabia. The revolution in Iran pushed Paris to focus even more attention on Iraq and Saudi Arabia, and to rebuild relations with Algeria. The eastward tilt in French oil policy is evidenced by the fact that in 1981, 32 percent of all French petroleum imports came from Saudi Arabia and 21 percent from Iraq. The Iran–Iraq War has pushed the French even closer to Saudi Arabia.

French export strength has generally mirrored its import dependence. The most rapid export growth can be found in trade with Iran until 1979,

FIGURE 2.3.
**French Exports to Selected Middle
Eastern Countries, 1974–1984**

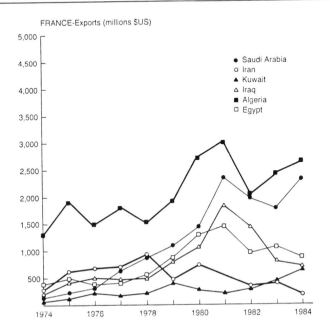

and since then with Saudi Arabia and Iraq (although, again, the Iran–Iraq War has resulted in fewer purchases by the latter). Paris still exports more to Algeria than to any other Arab state, but the rate of growth has been moderate, suffering from time to time as a result of difficult political relations. In absolute terms both the United States and West Germany now export more to Algeria than does France. French exports to Egypt are one case where oil dependence has not preceded rapid expansion. Paris took advantage of Sadat's open door policy to boost sales of French goods and to negotiate a number of lucrative contracts. The latter have included construction of a Cairo subway, development of a port at Damietta, expansion of the Cairo airport, and the building of two nuclear power plants.

British trade in the Middle East (Fig. 2.4) continues to reflect that country's historical ties to the region. With few exceptions, trade volume has been the largest and rates of growth the fastest in the Gulf and in non-Mediterranean African countries. British traders in French-speaking North Africa have repeatedly shown an unwillingness or inability to pene-

FIGURE 2.4.
British Exports to Selected Middle Eastern Countries, 1974–1984

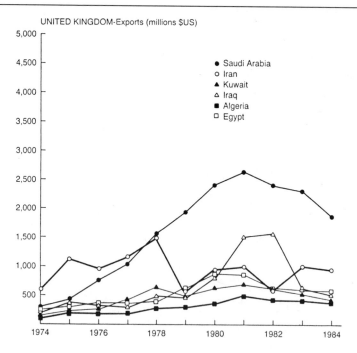

trate these markets. The production of North Sea oil, however, has reduced British dependence on Middle East supplies and given the British a position in Arab markets quite different from that of the French. British imports from all OPEC countries increased marginally from $8.7 to $9.9 billion between 1974 and 1980, while exports to the same states grew much more rapidly, from $2.6 billion to $10.8 billion, due largely to the expanding market in Saudi Arabia. While diminished oil dependence gives greater flexibility to British policymakers, it also reduces the incentive to promote exports.

Saudi Arabia is far and away Britain's largest trading partner in the region, taking $1.9 billion in British exports in 1984, an eightfold increase over 1974. Exports to Kuwait and Iraq also increased steadily if less dramatically. British exporters also did a booming business with Iran prior to 1979, and it is significant to note that British exports to that country were approaching $1 billion in 1980. Exports to Egypt have also shown steady growth. The most disappointing performance has been in French-speaking North Africa, where exports to Algeria in 1980 totaled only $331 million, about half the amount sold to the tiny state of Kuwait. Despite overall increases in volume, British market shares have fallen in almost every Middle Eastern country.

Although facing many historical obstacles, West German trade with the Middle East increased sharply in the 1970s and shows little sign of slowing in the 1980s. (Fig. 2.5). Like the French, the Germans import most of their oil from the Middle East, although they have reduced OPEC's share of oil imports from 95 percent in 1973 to 70 percent in 1982. Twenty percent of German export earnings go to cover the costs of energy imports.

German exports have shown remarkable growth in a number of Middle Eastern states. The most spectacular rise in the early 1980s was in Iraq, where German sales reached $2.9 billion in 1981, and $3.1 billion in 1982, nearly four times the 1978 figure. The 1981 amount was larger than German exports to Saudi Arabia, which at $2.6 billion were 40 percent higher than the previous year. German successes in Iraq are due in part to the willingness to continue business after the war with Iran began in 1980, when most Italian and Japanese firms departed. Iraqi trade dropped off sharply, however, as the effects of the war and oil glut were felt; in 1984 total German sales were down to one-third those of 1981.

German trade with Iran has also shown signs of vigor since 1979, suggesting that the Germans may be well positioned to take advantage of any eventual normalization of relations between Iran and the West. German firms have also taken advantage of troubled political relations between Algeria and France to make inroads into Algerian markets. German trade with Kuwait and Egypt has grown steadily but at a more moderate pace

FIGURE 2.5.
West German Exports to Selected Middle
Eastern Countries, 1974–1984

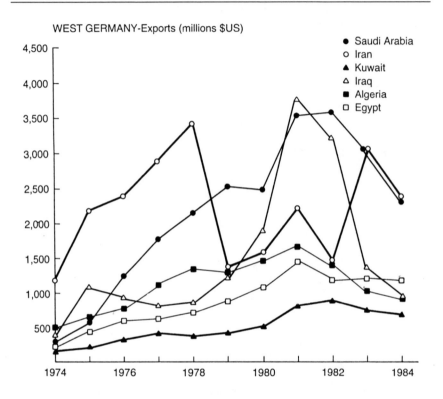

WEST GERMANY-Exports (millions $US)

● Saudi Arabia
○ Iran
▲ Kuwait
△ Iraq
■ Algeria
□ Egypt

than for the other four countries. Libya has also been a consistent and growing market for German goods. Remarkably, German efforts yielded a trade surplus with the Middle East in 1984 approaching $3.5 billion, an impressive accomplishment in view of Germany's oil import requirements.

By virtue of geography, Italy is better positioned to expand trade in the Middle East than any of its West European allies. Italian dependence on Middle Eastern oil and natural gas made it imperative that Italy aggressively expand its exports to the region in order cover its import costs. Like the French, the Italians have been open to "special relationships" and have cultivated close ties with Libya for some time. In 1979 Libya took $1.92 billion in Italian exports and was Italy's leading market in the region (Fig. 2.6). Prior to 1979, Italy imported oil principally from Saudi Arabia, Iraq, and Iran, in addition to Libya. The decline in Iranian imports pushed the Italians to greater and greater reliance on the Saudis, with a

FIGURE 2.6.
Italian Exports to Selected Middle
Eastern Countries, 1974–1984

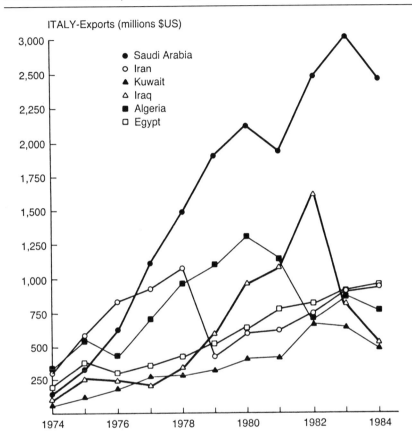

ITALY-Exports (millions $US)

- Saudi Arabia
- Iran
- Kuwait
- Iraq
- Algeria
- Egypt

leveling off of Iraqi sales in the context of the Iran–Iraq War. At the same time, the Italians and their giant energy firm ENI negotiated with Algeria for the construction of a natural gas pipeline, the Transmed, which is to provide Italy with 30 percent of its natural gas needs. As a result, imports from Algeria have been rising slowly but steadily.

As in the case of France, Italian export markets tend to mirror the pattern of energy imports. Libya traditionally purchased the largest share of Italian goods in the region until 1982, when Saudi Arabia became the major Italian customer. Sales to Iran and Iraq have also been substantial, although they have been characterized by wide fluctuations in the years since the beginning of the war between them. Like Germany, Italy's export gains have been widely distributed throughout the region. Thus, steady growth can also be found in Egypt, Kuwait, and smaller markets such as Jordan, Lebanon, and the UAE.

Japan was a latecomer to the Middle East, but has been the most successful of the industrialized countries in expanding its exports to the region. Between 1974 and 1980, Japan saw large absolute increases in total sales to virtually every Middle Eastern country (Fig. 2.7). In most instances the same can be said for the period through 1984. Iran and Iraq were extremely important and growing markets, but the drop-off in sales to Iraq since 1981 was dramatic, while exports to Iran were uneven following the 1979 revolution. As with most of the other major industrial countries, Japan finds its largest and most rapidly growing market in the region to be Saudi Arabia. Japanese exports to the Saudi Kingdom increased nearly tenfold in the decade 1974–1983. Kuwait and the UAE have been steadily expanding markets, and Japan also enjoys more than 20 percent of the market in smaller countries such as Oman, Qatar, North Yemen, and South Yemen.

Overall, the bilateral trade data tend to reflect the broader patterns of relations between the two regions. Saudi Arabia is the major and most rapidly growing market for most countries. Slower and steady growth can be seen in countries like Egypt, Kuwait, and generally Algeria. Iran and Iraq have been lucrative trading partners for some states, but patterns of trade have shown considerable fluctuation. Yet within this broader picture, it is clear that aggressive exporters such as Japan, West Germany, and to a lesser extent Italy have made impressive inroads into almost all markets in the region, regardless of the political disturbances that have discouraged other exporters. The United States tends to develop trade patterns that directly reflect its political interests in the region far more than economic opportunities. Much the same can be said of France, although its regional interests tend to be more focused on Algeria, whereas those of the United States have been centered on Saudi Arabia, Egypt, Jordan, and Israel. Britain has shown growth in virtually all markets in the region, but at rates behind those for most of the other industrial countries.

Product Specialization

Country-by-country trade statistics show only one dimension of technology transfer, although undoubtedly they account for a very high proportion of total transfers. When one examines specific product sales, the diverse character of the transfers taking place becomes even clearer. Just as the individual supplier countries demonstrate different strengths or weaknesses in their total trade with the several countries of the Middle East, so too have they shown unequal abilities in exporting different

FIGURE 2.7.
Japanese Exports to Selected Middle
Eastern Countries, 1974–1984

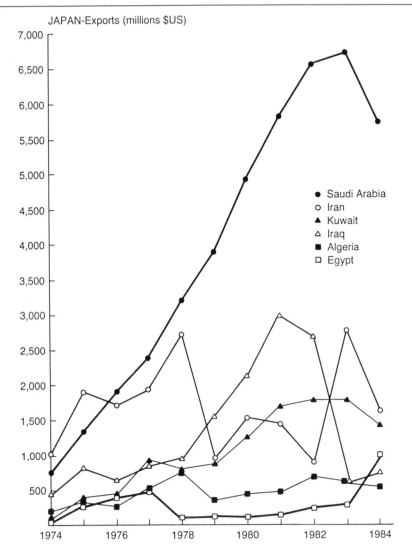

JAPAN-Exports (millions $US)

- ● Saudi Arabia
- ○ Iran
- ▲ Kuwait
- △ Iraq
- ■ Algeria
- □ Egypt

products. This becomes evident through an examination of six different product areas that we believe are a good representation of the range of technology transferred to the region: nuclear plants, machinery, telecommunications, medical equipment, aircraft and air transport equipment, and arms.

The sale or purchase of nuclear power technology is perhaps the most vivid example of large-scale, high-visibility technology transfer. The exporter of a nuclear power facility must provide not only highly sophisticated hardware and accompanying operational technologies, but also training programs for indigenous engineers and technicians who will operate and maintain the equipment. With the successful delivery of such a technological package comes a lucrative payoff. What is most surprising, given the general scope of technology transfer between the industrial countries and the Middle East since 1970, is that trade in reactors has remained at such modest levels despite the desire of many Arab countries to acquire such technology. Germany and France were in the formative stages of nuclear projects with Iran when the fall of the Shah brought about their termination. The French also pursued a nuclear program in Iraq that resulted in reactor sales in 1979, but that program, too, was temporarily shelved after the Israeli attack on the power plant in 1981. Both the French and Germans have preliminary nuclear technical assistance programs in a number of Middle Eastern countries, with the expectation that sales of nuclear power plants will follow in due course. The French are in the final stages of negotiations for the sale of two plants to Egypt, the first of eight proposed by the Egyptian government. Talks have also been held with representatives from Iraq, Algeria, and Morocco. While both Kuwait and Saudi Arabia have at various times expressed interest in nuclear technology, neither appears prepared to move forward in the near future. Italy, through the Italian Nuclear Agency, has provided Iraq with considerable nuclear assistance, including a range of laboratory-scale processing facilities. Given Libya's stated interest in acquiring nuclear weapons and Italy's close ties to that country, the potential also exists for expansion of sales between these two countries.

For various reasons, Britain, the United States, and Japan have taken a much less active role in the export of nuclear power equipment. With the nuclear industry in decline at home and a highly regulated export sector, U.S. industry has largely surrendered nuclear sales in the Middle East to foreign competitors. For reasons of both economic profitability and political difficulty, the British industry has chosen a similar course. Japan, despite a potential capacity to do so, has not yet entered the nuclear export market.

The export of nuclear technology probably represents the greatest range of difficulties for potential suppliers, although the payoff can be substantial. Most estimate that a successful export program takes ten years to complete, taking into account such tasks as training local personnel, establishing experimental reactors, and then building and servicing a modern nuclear power facility. The economic and political hurdles are many, as domestic experience in the United States has shown, and ten years is a long time to maintain a favorable working relationship with importing countries and neighbors concerned about the proliferation of nuclear weapons. The French appear most prepared to make this long-term commitment.

Far less drama, but perhaps a much greater long-term impact, can be found in the area of machinery and equipment sales, which comprise by far the major category of export from each of the industrialized countries to the Middle East. In 1978 this category accounted for 46 percent of total exports from the industrialized countries to the Middle East; in 1982 it was 57 percent. Roughly equal shares of 20 to 23 percent of the total machinery and equipment market are currently held by the United States, Japan, and West Germany. Germany and the United States have retained roughly comparable shares since 1970, while Japan's current share shows a striking increase, from 9 percent to 23 percent over the past decade, due primarily to Japan's success in exporting road vehicles, telecommunications, and consumer electronics. By 1982 Japan had moved into first place in total machinery exports, passing the United States.

Italy's total share of the machinery market is a smaller 15 percent, but this too shows an increase from a 10 percent share in 1970. France and Britain have each recently managed to secure only about 9 to 10 percent of total Middle East purchases of machinery and equipment, reflecting substantial declines from 18 percent for France and 16 percent for Britain.

One is also struck by the extreme volatility of sales of machinery. Fluctuations are largely explained by the fact that exports of such equipment are often closely tied to large contracts, which are generally concluded on an irregular basis. For example, the French exported a record $300 million in heavy machinery to Algeria in 1977, but following a freeze on French contracts in Algeria during a period of political difficulties, exports dropped to about $70 million in the following year. Similar fluctuations can be found in sales to Iraq, Kuwait, and to a lesser extent, Saudi Arabia. West German machinery exports to Egypt tripled from 1974 to 1975 and nearly tripled again in 1976, only to fall back close to the 1974 level two years later. Much the same happened to machinery sales from Italy to Iraq over the same period. In the first half of 1984, German machinery exports showed a dramatic increase over the previous year in Iran, while suffering sharp reversals in Kuwait, Saudi Arabia, Iraq, and Algeria.[3]

Telecommunications trade reflects many of the same traits as machinery. Most of the Middle Eastern countries acquired their first generation of telecommunications equipment from their colonial rulers and continued to be supplied by those countries for many years. France and Britain were thus the major beneficiaries. However, the expansion and modernization of these systems from analogue to digital technology reopened competition in the telecommunications sector to other potential suppliers. Similarly, the range of new products developed in telecommunications has expanded dramatically, now including everything from massive nationwide switching networks to telex, mobile radios, and radio and video broadcasting equipment. The result has been great volatility in what is now a $2.5 billion market.

In the last decade, the key development in telecommunications has been the rapid surge in Japanese sales. One set of data suggests that Japan's market share rose from 13.6 percent in 1971 to 21.4 percent in 1981. More recent data shows Japan selling 44 percent of all telecommunications equipment in the region in 1982.[4] Japan also won the lion's share (almost 80 percent) of the communications construction contracts between 1978 and 1982. Tokyo's greatest successes have been in Egypt, Saudi Arabia, and Kuwait. Among the other suppliers, only France has been able to increase its total market share, rising modestly from 5.4 percent to 6.5 percent between 1970 and 1980. The United States, Britain, and West Germany all registered declines in market share with Britain experiencing the largest losses.

Within this broad picture, a few bilateral trends in telecommunications trade deserve mention. The Germans have managed to acquire or retain large market shares in Algeria, Iraq, and Iran consistent with their broader trade patterns. French success has been most marked in Iraq and Egypt. Britain's most lucrative markets have been in Egypt, Iraq, and Algeria, while the United States has done well in Saudi Arabia and Egypt. Italian performance in telecommunications has been uneven country by country and has remained modest overall.

Medical equipment and supplies form a vital and rapidly expanding technological demand for the countries of the Middle East. The market in medical equipment and supplies (exclusive of pharmaceuticals) in the six largest Middle Eastern countries (plus Qatar, Oman, and the UAE) has been estimated at $250 million for 1980, up by an annual rate of approximately 20 percent from the $95 million market of 1975. Steady growth, rather than the wide annual swings found in heavy machinery and telecommunications, characterize trade in this sector.

For many years, the United States held the technological advantage over all other potential suppliers of medical equipment, but this has been eroded in recent years largely as a result of poor after-sales services. Today, Germany is the leading supplier of medical equipment to the region, with about 25 percent of the market. Saudi Arabia is Germany's largest customer, while Egypt has shown the most rapid increases. With some 18 percent of the market, the United States now ranks as the second largest supplier of medical equipment. Britain, France, and Japan all follow the top two with shares of 12 percent, 10 percent, and 7 percent, respectively. The British have recorded strong export performances in countries of traditional strength (namely Egypt, Iraq, and Saudi Arabia), while France has shown some gains in Iraq and Saudi Arabia, and holds strong positions in Egypt and Algeria.

It is worth adding that the United States has done extremely well in bidding on contracts for both technical services and equipment supply in the medical area. So too has Britain, although at generally lower levels. France has been particularly successful in winning construction rights for medical facilities.

The story of commercial aircraft exports is essentially an American tale. In 1978 the United States accounted for 55 percent of all aircraft sales and 63 percent of all aircraft parts sales in the region. Britain accounted for a much smaller 23 percent of aircraft sales, followed by Italy with 12 percent. U.S. aircraft sales in 1982 represented 63 percent of the total, with Italy taking 15 percent and France 13 percent of the market. Italian sales have been highest in Iran and Kuwait, while France has done reasonably well in Egypt, Iran, Iraq, Kuwait, and Saudi Arabia. French sales of aircraft and parts have been paralleled by its success in bidding on contracts for the construction of commercial aircraft support systems. For technical services associated with the aircraft industry, however, the United States has again been dominant, winning virtually all announced Mideast contracts between 1978 and 1982. The European airbus has had some modest success through the early 1980s, but sales remain a small fraction of those won by U.S. suppliers. And as was the case in nuclear exports, Japan has chosen not to enter the export market for commercial aircraft, aircraft parts, or support systems.

The United States has also been the major supplier of arms to the region. U.S. arms transfers to the Middle East (including Israel) from 1946 to 1981 totaled nearly $30 billion. In recent years, Saudi Arabia, Egypt, and Israel have been the principal recipients, although Iran was a key target of such transfers prior to the revolution. Jordan also continues to receive substantial aid, particularly in proportion to its small size.

France has ranked a distant second to the United States in arms sales, but such exports have been an important component of French technology transfer to the region. French supplies of arms to the Middle East quadrupled between 1974 and 1980, and of $4.8 billion in military sales worldwide in 1981, 72 percent went to Mideast countries, up from 18 percent in the decade 1963–1973. Since the late 1970s, arms sales to Saudi Arabia and Iraq have been an effective way to pay for burgeoning petroleum imports. Egypt and Libya have also been substantial recipients of French arms. Undoubtedly, French sales of military hardware in the Gulf have also assisted in efforts to export more nonmilitary goods to these countries, a region that has long looked to British suppliers.

Britain, too, has benefited from arm sales to the Arab states, although not nearly so much as France. Of military export sales of £537 million in 1981, one-third went to Middle East purchasers. As with the larger pattern of British trade, the Gulf states remain the biggest customers, where Saudi Arabia is the leading buyer. A four-year, £800 million agreement was signed in 1977 and renewed in 1981 to provide training and maintenance functions for the Saudi Air Force. Iran was also a major purchaser of British arms until 1979.

For the most part, Italy, Germany, and Japan have not been involved in substantial arms sales to the Middle East. In the cases of Japan and Germany, however, there has been growing pressure to engage in such sales, and some currently traded items have military applications following simple adaptations made by the recipient.

As was the case in the bilateral data, the product-specific transfers between the industrialized countries and those of the Middle East reflect some important variations. By far the single most important product category for transfer among those reviewed has been machinery and equipment, with important exchanges also in telecommunications. The record of Japanese and German firms has been most notable in these areas. U.S. successes have been in arms and civilian aircraft, while U.S. shares have fallen in medical equipment, a field it once dominanted, and in nuclear power exports, a sector it might be expected to control. Meanwhile, France has established the largest presence in nuclear plant exports and holds a firm second place behind the United States in arms transfers to the region. The image of Britain, sector by sector, indicates its declining role in this region, where few product categories are dominated by British exports.

ADDITIONAL TRENDS IN TECHNOLOGY TRANSFER

Besides direct trade, there are many other ways by which technologies are passed from one society to another. Among the most prominent are direct foreign investment and joint ventures, development assistance, and personnel transfers (which includes placing experts in a developing region and training local personnel). In addition, transfers occur through the direct provision of services, typically on a contractual basis.

These other channels, particularly those involving acquired knowledge and skills by local personnel, may be as effective or more effective in transferring technology than straightforward commercial exchange. Evaluating such transfers, however, is more difficult because they are harder to detect and quantify. Data is most readily available for direct foreign investment, although even here it is incomplete or lacks sufficient detail. By and large, levels of direct foreign investment have remained modest in the Middle East and have been concentrated in petroleum-related sectors. U.S. and Japanese firms have been most active. In the early 1980s, the U.S. firms, with a total of $227 billion invested abroad, had only $3.3 billion invested in the Middle East, of which $2.2 billion was in petroleum-related projects. Of the $61 billion invested abroad by Japan in 1984, only $2.7 billion had gone to the Middle East, $1.1 billion of which was in petrochemicals. European firms have been even more reluctant to invest directly in the Middle East, preferring turnkeys or medium-term management contracts. Only recently have some begun to be coaxed into joint ventures (see chapters 3–5).

Political instability in the Middle East no doubt contributes to the reluctance of foreign investors. The negative experiences in Iran, especially the Japanese troubles with the enormous Bandhar Khoumeni petrochemical plant, have surely reinforced concerns about the security of large-scale investments. The collapse of Lebanon, the rise of conservative religious movements in a number of countries, and the wave of terrorism have done little to increase the confidence of international business. Economic conditions also argue against direct investment in many of these countries. Domestic markets are small or undeveloped in all but a few countries; labor pools are generally small and lacking sufficient skills; domestic infrastructure remains inadequate. It is understandable that suppliers are more attracted to turnkey ventures or fixed-length contracts for goods and services.

With a couple of exceptions, development assistance also contributes little to technology transfer in the region. Indeed, many of the oil-rich nations are themselves aid donors, and relatively small amounts of aid flow into the region from the industrialized countries. Of a total of $25 billion in Development Assistance Committee (DAC) aid allocated in 1980, less than 5 percent went to the entire Middle East. The United States sends about one-third of its total Overseas Development Assistance (ODA) to Egypt and Israel. But no other industrialized country provides more than 5 percent of its overseas aid to any country in the Middle East. Another perspective on the relative insignificance of aid as a vehicle of technology transfer can be gained by realizing that the number three recipient of DAC aid in the Middle East is Morocco, which in 1979–1980 received only 0.8 percent of total DAC aid worldwide. As with direct investment, pockets of influence can undoubtedly be identified, but as a general transfer mechanism, aid has been a far weaker vehicle than exports. A small amount of project aid is also channeled to the Middle East through multilateral institutions such as the European Community and various UN agencies (see Chapter 7).

Another vehicle of technology transfer is to train scientists, engineers, managers, and technicians, either in the supplying or the receiving country. Extensive training is increasingly being included as a feature of large-scale management contracts at the specific request of the Middle Eastern countries. While data are hard to come by, it appears as if the Germans, with their strong history of technical education, and to a lesser degree the French, are the most sensitive to training needs. The United States also provides substantial assistance through its college and university system. In the early 1980s some 75,000 students from the region were studying in the United States, with the largest numbers coming from Iran, Saudi Arabia, and Lebanon. The specific programs of the various industrialized nations to provide training are explored more fully in chapters 3-6.

Technology transfer may also be achieved by the employment of foreign experts as advisors at various stages of industrial development. Often such advisory services are also made part of large contracts. Experts typically assist in the design and construction of projects, and in the management of plants and facilities once construction is completed. Middle Eastern countries have increasingly asked for comprehensive packages of such technical assistance as management and maintenance problems of technologically complicated ventures have become more apparent. The Germans, the French, and the Japanese appear most sensitive to these needs and most prepared to meet such requirements.

Another kind of consulting service precedes the signing of a large contract. Experts, generally engineers, are frequently retained to conduct feasibility studies and then to advise their clients regarding the choice of contractor. As noted earlier and discussed more fully in Chapter 3, British consultants have won a decisive share of this business, based largely on their reputation for competent work and objective and independent advice to their clients. While data are incomplete, the work of consultants is a lucrative business in all European states, but is one area where the British retain a strong lead.

Finally, one can point to the role played by service contracts. During the last decade or so, the provision of specific technical services has taken an increasingly important place in major contracts between nations of the Middle East and the industrialized suppliers. This seems to reflect a shift in several Arab nations as they move from a need for infrastructural and industrial hardware provided through heavy construction to a wider range of management and maintenance services for completed projects. Particularly in areas such as medical services and commercial aircraft systems, services have come to occupy a larger role in international transfers. Between 1978 and 1982, for example, technical service contracts in the medical area accounted for $1.2 billion, most of which was provided by the United States. Such service contracts, while a small share of total transfers, appear to be a source of potential growth for the countries of the Arab world.

CONCLUSION

No regional transfers of technology expanded more rapidly in recent years than those between the industrialized nations and countries of the Middle East. The sudden increase in purchasing power available to the OPEC countries combined with the desire of oil importers to balance their trade accounts and ensure stable supplies of oil, gave great impetus to technology trade.

The breadth of exchanges and the rapidity with which they have been made provide an interesting microcosm of many of the broader issues of technology transfer raised in Chapter 1. A major message that emerges is the importance of a congruence between need and capability for both exporters and importers of technology. This is seen dramatically in the sudden interest shown by oil importers in transferring technologies to the oil-rich countries of the Middle East, once their supplies of this vital commodity were threatened. But even more telling has been the drop-off in technology transfers in the years of oil glut and lower oil dependency. Just as the countries that were most dependent were the most aggressive in attempting to sell and transfer technologies to the Middle East, so too they were the countries whose transfers showed the most significant reductions once oil became cheaper. In short, once technology transfer begins, there is no guarantee that it will continue unless both sides are willing and able participants.

Within this broad pattern, however, it is clear that some countries show widely different strengths and weaknesses, both in terms of products transferred and countries to which they have greater access. The firms of some countries appear to be guided only by economic calculations, trading with all countries able to pay for their wares; others pick and choose their clients with one eye on political relations, in addition to calculations about profits and losses. Not only firms but governments act in ways that may promote or retard technology exchange. Some have actively and aggressively intervened in the process of transfer; others have chosen to remain on the sidelines. Some have acted for political reasons, others for largely commercial motives. And the differences in relative success and failure indicated by the broad trends outlined in this chapter can in large measure be traced to the individual combinations of public and private strategies pursued by the major supplier countries. It is to a deeper understanding of these national difference that chapters 3–6 are devoted.

3

BRITAIN: TRADING TECHNOLOGY IN THE POSTCOLONIAL ERA

Our purpose in this and the three succeeding chapters is to examine how each of four countries has approached the challenges and opportunities of technology trade and transfer to the Middle East. None of the countries has developed an explicit policy regarding technology transfer either to third world countries in general or to the Middle East in particular. Yet, a range of policies directed at different political and economic issues affects the process of transfer. It is this combination of influences emanating from both the public and private sectors, some consistent with one another and some not, that we are calling a country's strategy regarding technology flows. Where inconsistencies and conflicts among policies are particularly numerous, it may seem inappropriate to use the term *strategy* since it generally implies rational calculation and planning. However, our view is that a nation's strategy regarding this aspect of foreign economic policy derives from two sources: first, how the country defines larger foreign policy objectives (in this case, objectives directed to the Middle East), and second, from historically rooted patterns of economic relations between the government and the private sector.[1] Strategies are bound to be both less coherent and less effective where larger foreign policy interests clash with the objectives of domestic economic actors. Similarly, where relations between the government and the private sector are not mutually supportive, the result may be that government and private-sector actors operate at cross purposes. In other words, these national approaches are not highly malleable tools in the hands of able policymakers. Rather, they are slowly evolving instruments determined both by stable or slowly changing national interests in international affairs and by domestic institutional relationships between the state and society. Both give shape to the way national interests will be addressed. Such strategies can and will change as national interests are redefined and domestic institutions evolve. But the more striking feature is their continuity over time.

As we argued in Chapter 1, some national strategies may be more suitable for taking advantage of certain features of the process of technology transfer than others, but no one approach is likely to capture all of the benefits. Our view is that it makes more sense to direct attention to where the strategy is likely to pay greatest dividends, rather than trying to replicate the approaches of others.

In order to ensure some measure of comparability country by country, each of the four chapters follows a similar pattern of organization. We discuss first the larger historical context of relations between the supplier country and the Middle East. In this section, we seek to identify the general foreign policy objectives of each nation-state and to examine how these objectives have been pursued in the recent past. A second section explores trade and foreign investment initiatives by both government and the private sector that have consequences for technology transfer. Trade and investment policy sets the general framework for technology exchange and gives insight into the more general character of the relationship between the government and private sector on economic issues. The third section treats a variety of activities that support trade and investment policy and the process of technology transfer. Included are foreign aid policies, support of scientific and technical agreements, financing and insurance schemes, manpower programs, and other services.

There has been a tendency for supplier countries to compete with one another to come up with the best package of supportive measures in order to give special advantages to their national firms. International agreements have been negotiated among such countries to limit this competition and narrow the differences among national policies. In 1976, in the face of growing competition to provide the most attractive export credit terms, the Group on Export Credits and Credit Guarantees (ECG) of the OECD Trade Committee negotiated an information "consensus" on credit terms.[2] The rules were finalized in April 1978 as an Arrangement on Guidelines for Officially Supported Export Credits. It specified floors under permitted interest rates and ceilings on maturities, as well as minimum down payments and maximum local-cost financing allowances for most officially supported export credits of two years or more. The arrangement requires that any member state intending to offer terms more favorable than those permitted must first notify other members of its intention to do so and explain its reasons for the action. The terms vary for different receiving countries, depending on their relative economic strength. The so-called Berne Union, founded in 1934, performs a similar harmonization function for national policies relating to credit and investment insurance.[3]

A final section in each chapter assesses the national strategy in light of the generic process of technology transfer and tries to account for distinctive national features.

HISTORICAL CONTEXT

Britain's interest and involvement in the Middle East is closely tied to its fortunes as a great power in international affairs. Elizabeth Monroe speaks of "Britain's moment in the Middle East," corresponding to the years when its political influence was truly global and its economic might was second to none.[4] Economically, the Middle East became important in the nineteenth century when the British Empire established a presence in Asia, particularly in India. Monroe and others argue that India played an extremely important part in Britain's role as a global power, and the Middle East was a vital link between London and the Indian subcontinent.[5] Indeed, if one looks at the pattern of British colonization in the region from Egypt to Iraq to Transjordan to the lower Persian Gulf, one is constantly reminded of the need to ensure passage by land and later by sea to this vital colony. This commercial association with the region is the earliest of any of the European states, and provides a network of business relations that Britain continues to draw upon today.

At the same time that British economic and commercial interests focused on the Middle East, political changes in Eastern Europe and North Africa underlined the importance of the region for British strategic purposes.[6] The decay and collapse of the Ottoman Empire in the nineteenth and early twentieth centuries, and the Russian interest in filling any power vacuum to its south, increased British resolve to keep the region free of unfriendly foreign influences. Growing French colonial interests in North Africa and a desire to extend French influence east from Algeria and Morocco brought on a determination in London to resist such moves and keep Egypt and East Africa out of the hands of other European colonizers. In other words, both the decay of the old East European empires and their final dismantling by the battles of World War I, combined with the new imperialism of West European powers in Africa and elsewhere, increased the strategic importance of the Middle East for British policymakers. As a global power with economic interests to protect and strategic and political objectives to advance, London looked upon the Middle East as a key region in which to project its power.

The outcome of World War I both solidified British presence in the short term and helped to undermine it in the long term. The settlement prescribed that London administer a number of territories as League of Nations mandates including Iraq, Transjordan, the Anglo-Egyptian Sudan and, most problematically, Palestine. The British also continued to rule most of the Persian Gulf territories and the Aden protectorates. Special treaty relations linked Britain with Egypt. In short, London was most successful in paving the route to India with friendly governments or regimes under their control.

Problems began to appear in the 1930s over the question of Jewish emigration to Palestine coupled with emerging Arab nationalism. Jews complained that the pace of immigration was too slow; Arabs wanted to halt it altogether. Neither side was happy with the proposals for a partition, and London was increasingly seen as the principal obstacle to a satisfactory resolution of the problem. Other states too began to be restive under foreign influence or rule, eager to speed along the process of decolonization and British departure. The diminished status of Britain as a global power in the interwar years both encouraged such domestic unrest in the region and made it difficult for British policymakers to make a convincing response.

After World War II, the continuing decline of Britain as a global power was paralleled by a steady retreat from the Middle East.[7] Indian independence in 1947 and the British withdrawal from other outposts in Asia caused the passageway through the Middle East to decline in commercial value to London traders. Moreover, the economic difficulties endured by Britain after the war, the vulnerability of the once proud pound sterling, the hardship caused by the withdrawal of Lend-Lease aid, and the need to rely on American Marshall Plan assistance to rebuild its economy made it steadily more difficult for Britain to underwrite economic and strategic policies in the region.[8] These tasks were certainly not helped by the political desire on the part of individual countries to rid themselves of foreign dominance. Nationalist forces gained popularity in Egypt and Iraq, while the lingering frustrations in Palestine resulted in the British departure in 1947.

In some respects, the British retreat was made easier by the growing U.S. presence in the Middle East. As was true on questions of security in Europe, U.S. and British interests were not dissimilar. As it gained in global power, the United States too saw the "gateway to Asia" as of vital importance in its growing confrontation with the Soviet Union. Washington's containment policy gave prominence to close relations between the northern rim of Middle Eastern countries, particularly Turkey and Iran, as a barrier against Soviet designs to the south. And while Washington saw a commercial route to the Far East as less compelling for its own economic purposes, the growing commercial and strategic importance of Middle East oil both to the Western allies and to large U.S. oil firms became a new reason for a sustained U.S. involvement. The Americans also inherited the British problems in Palestine and cemented this commitment in the region by undertaking the defense of Israel. Thus, while political withdrawal from the region was inevitable as British power declined, the retreat was cushioned by the knowledge that Washington would generally act as a surrogate for British interests.

Virtually all students of postwar international politics point to the 1956 Suez crisis as a crucial turning point for British foreign policy.[9] It brought home two lessons regarding the Middle East. First, it indicated that while broader British and U.S. interests were similar in the region, their methods and approaches for realizing those objectives were often at odds, and where these strategies clashed, the Americans were likely to prevail. Second, Suez forced a rethinking of British colonial policy and was undoubtedly a major factor in forcing the British to adopt a more modest role in third world politics. Lingering financial problems at home in the late 1950s and through the 1960s made the deployment of British forces abroad and the maintenance of foreign bases more and more difficult. In 1962 the decision was made to withdraw British troops from Aden, followed by a withdrawal from the Persian Gulf in 1971.[10]

While political disentanglement was in some respects helped along by the U.S. presence (which is not to imply that devolution was easy and painless, although it was by comparison to French withdrawal from Algeria), new economic interests made commercial separation much more difficult. As luck would have it, one author suggests, petroleum lay under the sands of many of those former British colonies on the route to India.[11] And the postwar British economy increasingly ran on Middle East oil. Oil dependence grew as political influence declined. Thus, economic ties with the region became more important through the 1950s and 1960s, although on terms that were less under London's control.[12] It is fair to say that in the short term the presence of the United States and the large petroleum companies was adequate to ensure ample supplies at low prices. Indeed, price and availability made possible the European conversion from coal to oil in the 1950s. Yet the consequences in the 1970s were dependence and vulnerability. Moreover, the low petroleum prices that prevailed until 1973–1974 gave little incentive for the British to expand their own commercial activities in the region, since oil import bills remained modest and could be covered by expanded trade elsewhere. As a review of postwar British trade accounts shows, there was a major shift under way from the 1950s to the 1970s, as exports formerly designated for the Commonwealth were directed to markets in Western Europe and the United States. In 1954 the former colonial area accounted for 45 percent of British exports, with only 28 percent going to all of Europe. By 1970, Commonwealth exports amounted to only 27.5 percent compared with 20 percent purchased by the six members of the EEC. By 1973, the expanded EEC took 32.8 percent of British exports, compared with 17.8 percent sold to Commonwealth countries. This shift was reflected in a change in policy regarding membership in the European Economic Community. In negotiations in the late 1950s, London had argued against the idea of a European Common Market, preferring instead a free trade area that would permit access to its sizable Commonwealth trade. By the early 1960s, the Conservative government made application for EEC membership, convinced that the future of British trade lay with Europe.

The quadrupling of oil prices in 1973–1974 produced a response in Britain quite unlike that in the other hard-hit countries in Europe. In France and Germany, the rising cost of imports and enormous trade deficits with the Middle East stimulated efforts to promote exports to the region to reduce those deficits. With few other energy options, these countries had little choice. For Britain, the boost in prices, while costly in the short term, provided incentives to develop more rapidly Britain's newly discovered petroleum reserves in the North Sea and to pursue the route of energy independence rather than becoming more economically entangled in the Middle East. In this respect Britain shares some similarities with the U.S. energy position and the economic response.[13] Blessed with energy options over the medium term, Britain's response to the oil exporters was to diminish rather than intensify economic contacts over the next decade. Conversely, the continuing U.S. political presence in the region mitigated against any American temptation to withdraw economically, recognizing, as the British did in an earlier time, that economic involvement and exchange are frequently useful tools of political influence. Ironically, in the British case, the energy crisis may be viewed as an incentive for Britain to follow its political disengagement from the region with an economic withdrawal, or at least not to pursue expanded economic relations as vigorously as its trading partners in Europe.

In summary, the legacy of British involvement in the Middle East, while long, has been one of steady decline since World War II. If one is prepared to argue, which we are not, that economic benefits always go hand in hand with political and diplomatic influence, then one should observe a declining ability to secure the economic rewards of technology trade. Moreover, if national economic policy, an important component of which is energy policy, is revised and redefined in ways that diminish the role to be played by Middle East trade, one might expect few public resources to be allocated to stimulate such trade or few efforts of public and private sectors to work together to promote this commercial exchange. The legacy of postwar British involvement in the Middle East would lead us to expect only moderate and probably declining official support of technology trade to the region. Only to the extent that the British government is seeking to find markets for high-technology goods will export promoters be attracted to the Arab states.

One commercial remnant of British strategic influence in the region has been the sale of arms to Arab countries as discussed in Chapter 2. While the British totals lag behind those of the French, the Thatcher government has identified Arab markets for increased attention and has sought to build London's share by going head to head with Paris for contracts.[14] Currently Britain has about 7 percent of the Middle East arms business. Iran was one of Britain's leading customers before 1979, and it was estimated that the fall of the Shah resulted in the cancellation of contracts worth £2 billion. Egypt became another valuable customer after 1974, when Sadat discontinued purchases from the Soviet Union and the Americans were fearful of antagonizing Israel with a rapid buildup of sales to Egypt. Saudi Arabia and other Gulf countries are the biggest purchasers of British weapons. In 1977 the Saudis signed a contract with London worth £800 million over four years, much of it for training and maintenance services; that contract was renewed in 1981.

However, it is also important to focus briefly on nongovernment relations, relations between private citizens and business associates that began during the long period of colonial rule. Some make a sharp distinction between the state of official and private relations, arguing that the rate and extent of decline in the former far outpaced changes in the latter. While discussing the growing tensions between Britain and various Arab governments after World War II, Monroe contrasts the state of relations in the private sector:

> British consultants and commercial firms, on the other hand, were freely used; when hired on the local government's own terms, and the basis of an ordinary professional or commercial contract, their presence was unconnected with dominance, and their familiarity with local conditions was valued. For instance, a firm of British engineering consultants—Sir Alexander Gibb and Partners—advised Persia on municipal water supplies all through the British quarrel with Mussadeq, over oil, and served Egypt as consultant on the Aswan dam no matter where the money for it was coming from, or what the relations between the British and the Egyptian governments.[15]

At the individual level, the English and Arabs have shown general interest in and affection for each other from the earliest contacts. To some extent this was a product of Arab admiration for the modern ways of their colonial rulers, a not unusual consequence of social and cultural dominance, but it was also accompanied by considerable British curiosity about Arab ways.[16] There has always been a large English community living in Arab countries since the time of British rule, a community that has settled there by choice and considers the arid land to be home. The Germans, by contrast, have shown much less interest in Arab cultures, and recruiting German workers and managers to live abroad has often been difficult.

One of the most enduring aspects of these strong Anglo-Arab personal relations has been the willingness to do business with one another. The Arabs have repeatedly relied on British personnel for guidance and advice on economic projects and business undertakings. A reputation for competence and honesty among the English deepened the trust between the parties. However, there are limits to these good feelings. The attraction of British culture and society has made London a favorite place for oil-wealthy Arabs to visit, and one observer notes that the new circumstances of Arab affluence amid British economic decline have not always been easily accepted by the hosts:

> The changing economic and social conditions of both the Arabs and the English in the second half of the twentieth century seem to have threatened British self-esteem. Britons, although ready to accept the support of Arab money, viewed the Arab presence and their wealth as a danger signal and as a reminder of Britain's falling place in the world.[17]

The long association between Britain and the Arab world gives us mixed signals in assessing its impact on technology transfer and trade. Foreign policy since World War II gives every indication that the British moment in the Middle East is history, that government leaders in London are content largely to follow U.S. diplomatic initiatives and to make only modest and cautious overtures of their own. Diminished dependence on oil imports has further lowered the stakes in the region and lessened Britain's need to expand rapidly its sale of goods and services. In the mid-1980s Britain was running a balance-of-trade surplus with Arab states. There are not, in short, strong reasons (derived from larger foreign policy objectives or energy policy) for the government in London to take up the cause of expanded Middle East trade generally or technology trade in particular.

At the same time, the industrial decline that Britain has endured in the postwar era has made improved economic performance both at home and abroad a high priority of British policymakers. Much attention has been directed toward the cultivation of new, or the rejuvenation of aging, high-technology industries at home, and to the establishment of new markets for the products of such industries abroad. The suddenly increased purchasing power of the Arab states makes them a logical target of these policy initiatives. More important, the rich history of strong personal and business relations between Arabs and the British provides a good foundation on which to build such initiatives. While the British government contributes some support, the strength of this association continues to be the activities undertaken by the private sector.

TRADE AND INVESTMENT POLICY

As indicated above, there is no officially stated British policy regarding technology transfer generally or to the Middle East in particular. Rather, the implicit policy (or what we are calling strategy) is given its principal shape and direction by the interwoven features of the country's foreign trade and investment policies. In Britain, these policies derive fundamentally from the historical process of industrialization, which was informed by the tenets of economic liberalism.[18] British liberalism assigned the primary tasks of economic development to the private sector, which was expected to respond to changes in supply and demand in the marketplace. In these early days, the government's economic role was to do little more than ensure that the rules of fair competition were observed. The division of labor between the public and private sectors was similar in foreign economic affairs. Free trade among private producers was to be encouraged by the reduction or elimination of government-imposed tariffs and quotas. Public officials were to intervene, not to direct foreign trade but only to ensure that the rules of free trade operated for all. At home and abroad, economic initiative rested in private hands; the state assumed the role of regulator and commercial arbiter.

In the nineteenth century, the years of the *pax Britannica,* the British were blessed with a superior navy and a powerful economy, and they prospered under a system of free trade and investment.[19] However, even through the years of industrial decline in the twentieth century, classical liberal principals remain embedded in much of current policy. Yet, the economic inequities that seemed to be aggravated by liberal economies in Britain and elsewhere early in the twentieth century and by the declining competitiveness of British industry (particularly after World War II) encouraged many to seek a wider role for government in the management of domestic and foreign economic affairs. Pushed along by the election of a Labour government after World War II, Britain adopted what came to be known as a "mixed economy," in which the state took on a variety of social welfare functions, nationalized selected industries, and engaged in a limited and unique form of economic planning. Successful postwar modernization and revitalization in France under the guidance of economic planners attracted the British to this experiment. However, where the French gave to the state the tools for directing economic activity, the planner's role in London was defined more narrowly as facilitator of activities already initiated by the private sector. This modest planning exercise has also given attention to the difficulties of British exporters seeking ways to boost their fortunes in international markets.[20] The National Economic Development Office (NEDO), the British implementing administrative agency, was charged with improving the climate in which business decisions are made and with instituting a tripartite (business, labor, and government) forum for discussion of the problems of particular industries. The generation of useful information, improved communications, and the reduction of conflict between management and labor are key objectives of this forum, which also holds fast to the liberal belief that final economic decisions must remain in private hands. While NEDO's work was given strong support in the early stages, most agree that the results of the tripartite process have been disappointing.

In sum, liberal notions about the proper roles for government and the private sector in economic activities at home and abroad still prevail in Britain, although the state has been given greater prominence in the redistribution of domestic wealth and welfare and in the facilitation of private-sector initiatives in both local and foreign markets. This distribution of public and private authority is very much in evidence in trade and investment policies affecting technology transfer. More specifically, with the exception of products defined as strategically sensitive (arms and military equipment, nuclear power, and industrial goods with military applications), the private sector is strongly encouraged to pursue technology trade with and investment in the Middle East. Where appropriate, it is presumed that government officials should make every effort to facilitate such exchange. Even so-called sensitive exports are permitted, so long as the proper assurances are given and safety precautions observed.[21]

One can go further and claim that the promotion of trade to and investment in the Middle East in technology-intensive industries has assumed a high priority over the past decade in Britain, offering as it does the prospect of considerable economic return in one of the few areas of national strength in trade and services. While the growth of direct foreign investment is less dramatic, the rapid expansion of British exports to the Arab nations over the past decade would appear to confirm this view. Exports to all OPEC countries grew from $2.6 billion in 1974 to $10.8 billion in 1980 and nearly $12 billion in 1981, before falling off somewhat over the next three years. Imports increased from $8.7 billion to only $9.9 billion at their peak in 1980, falling dramatically over the next four years. By 1984 British exports were more than double British imports from the region.

The book value of British direct foreign investment in the OPEC countries (excluding oil, banking, and insurance) was £319 million in 1974, jumping to £790 million in 1978. But as a percentage of total direct foreign investment, the OPEC share actually dropped from 4.7 percent in 1962 to 3.1 percent in 1974 (perhaps a reflection of British political withdrawal from the region), before rising slightly to 4.1 percent in 1978. A measurement of annual outward flows of foreign direct investment shows Britain sending out £44 million in 1974 and £177 million in 1977, before dropping back to £69 million in 1979.[22]

Depending as the British do on the initiatives of their private firms, what has been their record over the past decade? The greatest successes can be found in the work of British consulting firms (architects, engineers, and managers), who draw on their close personal relations with local leaders and years of experience in regions such as the Persian Gulf to win contracts for the design of large projects of all sorts. One such firm mentioned above is Sir Alexander Gibb and Partners, one of Britain's leading groups of consulting engineers.[23] Gibb employs over 100 engineers in the lower Gulf region alone who do feasibility studies, project planning, and design and supervision of airports, hotels, hospitals, roads, harbors, and industrial projects. The firm's success has been the result of professional competence and close attention to personal relations. As one company official put it, "The consulting engineer is still akin to a local doctor; people want to know they can ring the local man for help."[24] Watson Hawksley, another consulting engineering firm, undertook its first Middle East job in the early 1950s, the design of a sewage facility for the Anglo-Persian Oil Company; its work was halted by the Mossadeq revolution in Teheran in 1952.[25] Since that time the firm has been a trusted designer of desalination and waste treatment facilities throughout the Gulf region. Another prominent firm is John R. Harris, an architectural and planning firm that has been designing buildings in the Middle East since 1951.[26] The Dubai International Trade Center, Continental Bank of Bahrain, and the state hospital in Doha are among the projects designed by Harris.

While data is hard to find, it is estimated that British firms regularly win about 50 percent of the consulting business in the Middle East. Thirty thousand British consultants are believed to be working in the lower Gulf region alone. Some British exporters complain that such firms should steer more of their clients to British suppliers, but the consultants argue that their success is due in large part to their reputation for serving their clients' interests faithfully and providing objective and reliable advice, regardless of whose business it benefits.

If the strength of private-sector initiatives has been in consulting and related services, the weakness has been in a failure to bid on and win major turnkey and capital goods contracts. Margaret Thatcher noted this deficiency in a 1981 speech: "Why don't the contractors bid? We've got to crank the contractors up."[27] Several reasons have been cited for this reluctance to take on the other international competitors. First, effective bidding on contracts of this sort often requires close cooperation and coordination among a number of large national firms to enable the lead firm to submit a competitive bid. British firms have traditionally shied away from consortia arrangements, preferring "not to get in bed with one another."[28] Second, competitive bidding often requires ready access to financing and close ties between large firms and major banks. In countries such as Japan and West Germany, banks are permitted to take equity positions in major companies, and as a consequence take a very active role in the projects undertaken by those firms. Banks in Britain are forbidden by law to become stockholders in major corporations, and the links between the financial and productive parts of the economy are fewer.[29]

Finally, Lord Selsdon, chairman of the Committee for Middle East Trade (COMET, discussed below) criticizes senior business managers in Britain who have neglected to become informed about the Middle East and have not provided the resources necessary to increase their knowledge and position themselves to take advantage of opportunities.[30] One Western banker contrasted the approach taken by British and Japanese firms:

> When a UK company sends someone to Saudi Arabia, a man arrives having been told of a potential contract—but unsupported and with instructions to just get on with the job. His Japanese opposite number, in contrast, arrives with a full supporting team and administrative and financial back-up from Tokyo.[31]

The lack of attention to the organizational requirements necessary to win such large contracts may be a legacy of the colonial years, when the British option was all the importing country had. Given the fact that such organization often requires the intervention of government in other countries, British failures may also be a function of liberal notions about how the state should act.

Those who absorb the criticism about British failures to win the big contracts are quick to point out that what such firms lose by not bidding, they frequently recapture as subcontractors and suppliers for their international competitors. Those who are encouraged by the rapid gains turned in by British exporters over the last decade and a half point to business done by small- and medium-sized suppliers, who not only subcontract to large infrastructural or industrial projects, but also become long-term suppliers of parts and equipment once those projects are completed. Between 1974 and 1980, British exports to Saudi Arabi increased from $280 million to $2.4 billion; to Kuwait from $140 million to $601 million; to Iraq from $140 million to $748 million and to $1.5 billion in 1982; to Egypt from $122 to $806 million. The only areas of disappointment were the former French-controlled territories, where British exporters have shown very little initiative and have recorded only marginal trade gains. In the large and lucrative Algerian market, for example, British exports stood at only $128 million in 1974 and had increased to only $331 million in 1980. Over the next four years they inched up only marginally. The disinterest in these markets shown by national firms has drawn strong criticism from public officials determined to find new markets for British goods.

To restate, the British strategy of trade and investment relies principally on the private sector, which in turn has drawn upon its experience and network of close relations built up during the British colonial period to expand its export base of goods and services. To date, the private sector has been particularly successful in landing consultancies and in securing supply and subcontracting business. It has been largely unsuccessful in cracking new markets or in winning large capital goods contracts where international competition is keen.

The private sector gets help in its efforts to promote trade and investment generally, and in high-technology areas in particular, by public and private institutions and associations. NEDO, in its planning efforts, has repeatedly pointed to the need for developing high-technology industries as an area of potential export growth. The British Technology Group, the product of a recent merger of the National Resources Development Commission and National Enterprise Board, is charged with stimulating technology investment in Britain.

Trade promotion activities are formally supervised by the British Overseas Trade Board (BOTB), a curious body created in 1972 with membership drawn from government and industry. The BOTB president is the Secretary of State for Trade and the chairman is a leading industrialist. Its responsibilities are to advise the government on a strategy for overseas trade, to direct and develop export promotion services, and to encourage the exchange of views between government and the private sector. As a forum for facilitating economic activity by generating information and fostering communication between public officials and businesspeople, the BOTB is a typical British response to economic difficulties.

The BOTB meets regularly to discuss problems and annually allocates funds for export services.[32] Among other things, these funds have been used to establish a central data base of product and industry information, to provide technical assistance to exporters, to underwrite a substantial portion of export marketing research costs when companies are exploring new markets, to sponsor missions and trade fairs, and to grant assistance for travel costs.[33] BOTB has also devised a market entry guarantee scheme (MEGS) for new smaller and medium-sized firms entering new markets. Further, it supervises the Overseas Projects Fund, which assists British companies seeking major overseas contracts. It also helps to identify export opportunities that arise from British foreign aid programs.

Most of the day-to-day work of export promotion is supervised by the Department of Trade (DOT). Other departments, such as the Foreign Office (strategically sensitive exports), the Department of Industry, and the Department of Health and Social Security (export of medical equipment and services), become involved periodically. Prior to 1982, export promotion services were handled by industrial groups that had little regional expertise and were physically separated from the DOT's headquarters in London.[34] In 1982 these services were reorganized into branches that addressed particular geographical regions, and these new units were housed at DOT's main headquarters. Of relevance to this study are the Middle East branch and the North African, Caribbean, and Latin American branch. All branches are expected to respond to business inquiries, to work to maintain a satisfactory political climate for exports, and to sponsor trade missions, fairs, and exhibits. A special division is charged with looking after large projects and contracts. The arms of the department abroad are the commercial sections within British embassies, and it is generally agreed that they are particularly helpful in assisting British firms with foreign business.

"Close" and "congenial" are the adjectives used to describe relations between the BOTB and the DOT.[35] With its hands-on experience, the latter regularly makes suggestions and recommendations to the former, which are generally accepted. Technically, the personnel of the regional branches are employees of the BOTB, but on routine matters they receive their principal direction from the DOT. Trade promotion assistance is enlisted from other departments when necessary. The Department of Industry, which is charged with looking after the interests of domestic industries and which retains an industrial-sector organization with important industry-by-industry expertise, is often involved if exports are key to the firms in question. In a recent case, one department official organized several trade missions to the Middle East, resulting in a number of small contracts.[36] The Foreign Office, too, plays a frequent role in trade promotion, a clear recognition that satisfactory political relations are often a prerequisite for strong commercial ties. A visit several years ago by Lord Carrington to Iraq that resolved some outstanding political difficulties is generally credited with paving the way for improved commercial ties and expanded British–Iraqi trade. Alternatively, Margaret Thatcher's views on the PLO resulted in the abrupt cancellation of a visit by the Foreign Secretary to Saudi Arabia. This was expected to damage future prospects for British exporters. While British political leaders have made frequent visits to the Middle East in recent years, their activities have seldom gone beyond the maintenance of acceptable political relations; they have rarely assumed the role of salesman for British goods. Such leaders serve as public support for private initiatives rather than promoting deals of their own.

The BOTB is also assisted by a number of regional committees composed of representatives of business and government. The Committee for Middle East Trade (COMET), set up in 1963, is one such quasi-public body whose main purpose is to provide advice for the formulation of Middle East trade policy. To this end, it brings together high-ranking officials from affected government departments and a wide array of private-sector spokespersons from leading British corporations, banks, and consulting companies prominent in economic affairs with the Arabs.[37] A second objective is to create an awareness among British firms of the features of and opportunities in Middle East markets. To increase awareness it sponsors a program of conferences on trade, investment, and project development, and it prepares extensive reports that highlight specific markets or new potential business. The general view is that COMET does an admirable job with very limited resources.

British arms trade has been promoted by two specialized institutions. The Defense Sales Organization (DSO) is managed by government officials and military personnel attached to the Ministry of Defense. International Military Services (IMS) is a British company owned by the Defense Ministry that is run by "export agents." The Middle East has been the principal focus of both these arms merchants over the past decade. The two work closely together, with the IMS serving as the commercial arm of the DSO.

Trade and investment in the Middle East is also facilitated by the work of a number of private-sector trade associations. The oldest and best known is the Middle East Association (MEA), which was founded by a group of British companies in 1961 and now boasts a membership of 500 firms. It operates in a fashion typical of most trade associations, facilitating the exchange of expertise and market intelligence, so that members are informed about the complex markets in the Arab countries and kept abreast of changing political and economic circumstances. MEA is supported by firms who have a long history of doing business in the area. The Confederation of British Industries (CBI), the industrywide British trade association, as well as sectoral associations representing chemicals, construction, electrical equipment, process plants, and oil technologies, have also directed attention to the Middle East.

A newer and intriguing organization, the Arab-British Chamber of Commerce (ABCC), is one of several trade associations founded by the Arab League in Europe and North America. Established in 1975, the ABCC already dwarfs the more established MEA.[38] Virtually all British firms doing business in the region have joined since it has taken over from Arab embassies the task of certifying all British goods exported to Arab countries. The fees collected from such services have enabled the organization to grow and prosper and to provide a broad range of services to potential exporters and importers. Staffed almost entirely by Arab nationals, the ABCC has become the envy of the MEA.

SUPPORTIVE POLICIES FOR TECHNOLOGY TRANSFER

Each of these public and private instruments makes similar assumptions about how trade and investment should be promoted. Individual British firms are expected to initiate and conduct business abroad; government policies and the work of quasi-public organizations are designed principally to alert such companies to market opportunities and to create an environment in which they can do business successfully.

Like other supplier countries, the British have also employed a number of other tools to enhance the attractiveness of their technology exports. We look in turn at financing and insurance, training opportunities and foreign aid, and scientific and technical cooperation.

Financing and Insurance

There is no specialized British institution to provide financing for technology exporters, but the Export Credits Guarantee Department (ECGD) intervenes through refinancing arrangements with private bankers to ensure adequate funding at competitive rates.[39] In other words, British banks are able to provide export credits on terms as favorable as other OECD countries because the government pays the banks a direct subsidy to cover the difference between the credit terms extended and the normal bank lending rate. From 1961 to 1972, the Bank of England maintained these refinancing facilities for clearing banks. From 1972, ECGD agreed "to refinance any fixed-rate export lending by the clearing banks in excess of an agreed percentage of their deposits" (24 percent in 1978), and assured the banks an "agreed rate of return" on their unrefinanced lending.[40] In 1980, refinancing for sterling fixed-rate export finance was withdrawn for new business, but for exports on credit terms of two years or more, exporters and overseas borrowers continued to get financed at fixed rates determined according to international guidelines. The interest subsidies are provided from public funds and totaled £357 million in fiscal year 1980.

Most agree that the financing available through this arrangement is ample for British exporters and that it is offered on terms competitive with any other supplier country. If there is a weakness in this approach, it derives from the broader restrictions in law discussed above that prohibit close collaboration between British corporations and banks. In response to similar schemes in other countries, London has also made export financing available through its foreign aid program. The Overseas Development Association (ODA), which administers British foreign aid, has channeled 5 percent of its budget through an export credit facility since 1980. The program permits exporters to mix regular financing with foreign aid funds. The package provides cheaper financing for poorer countries in the third world that could not otherwise finance necessary imports. The aid allocated in 1980–1981 was £6 million, in 1981–1982 it was £2 million, and in 1982–1983 it was £4 million. Little of this form of financing was available to the relatively affluent countries of the Middle East.

Export insurance and bank guarantees are the principal responsibility of the ECGD.[41] The ECGD was established in 1919 as a separate government department, accountable to the Secretary of State for Trade; it currently derives its powers from the 1978 Export Guarantees and Overseas Investment Act. By statute, the undertakings of the ECGD are all subject to the consent of the Treasury, but in practice most of the department's activities are recommended by an Advisory Council composed of bankers and businesspeople appointed by the Trade Secretary. The Council's main task is to give advice on the acceptability of risks for insurance coverage.[42]

ECGD offers cover for both buyer and supplier credits, in effect insuring exporters against the risk of not being paid and providing guarantees of 100 percent payment to banks. Two categories of export trade are covered: trade of a repetitive type in standard or near-standard goods, and projects and large capital goods business of a nonrepetitive sort. In the first category, cover is provided under comprehensive policies; in the second, specific terms are negotiated for each contract, and the department will cover 90 percent of the insured loss.[43] There is no official program for coverage of losses due to foreign exchange changes.

By statute, ECGD is required to set rates at levels that will preclude the need for public funding. The agency insured 8 percent of British goods in 1947, and the percentage has increased steadily to 33 percent in 1982. In 1981, £17 billion in exports were insured and £300 million in claims were paid out. ECGD offers a full range of insurance programs to British exporters on terms fully competitive with other OECD exporters. Among them are several special programs aimed at insuring large capital projects of the sort relevant to technology trade. A cost escalation scheme (CES) was introduced in 1975, providing some protection against cost increases for firms with capital goods contracts worth over £2 million and of over two years' duration. The supplemental Extended Terms Guarantee provides insurance in excess of six months for suppliers of production engineering goods—machine tools, machinery, contractor's plant. Cover is also available to British firms involved in consortia or joint ventures.[44] Nine regional offices in Britain serve exporters.

Training

British universities have long been a vehicle for the transfer of technological knowledge to the third world. The indigenous elites of colonial and postcolonial regimes have for years sent their most able young people to be educated at the best British schools. India, for example, has deepened its pool of knowledge and human capital both by sending its citizens to British universities and by establishing similar institutions in India. British schools abroad have also exposed many to the strengths of the English system. The British Council is an organization that teaches English language skills abroad and operates a full range of programs in the Middle East. Such training has helped to make the English language the primary vehicle of scientific and technical communication throughout the world. As a result, familiarity with English is often mandatory for technology suppliers in places like the Middle East. U.S. suppliers obviously benefit from the legacy of British education, and German and Japanese firms have learned the value of knowing English if one is to do business in the Arab world. This ease of communication in areas of former political influence also probably accounts in part for the British reluctance to move aggressively into French-speaking markets of North Africa. The Germans and the Japanese, accustomed to mastering new languages, have used their language skills to great advantage in North African markets.

The appeal of the British education has probably declined somewhat as opportunities for foreign students have expanded in other countries, particularly in the United States. Financial support for foreign students has declined in recent years in Britain as the costs of education have steadily risen. Thus in the late 1970s, there were nearly 40 times more Saudi students and 10 times more Iranian students in the United States than in Britain, and significantly more Egyptians in the United States, France, and Germany. Education at the prestigious British universities like Oxford and Cambridge also often turns out generalists rather than the highly specialized and technically competent students that are the product of the training one finds, again, more readily in the United States.

Much of the technical education for foreigners in Britain has been offered by private firms that operate schools or training centers to teach foreign customers how to cope with complicated equipment. In the communications field, International Aeradio (IAL) runs a program in English, mathematics, and telecommunications at Bailbrook College in Bath.[45] Nationalized British industries such as British Electricity International (BEI) also offer training opportunities in the Middle East. This ad hoc approach to training has undoubtedly produced good results in some sectors, but a better coordinated system that could become a vital asset in competing for large-project packages would almost certainly put British firms in a more competitive position. The trust that British personnel inspire in many parts of the Middle East and the belief that they are competent professionals, assets that have served the consulting firms well, would seem to offer similar possibilities in the realm of technical training and related services.

Foreign Aid and Scientific and Technical Cooperation

British foreign aid programs are not organized in ways that provide much assistance to technology transfer and trade in the Middle East. Overall, the levels of official aid as a percentage of GNP have steadily fallen from 0.56 percent in 1960 to 0.41 percent in 1970 and 0.38 percent in 1982.[46] Since 1979, official British aid has remained at about £1 billion, representing a real decline in the value allocated. Moreover, the geographical distribution of aid continues to follow British Commonwealth association, with the largest amounts going to India and sub-Saharan Africa. The Overseas Development Administration, which manages the aid program, has focused most attention on the poorest developing countries, with countries of per capita GNP of less than $370 receiving 68 percent of the funds in 1982.

On the whole, however, the British have devoted much less attention to scientific and technical assistance than either France or West Germany. London's technical assistance totaled $432 million in 1981, compared to $879 million for Germany and $1.5 billion for France.[47] The figures are particularly striking in the Arab world. In 1981, London provided only $9.9 million in technical assistance to North Africa (compared to $162 million from France and $38 million from Germany), $8.8 million of which went to Egypt. In countries east of the Suez Canal, the British allocated $12 million, compared to $22 million from France and $46 million from Germany. Moreover, the number of publicly financed technical personnel sent to developing countries from Britain has steadily decreased from 17,000 in 1970 to 11,000 in 1976 and 6,500 in 1981. The number of German personnel has remained reasonably steady in the same years, while the French personnel have declined from a much higher level (38,000 in 1970 to 23,000 in 1979).

As one OECD report notes, the British continue to give emphasis to nonconcessional flows to developing countries initiated by the private sector and facilitated by the ECGD.[48] These flows totaled $8 billion or 1.56 percent of GNP in 1981, down from $11 billion or 2.09 percent of GNP in 1980. Such an emphasis is in keeping with the British view that initiative for commercial exchange should come from the private sector, with the government providing only supplementary assistance in insurance and financing. As a country experiencing serious economic difficulties of its own in the 1970s and with global political commitments in the third world on the decline, it is not surprising to observe an overall decline in British aid, with remaining assistance focused on the poorest of the developing countries.

THE BRITISH STRATEGY ASSESSED

This chapter has suggested that the British strategy to promote technology transfer to the Middle East is more successful in some parts of the transfer process than others. Most notably, the British have succeeded in capturing a large share of the business associated with the first phase of the generic process, which addresses the planning and design of technology projects. By virtue of their long association with the region and an earned reputation for competence and objective advice, British architects, engineers, and managers have captured the lion's share of the consulting business in this rapidly growing area. The British government's declining political stake in the region over the past three decades has undoubtedly made it easier for such consultants to strike an independent posture, knowing that fundamental national interests are seldom at stake. Moreover, recipient countries are likely to trust such firms more, knowing that government officials in London are not pressing for particular outcomes.

Trade in services as opposed to goods has long been a strength of the British trade account, and this strength is reaffirmed in the Middle East. However, one can raise questions about the future of consultancies for Britain. The advantage that British consultants have enjoyed over their competitors was based in the first instance on a long history of personal relations with local personnel. In time, these relations will become less important as firms of other countries gain valuable experience in the region. Competence and performance are therefore likely to be the decisive factors determining the choice of firm, and only time will tell if British consultants will continue to outperform the rest.

The principal area of weakness of the British strategy is in landing large infrastructural or industrial contracts, those undertaken in the second and third phases of the generic process. A number of factors explain this poor performance. Most importantly, success in securing large contracts requires considerable organization and initiative, either by large private firms or by decisive supportive action by the supplier government. The overall decline of British industry, which has taken its toll on the confidence of large national firms, the reluctance of national firms to engage in cooperation or consortia with one another, and the legal separation of corporate and financial activities all contribute to a private sector without the organizational means or the confidence to pursue and win large contracts. The weakness of the private sector is reinforced by a belief in government and society at large that the state may seek to improve the business climate for the private firm, but it should stop short of organizing private-sector activities or taking the initiative on its own. British views about the proper role for the state in the economy are deeply embedded in all the institutional arrangements and procedures designed to promote trade and investment; and those institutions give initiative to the private firm and cast the state in a supportive role. The combination of a declining industrial base and a state determined to play a limited role has ensured minimal success in the race for big contracts. Political withdrawal and diminishing dependence on Middle East oil further argue against a more assertive stance in these phases of the transfer process.

Finally, the British strategy is reasonably well suited to the fourth phase of the generic process, which offers opportunities for smaller firms and more specialized suppliers. These firms have already performed well as suppliers to large contractors in infrastructural and industrial projects. The rapid gains in British exports to the Middle East over the last decade testify to the competitiveness of such suppliers. The same institutions and government policies that were not very helpful in organizing large firms to bid are much more appropriate for putting small and medium-sized buyers and sellers together, who then can negotiate their deals. Generating information and publicizing market opportunities are what British quasi-public committees (COMET) and private trade associations (MEA, ABCC) do best. As one looks to the day in the Middle East when many large-scale projects are complete and the majority of technology trade is in more specialized projects and processes, the British strategy may become increasingly successful. The greater reliance on long-term contracts that calls for extended use of management services and training options could offer lucrative opportunities for Britain.

In conclusion, the British place great faith in the private sector to secure the gains from technology transfer. The government provides helpful supportive services, but without private initiative such services are likely to count for little. Where the private sector has remained competitive and built on past associations (as in the consulting business), the returns have been encouraging. However, one would expect continuing frustrations in the large contract market. It makes much more sense to play to the strength of smaller suppliers and draw on existing state policies and to facilitate practices to bolster such trade.

4

FRANCE: TECHNOLOGY TRADE, POLITICS, AND THE STATE

HISTORICAL CONTEXT

French involvement in the Middle East and North Africa predates even the British presence. As a Mediterranean power, the French have long had strategic and economic interests in the region. However, while the British viewed the western Mediterranean as central to their interests in India, the French regarded the Maghreb countries (Algeria, Tunisia, and Morocco) as both their "gateway to Africa" and their base from which to expand eastward into the Middle East.[1] From the early nineteenth century, when French colonization began, Algeria became the cornerstone of French imperial designs. Expanding French settlements and the growth of trade drew the two countries together. From the earliest days, Paris treated its colonies as extensions of the French nation, and undertook to assimilate foreign peoples and cultures into the French way of life. This view of the empire as merely an extension of the French nation would eventually make the process of decolonization particularly painful. And even though vast differences remained between French and Moslem cultures, the bonds between France and its Arab colonies were particularly strong.

After World War I, the French extended their control over Arab territories into the eastern Mediterranean by taking charge of mandates in Lebanon and Syria. This influence was short lived, however, as the mandates were discontinued after World War II, and France again focused attention on the Maghreb. Unlike the British, who embarked on a steady political withdrawal from the region following Indian independence and the departure from Palestine in 1947, the French made an effort (ultimately unsuccessful) to intensify their links with their colonies by forming a French Union. The first indication came at the Brazzaville Conference in 1944, when the Free French under Charles de Gaulle devised the institutional arrangements that would govern relations with the colonies. The conference called for the extension of French citizenship to colonial subjects and the establishment of colonial political institutions under the new French constitution. Brazzaville indicated a commitment to integration and unity among French-controlled territories and rejected the option of local autonomy and political independence.

However, the French desire to maintain its global presence clashed repeatedly with the forces of nationalism in the colonies. Slowly and painfully the French were forced to retreat, first from Indochina (1954), then from Tunisia (1955) and Morocco (1956), and then from various parts of sub-Saharan Africa. The most difficult disengagement was the long and bloody withdrawal from Algeria, which undoubtedly was a major factor in the collapse of the Fourth Republic and the return of de Gaulle to power.[2] The close relations that had prevailed between the two countries for over a century and the image that the French had of Algeria as an integrated part of the French nation prolonged the disengagement.[3]

Relations with the Arabs under the Fourth Republic were further damaged by the French support of Israel during the 1956 Suez crisis. In the aftermath of the crisis, virtually all Arab governments broke off diplomatic relations with Paris. By the time de Gaulle assumed power in 1958, relations with Arab states were at an all-time low. However, rather than digging in his heels as the leaders of the Fourth Republic had done, or beginning a step-by-step withdrawal from the region as the British chose to do, de Gaulle took a novel route. As Edward Kolodziej puts it:

> The delicate task confronting the Gaullist Fifth Republic was to marry necessity with a national opportunity: to inter the remains of the French empire and create a new image and source of influence among the developing states while avoiding its predecessor's unfortunate fate.[4]

Recognizing the futility of the Algerian struggle for France, de Gaulle worked to achieve satisfactory terms for French disengagement and Algerian independence. The political settlement, the so-called Evian Accords of March 1962, called for complete Algerian independence following referenda in France and Algeria, the complete withdrawal of French troops over a two-year period, and the provision of economic and technical aid in return for the safeguarding of French economic interests in the new nation. Even though the Algerians failed to live up to many of their obligations under the agreement, the French provided all of the assistance required of them and worked hard to maintain good relations with the new government.[5]

Algerian independence freed de Gaulle of the colonialist yoke under which French prestige suffered in the third world in the 1950s and early

1960s. Ironically, however, Algeria would continue to play a key role in the French president's new strategy to align France with the third world. To understand this role, it is necessary to view it in light of his broader foreign policy objectives.[6] De Gaulle inherited a French nation in 1958 that was on the verge of bankruptcy, had endured a humiliating occupation during World War II, and had seen its postwar economic and political recovery undermined by the weaknesses of the Fourth Republic. The new president was determined to restore France to a position of rank internationally. For de Gaulle this meant foreign policy independent of the superpowers. His withdrawal from NATO, his vision for the European Community under French leadership, and his modernization of the French economy were among the tools for this independent posture. He likened this French quest for independence to the aspirations of the third world in the postcolonial era, and he saw in these common urges an opportunity for France to exercise leadership among the new nations. Only a short time after unburdening himself of the label of colonial master, he became the champion of the weak. He criticized the superpowers for their interventions in third world affairs, increased economic and technical assistance necessary to the process of industrialization, and supported preferential trade arrangements that would increase access for developing countries to northern markets. By acting as a leader and supporter of the independence of others, he expected to enhance French standing in international affairs.

Ironically, good relations with Algeria were viewed in Paris as a prerequisite to French legitimacy in the third world. Some have noted the lengths to which the French were willing to go to woo the regime in Algiers at a time when they paid much less attention to the governments in Tunisia and Morocco.[7] A full 25 percent of all French aid went to Algeria in 1964. In part, the radical views of the Algerian government were what attracted the French. With credibility among such leaders, it was calculated that French standing in the eyes of the third world would certainly rise. Arms sales to Libya in the late 1960s and expanded trade with Iraq, including the sale of a nuclear reactor, might be viewed as motivated by similar considerations. As in the past, Algeria was important as a door to the larger Middle East and to sub-Saharan Africa.

In addition to these political and symbolic attractions of Algeria, France also had economic and strategic interests to be served. Like the British, who came to need the oil discovered in their former colonies, the French too became dependent on Algerian oil and gas resources, and French petroleum firms made large investments in the Algerian fields. The country was also France's fourth largest trading partner, and participation in Algerian modernization and development was not only bound to be a source of future export earnings, but also a means to pay for oil and gas imports. Finally, the independent strategic posture pursued by de Gaulle in the 1960s assumed a French willingness to look after its own defense to the east, west, and south. As a Mediterranean power, vulnerable to attack by sea, France needed to pay close attention to relations with her Mediterranean neighbors. The former French colony was a key actor in the western Mediterranean.

Courtship of Algeria resulted in a five-year oil agreement in 1965 under which the French agreed to provide 1 billion francs in aid. Algeria also continued to depend heavily on France; about 1 million Algerian citizens were employed in the French work force and provided remittances crucial to the growth of the Algerian economy.

The most striking turn in French policy toward the Arab states came after the 1967 war in the Middle East when de Gaulle condemned Israeli action and called for withdrawal from all occupied territories. This growing French support for Arab states had been previewed in 1963, when de Gaulle negotiated the reestablishment of diplomatic relations with all of the Arab states that had severed ties with Paris after the Suez crisis. Nevertheless, the policy shift in 1967 undoubtedly shocked the Israelis and the large Jewish community in France. However, both the desire to increase French influence among third world countries and calculations about oil dependence figured prominently in the move. Support of the Arabs also gave greater substance to the French claim of independence from the United States, wedded as the latter was to the support of Israel. Some have argued that the French position actually enhances the interests of the Western Alliance in the Middle East, by giving Arab states a western alternative to the Soviet Union that is not closely tied to Washington.[8] Some radical governments have felt comfortable dealing with France on a variety of issues precisely because the country had maintained its independence from the United States.

This role of broker between North and South was part of the Gaullist vision. As an industrialized power with credibility among third world leaders, the French could play a pivotal role in the political and economic negotiations that would eventually surpass East-West issues in importance. Much of the French ability to play such a role was built on the personality and charisma of de Gaulle; when he left power in 1969 and was replaced by Georges Pompidou, this vision was narrowed significantly.

Pompidou viewed France as a regional rather than a global power, and focused his attention on the Mediterranean as the appropriate arena for French influence.[9] This view was consistent with de Gaulle's courtship of the Arabs, which was continued by both Pompidou and his successor, Giscard d'Estaing.[10] Relations with Algeria did not come any easier in the early 1970s, when a crisis over a renewal of the oil agreement of 1965 prompted an Algerian nationalization of pipelines and gas-producing installations and the seizure of 51 percent of French oil interests in the country. When an oil accord was finally reached in 1971, the French were more convinced than ever of the need to diversify their sources of petroleum within the Middle East.

New diplomatic overtures in the eastern Mediterranean and the Persian Gulf paid dividends during the 1973–1974 oil crisis. Paris was quick to capitalize on such good feelings by negotiating swaps of oil for technology with several of the major producers.[11] Yet, this "stooping for oil" was hardly an image consistent with de Gaulle's view of French influence in third world affairs.

Giscard d'Estaing did little to alter French policy toward the Arab world.[12] In the mid-1970s leaders in all Western states had less and less time for political posturing and thoughts of grandeur, concerned as they were with the economic ramifications of high oil import bills and recession at home. Giscard did speak of a "trialogue" between Europe, Africa, and the Arab world in which France would be expected to play a central role, but it generated little outside support.[13] The French were also active in the Euro–Arab dialogue (see Chapter 7), which envisioned close relations between the European Community and the Arab League, but which also required an elusive political consensus among all the participants.

In most respects, the French efforts to use restored relations with the Arab world as a vehicle to political influence (either globally in the context of North-South relations or regionally in the Mediterranean basin) yielded very marginal returns. However, the economic benefits from improved relations were more substantial. Closer ties with countries in the eastern Mediterranean and the Gulf permitted the French to secure new sources of oil that lessened dependence on Algeria. Such ties also encouraged French exporters to seek entry into new markets, broadening their sales from the old colonial markets into new and faster-growing economies. Expanded technology flows were also a consequence of these improved political relations.

In a fundamental respect, the British and the French differ in their assumptions about the proper relationship between diplomacy and commercial affairs. As we argued in the last chapter, commercial affairs are the province of the private sector in Britain, and diplomacy smoothes over rough edges in political relations or offers various means of support for economic ventures. Initiative comes from the private sector and the state provides support as needed. In France, the view is that political and economic relations must go hand in hand and that the state must use diplomacy to initiate the growth of commerce. As a former French trade minister put it, "There is no gap between diplomacy and commercial relations."[14] Where the diplomat succeeds, so too will the exporter. Where the statesman fails, there will be an accompanying decline in trade. When there were strains in political relations between France and Algeria in the mid-1970s, French exporters found the trade waters poisoned as well. Alternatively, the attention that Giscard showed to the Gulf by making several trips to the region in his last two years in office certainly is reflected in rapidly growing exports.[15]

There was considerable speculation that François Mitterrand's election in 1981 would bring a new direction to French Middle East policy.[16] The new French president, who had long been a strong supporter of Israel, emphasized those sentiments in his election campaign and was the only presidential candidate to endorse the Camp David accords. Mitterrand was tested shortly after assuming office when Israeli warplanes attacked the French-built nuclear reactor in Iraq in June 1981. The new government attempted to walk a line between two contradictory positions, supporting the UN Security Council resolution censuring the Israelis, while at the same time refusing to honor the Iraqi call for sanctions. After his election, Mitterrand took a number of steps to correct Franco–Arab relations. Saudi King Khaled was the first head of state to visit France after the Socialist victory in 1981, and Mitterrand went to Riyadh in August of the same year. The French president also named his brother Jacques special envoy to Saudi Arabia. Moreover, the new government assured those Arab states that had contracted to buy French arms that all contracts would be honored and new deals could be negotiated. And while Mitterrand campaigned on a platform of slowing or ending altogether the construction of new nuclear power plants in France, he encouraged continuing sales abroad, including sales of two plants to Egypt that were in the final stages of negotiation.[17] The importance of exports, particularly technology exports to the Middle East, was noted by former Minister of Research and Industry, Jean-Pierre Chevenenment, who targeted sales to Egypt, Iraq, Algeria, and Morocco.[18] Continuing dependence on Middle East oil and the importance of Arab markets for French goods made any radical shift in policy very unlikely.

At the political level, the Mitterrand government has pursued what one observer has called "double-edged diplomacy," seeking both to be Europe's most vocal spokesman for the rights of the PLO, insisting on Israeli withdrawal from occupied territories, and to support the Camp David accords and Israeli desires for a negotiated peace settlement in the Middle East.[19] As Marie-Claude Smouts argues:

Mitterrand's policy in the Middle East provides the most significant example of the high risk diplomacy which the pursuit of a balanced position based on moral principles constitutes. Because he has given signs of friendship to Israel by going to Jerusalem and by breaking with the foreign policy smelling strongly of oil conducted since 1967, François Mitterrand considers that he can proclaim the right of the Palestinian people to have a state without Israel feeling betrayed. Because he has accepted the Camp David agreement, he considers that he can seek with Egypt, ways of rescuing the negotiations over Lebanon from deadlock with a formula which permits the disengagement of forces while avoiding the crushing of the PLO.[20]

In many respects, such an independent and important role for France is in keeping with de Gaulle's aspirations since 1967. Because of its influence and credibility, France would play a significant role in international diplomacy apart from that played by the superpowers, and thus constitute an effective third force in international affairs. However, these lofty ideals are frequently compromised by practical realities, often owing to weaknesses in the French economy and declining political support at home. Just as de Gaulle's vision was clouded by economic difficulties and declining domestic support in the late 1960s, so Mitterrand's strategy confronts similar troubles in the mid-1980s.[21] And the economic links that France has forged with the Arabs since the late 1960s may be the undoing of an even-handed policy.

Not only do the French continue to rely heavily on the Arabs for imported oil, but Middle East markets have become crucial for French exports. In addition to the value of civilian technology sales, which we discuss in the next section, Middle East countries have become vital markets for the sale of French arms abroad.[22] The rapid growth of arms sales to the Middle East can again be traced to de Gaulle's policy, following the conclusion of the Algerian war, aimed at improving relations with Arab states and diversifying sources of oil. The Defense Ministry's Direction Ministerielle à la Armement (DMA) has overseen the manufacture and sale of French arms since 1945, has been assisted by the formation in 1965 of the Direction des Affaires Internationales (DAI), which promotes sales and handles relations with foreign clients. French arms exports increased tenfold from ff2.4 billion in 1970 of ff24 billion in 1980, representing an increase from 2.5 to 5 percent of total French trade and making France the second leading exporter of arms to the region behind the United States. Between 1963 and 1973, 18 percent of French arms exports went to the Arab world; by 1981 that figure had grown to 72 percent. Between 1974 and 1980 sales to the Middle East and North Africa quadrupled. It was also apparent that arms sales were a key means of ensuring French oil supplies. As Saudi Arabia and Iraq replaced Algeria as the major suppliers of oil to France in the late 1970s, they also became among the most prominent purchasers of arms. Between 1978 and 1980,

Saudi Arabian orders alone constituted 20 percent of all French arms exports.

The booming arms trade is an undeniable asset to the struggling French economy.[23] The arms industry employs 300,000 French workers, 130,000 of whom are state employees and one-third of whom work to fill export orders. Besides its obvious economic benefits, the revenues from trade help to underwrite the research and development costs required for the modernization and improvement of France's own military forces. It is not surprising, then, that the Socialist government, like that preceding it, has been supportive of the arms industry.

Nevertheless, the rush to sell arms is not easily made compatible with a Middle East political strategy that gives considerable weight to moral principles. Indeed, the arms race in the region, pushed along by the aggressive salesmen in France and elsewhere, may regularly encourage nations in conflict to resort to force in an effort to resolve their disputes, rather than considering any peaceful initiatives advanced by outside powers like France. For de Gaulle, it is probably fair to say that political objectives in the Middle East and the third world ranked highest, while accompanying economic ties were seen as useful instruments in the service of those political ends. However, in the last two decades, France's economic interests in the region have grown immeasurably, and politics and diplomacy more often serve to advance those interests than the other way around. In his claim for a greater political role for France in the Middle East, Mitterrand harkens back to the early Gaullist era. But there is a certain hollowness in his rhetoric (as there was also with de Gaulle) when it is put face to face with vital French economic interests in the region. Smouts sympathetically refers to this dilemma as the difficulty of "reconciling the idea of justice with the exigencies of the balance of payments."[24]

TRADE AND INVESTMENT POLICY

The French strategy for promoting technology trade to the Middle East derives from a legacy of government–industry relations quite different from that in Britain. The patterns of nineteenth century modernization and industrialization in France and the accompanying historical evolution of the French state combined to produce a government role in post–World War II reconstruction and recovery that was both deeper and more direct than in Britain.[25] For reasons that have been explored and rank-ordered by many, the nineteenth century French economy never achieved the levels of growth or dynamism of the economies in Britain and Germany.[26] Rather than generating a vigorous and competitive private sector committed to the principles of liberalism, the French economy came to be dominated by small and inefficient family-owned firms, many of which had strong ties to the government. Seldom competitive with their international rivals, such firms argued not for a government commitment to free trade but for high tariffs and a focus on the much more limited domestic market. In other words, a strong commitment to liberal principles and heavy reliance on the initiatives in the private sector never developed in France. As the modern administrative state came to dominate French politics, it was the government, not the private sector, that was viewed as the appropriate instrument to fix what ailed the national economy.

The *dirigism,* or direction by the state, grew most rapidly after World War II, but it drew upon an administrative apparatus and societally accepted views about the role of the state that extended back to the *ancien regime.* However, one must be careful not to overstate the government's role in the economy, for it takes varied turns that are often misinterpreted by foreigners. In the words of John Zysman:

> Clearly, the French state, even in its most *dirigist* guise, is certainly not omnipotent in the economy nor does it even attempt interventionist strategies in all sectors. Yet equally important, the French do not see a sharp and clear-cut choice between state control or direction and a free market, a dichotomy that often creeps into British debate. For the French, there are three decisions, not two. The state can do (faire), incite others to do (faire faire), or simply leave be (laissez faire). Leaving things to private "forces," moreover, does not necessarily mean allowing free competition. It may imply, on the contrary, allowing *private* actors to negotiate market arrangements. This anti-market tradition runs deep in France, despite liberal protestations.[27]

The impetus for major change came after World War II. The process of decolonization brought to an end the guaranteed sources of cheap raw materials and the ready markets for French goods. Like the British, leaders in Paris saw trade with the empire decline over time as trade with industrialized countries filled the gap. Both participation in the General Agreement on Tariffs and Trade, which fostered free trade, and membership in the European Economic Community, committed to the formation of a common market, made it mandatory that French industries become competitive with their industrial rivals. To achieve the necessary modernization, which in retrospect some have called an economic miracle, Paris embraced "indicative planning," a government-led exercise designed to identify targets of economic attention for five-year periods.[28] Unlike the Soviet model, indicative planning is flexible and adaptable, offering guidelines for action and government assistance. In some areas the government became a very active participant, nationalizing some industries altogether, encouraging rationalization and mergers in others, and weaning firms from elaborate protectionist arrangements and exposing them to global competition.[29] The French state took charge of economic affairs, in these and other activities, establishing new ventures and making the hard decisions to close down others, rather than merely providing undirected assistance to the private sector, as in Britain. As the French state has incrementally nationalized more and more economic sectors (the last major nationalizations followed the election of the Socialist government in 1981), the distinction between public and private has been increasingly blurred. In the realm of high technology, virtually all of the key French firms are wholly state owned or operate with government as a major partner (nuclear power, telecommunications, aerospace, chemicals, consulting engineers). Moreover, the state underwrites much of the research and development in France, with careful attention paid to the commercial applications of ongoing research. Charles Kindleberger argues that it is this new concern for innovation and technological change that has given the French economy its postwar dynamism.[30] The importance of this link between technology and the economy was indicated by the Mitterrand government's decision to merge the Ministry of Research and Technology with the Ministry of Industry to form the Ministry of Research and Industry, and to give the new department considerable influence in the French Cabinet.

The close relations between government and industry are further cemented by the French educational system and the elite recruitment that follows from it.[31] A large number of business and bureaucratic elites are products of a small number of highly competitive government schools. Such officials and businessmen regularly speak of a relatively small network of individuals who come to know each other well at the same schools and develop good working relationships, whether in the public or private sector.

This postwar modernization with the active participation of the state brought about economic changes never before experienced in France.[32] That such economic strength was indispensable to the restoration of France as a country of rank was fully appreciated by de Gaulle: "Politics and economics are tied one to the other as action is to life."[33] The ability to negotiate effectively in the Middle East for supplies of oil or to exercise political influence required French economic muscle, often associated with highly sought-after technological goods and services. This prominent role played by the state in the French economy and the close links to French political objectives have important implications for policies directed to technology trade and transfer in the Middle East. Whereas in Britain the role of government continues to be secondary to the initiatives of the private sector, in France credit or blame in technology trade rests more directly with the state. While the French have no explicit or written policy regarding technology transfer generally or toward the Middle East in particular, the implicit policy is to encourage technology exports with a minimum of restrictions, and the French government takes an active role in the promotion of such trade.[34] Paris maintains a list of restricted exports that conforms with the NATO Coordinating Committee's (COCOM) list, but the French have generally sought a narrower definition of sensitive exports within the NATO group than either the United States or Britain. Moreover, the importance of French arms exports as well as the sale of nuclear power facilities abroad help to explain the French desire to avoid an unnecessarily restrictive policy regarding sensitive exports. French nuclear exports have drawn attention from other Western countries, most notably the United States, but Paris officials insist that all necessary safeguards are observed.[35]

The government's efforts to promote technology trade and investment in the Middle East have resulted in gains that follow the shifting patterns of French oil imports. French exports to all OPEC countries increased from $2.8 billion to $9.4 billion between 1974 and 1980, while imports grew from $9.9 billion to $24.5 billion. Both trailed off somewhat over the next four years, but imports fell far more rapidly, totaling $11.5 billion in 1984, compared to $8.7 billion in exports. France continues to import 70 percent of its energy needs from the Middle East, but some headway has been made in covering imports with increased exports. Further, there has been a growing eastward tilt in French oil dependence, with Saudi Arabia and Iraq combining for 51 percent of all French oil imports in 1981.

Unlike the British, who have concentrated on traditional markets in the eastern Mediterranean and the Gulf and have made little progress in French-speaking North Africa, the French have seen exports grow moderately in Algeria from $1.3 billion to $2.7 billion between 1974 and 1984, while witnessing rapid growth to the east during the same years. Exports grew from $215 million to $1.5 billion in Iraq (1982), from $120 million to $2.3 billion in Saudi Arabia, and from $258 million to $881 million in 1978 in Iran, although this dropped sharply with the outbreak of the Iran–Iraq War. The French have also been active in the Egyptian market following Sadat's declaration of an open-door policy, increasing their exports from $347 million to $1.3 billion in 1980 and $1 billion in 1984. French foreign investment in the OPEC countries also showed a steady rise in the mid-1970s before a freeze on new French deals imposed by Algeria toward the end of the decade.[36] The value of such investment flows grew from ff203 million or 4.8 percent of all French foreign investments in 1973 to ff1.3 billion or 16.6 percent of all investments in 1976.

The significant downturn in 1977 and 1978 resulted from a marked drop in petroleum and natural gas investments, many of which would likely have gone to Algeria. While foreign direct investment in OPEC countries still constitutes a relatively small proportion of overall foreign investment flows, the levels reached in 1976 actually exceeded by a small amount those flows to the United States.

The strengths and weaknesses of French technology trade appear to be the mirror image of the British. Where Britain does a booming business in consulting services and boosts national exports through subcontracting and the supply of specialized technology needs, the French have scored their biggest successes in large contracts, particularly those aimed at infrastructural or public works projects. Where the British strategy has failed to secure many large projects, the French have scored more modest gains in consulting services, in the export of industrial capital and equipment, and in supplying more specialized technologies from smaller French firms.

French consultants, particularly consulting engineers, have undertaken a growing volume of business abroad over the past decade, much of it in the Middle East. There are over 900 firms of consulting engineers in France, and their work abroad is frequently credited with steering clients to French suppliers of capital equipment and industrial plants. One government publication estimated that 44 percent of all exports of capital equipment in 1977 resulted from the initial work of consulting engineers, a figure up from 8 percent in 1971.[37] Consulting engineers also often pave the way for the signing of large public works projects.

Another spur to the growth of French consultancies is the business stimulated by the extensive program of technical assistance underwritten by the government and discussed more fully later in this chapter. Both the French and German governments have calculated that by putting engineers, technicians, and managers in contact with their counterparts in the importing countries, the result will be close personal relations that will encourage the recipient country to call for similar assistance over time.

However, in France, unlike in Britain, many of the consulting services are viewed as part of the government strategy to win business for French firms (indeed, one of the largest firms of consulting engineers, Technip, is partly state owned). In other words, such firms are expected to direct clients to French suppliers. Where importing countries are disposed to do business with the French, this situation may be attractive, but in a highly competitive market like the Middle East, such advocacy by consultants may impede the client's search for independent advice useful in the purchase of the most appropriate technology on the best terms. As noted in the previous chapter, this insistence on a posture of independence has been what has made consultants in Britain both attractive to foreigners and caused them to be resented by some of their own national suppliers. Language presents another difficulty for French consultants.[38] Ease of communication is particularly important in the planning and design phase of technology transfer, and use of English in most parts of the Middle East puts the French at a disadvantage. There are few language problems in the Maghreb countries, but consultants encounter greater difficulties in their attempts to penetrate other regions. The effort undertaken by the government to teach French abroad is one limited way to address the problem.

In sum, consulting services, which have proven in some instances to be an important vehicle to larger French capital exports, are likely to be limited in their appeal and are unlikely to be a major source of technology trade revenue in the foreseeable future.

The prominent role played by the state in the French economy is a particular help in the negotiation of and bidding for large contracts. Unlike in Britain, where the state depends on private firms to put together an offer (and most of them fail to do so), the government often takes the initiative in France, nominating a large firm to take the lead, bringing in smaller French firms as subcontractors and suppliers, arranging the financing and insurance, and even paving the way with some diplomatic overture to the host government. The close links between business and government elites and the fact that many of the large high-technology firms are state owned makes cooperation and coordination that much easier. The French have been particularly successful in landing large public works projects—nuclear power facilities, airports, dams, harbors, subway systems, telecommunications networks, roads, and hospitals. The construction of many of these projects has been undertaken repeatedly by the French state at home, and importing nations have an opportunity to see such systems in operation. The efficient Paris Metro was a model that the Egyptian government was persuaded that France could reproduce in Cairo. The Egyptians, too, were impressed with the operation of French domestic nuclear power plants and specified Electricité de France, the state-owned firm that manages operations of nuclear power installations at home, to be the lead firm in construction of two new facilities in Egypt. The Egyptians have also contracted with the French to develop a port at Darmietta and to modernize the Cairo airport. The French have undertaken a number of new large projects in Iraq and Saudi Arabia for road construction, desalination plants, and airports, although the continuing war with Iran has already limited Iraq's ability to sustain this pace of development. Algeria, Tunisia, and Libya have contracted for extensive telecommunications facilities.

The influence of the state is indicated in part by the dominant role played by a small group of large firms, most of which are state owned or partially state owned: Framatome in nuclear power exports; Thomson-CSF in broadcasting, civil aviation and telecommunications; CIT-Alcatel in telecommunications; Creusot-Loire in heavy engineering; Aerospatiale in military and civilian aircraft; Cogelex and Merlin Gerin in electrical power equipment; and Bouygues in housing and hospital construction. Industry leaders work closely with the same government officials time and again to nail down lucrative contracts.[39]

Some of these same firms have also been successful in securing contracts for turnkey transfers of industrial plants and equipment. Creusot-Loire has been active in the construction of chemical and petroleum plants, and Technip has been a successful vendor of oil refineries and related equipment. The Airbus, a civilian aircraft produced as a joint venture among the British, French, and German governments, has also sold well in Middle East markets. French firms have certainly been less successful than their German and Japanese competitors, but some have done a brisk business in capital goods exports.

While the big-contract business has been good to French firms, they have been less successful as suppliers of specialized and small-scale technologies, the kinds that are often provided by small and medium-sized firms. It is noteworthy that with all the success with large contracts, total French exports to the Middle East have fallen behind the British and were well back of the Germans, the Japanese, and the Americans. Even in Algeria, French traders have been surpassed by the Germans, the Americans, and the Japanese. As the British have realized, to be a factor in this smaller-scale and more specialized technology trade, one needs highly innovative and adaptable firms that can respond to the requests of buyers who have more particular needs. Such firms must eagerly search out such importers or rely on institutions and agencies who put buyers and sellers together, a function performed by private or quasi-public trade associations in Britain or Japan. With a state focused on the large contracts and a private sector more accustomed to following the state lead than initiating new trade of its own, it is not surprising that French performance in the last stages of the technology transfer process has been weaker. It is at this point in the process that a vigorously competitive domestic private sector is likely to be a great asset in the highly competitive market of the Middle East. The French private sector has never had such vigor.

In summary, the extensive state involvement in technology transfer in France has produced a particularly strong performance record in the second and third parts of the transfer process, where competing for and winning large contracts is vital. State assistance and coordination have proven extremely valuable in organizing a large number of economic actors and piecing together attractive packages. French fortunes in the consulting business have been more modest. Where French consultants have been employed they have often produced additional work for exporters of capital equipment, but their preference for French suppliers leads some to question the independence of this advice. The weakest performance has been in winning markets as suppliers of more specialized technology, where an active and vital private sector is likely to be indispensable.

Understanding the strategy of technology transfer in France requires first and foremost an appreciation of the activities undertaken by the state. In France, as discussed above, diplomacy generally precedes and is closely linked to economic policy. This has certainly been the pattern in the Middle East. Beginning with de Gaulle, the French have sought to carve out close political ties with all Arab states in anticipation of expanded economic relations. Where diplomacy has been successful, the economic harvest has been bountiful, as shown in Iraq, Egypt, and Saudi Arabia. Where political relations have soured, as they have from time to time in Algeria, a decline in economic fortunes has also quickly followed. Therefore, in France, the political activities of the Ministry of Foreign Affairs and even of the president define the setting for the transfer strategy more so than any other country we are examining.

French responsibility for the promotion of external trade and investment rests with the Ministry of Economic Affairs and Finance. Within this ministry, the Directorate of External Economic Relations (DREE; Direction des Relations Economiques Exterieures), which is headed by the Minister of Foreign Trade (Commerce Exterieur), is chiefly responsible for trade promotion.[40] The DREE is assisted in its work by the French Center of Foreign Trade (CFCE; Centre Français du Commerce Exterieur), a well-staffed agency that gathers data at home and abroad and publishes information useful to French exporters. Its weekly publication, Le Moci (Moniteur du Commerce Internationale), provides both regional and sectoral analyses of export markets.[41] CFCE has personnel located within France and abroad who gather data for French industry.

Policy designed by the Secretary of Foreign Trade and the DREE must conform in the first instance with the priorities and objectives of the French plan. In other words, exports are not promoted randomly, but certain sectors are targeted for attention, sectors that are likely to receive special policy attention at home. For example, the drive to modernize and expand the French telecommunications system in the 1970s has been paralleled by an export drive to sell the new system abroad.[42] Similarly, the decision to expand the use of nuclear power at home and the commitment of resources to develop a viable nuclear industry have been accompanied by efforts to export these facilities. And while the Mitterrand government has decided to slow the construction of new power plants at home, the president has not hesitated to act as a salesperson for the nuclear industry in developing countries.

The DREE is organized to provide a wide range of services. One division coordinates activities with French commercial attachés abroad, and a second supervises regional and sectoral studies and works closely with the CFCE. A third coordinates export credit, insurance, and financial negotiations as well as technical cooperation. Two final divisions focus on bilateral relations and multilateral institutional arrangements. The former has a separate section devoted to Near East and Mediterranean countries.

With the importance given to diplomacy in French trade, the DREE cooperates closely with the Economic and Financial Affairs Directorate of the Ministry of Foreign Affairs, which has a corresponding division devoted to bilateral relations and a section treating North African and Near Eastern countries. The Ministry of Cooperation and its Directorate of Economic Development also play an active role in DREE's program of export promotion, since there is a strong desire to link development aid to future export earnings. Technology trade also benefits from the activities of the Ministry of Research and Industry. Research and development in France is heavily underwritten by the state and carried out in a number of government research institutes. The Centre Nationale de la Recherche Scientifique (CNRS), an organization somewhat similar to the National Science Foundation, determines national research priorities, and specialized organizations such as the Commissariat à l'Energie Atomique (CEA) are linked closely to divisions within the DREE charged with promoting the sales of products that may originate in such research settings. While it is too early to evaluate the effects of the merger of the Research and Technology Ministry with the Ministry of Industry, it is a clear signal that the Socialist government is seeking to improve the links between research activities and industrial development.

In brief, the DREE acts as the central coordinating agency of foreign trade and investment promotion from the development of new technologies to the negotiation of final contracts. Close relations are nurtured with large private and state-owned industries, such that the organizational requirements for putting together a bid on a large contract can be met quickly and efficiently. And while the process probably seldom works as well as the organizational schematics of the French bureaucracy would have us believe, it undoubtedly accounts for some of the success the French have enjoyed in winning large contracts. We should note that good organization and support carry a country only so far in highly competitive markets, and most participants in this process argue that quality products and services are more important, particularly as importing countries become more knowledgeable and sophisticated consumers of technology.

Some aspects of French tax policy are also designed to aid exporters and to foster foreign direct investment.[43] Under safe-haven rules, income earned by French companies abroad is not taxable, nor is 95 percent of dividends received by French firms from foreign subsidiaries. Moreover, foreign losses are deductible from domestic taxes, even though foreign profits are not taxed. French companies are also permitted to establish tax-deductible reserves to cover export credit risks, development and promotional costs, and possible losses. French exporters also benefit from very liberal rules regarding transfer pricing and from tax agreements that some are able to negotiate with the government if they are designed to expand exports.

As one might expect, organizational and promotional activities in the private sector are much less well developed in France. Private trade associations and the French Chambers of Commerce are much smaller and weaker organizations than their counterparts in Britain, Japan, and West Germany. Whether organized by industrial sector or geographical region, these groups are generally understaffed and underfinanced, and carry little weight among the leading firms. In the chemical industry, for example, the weakness of the French Union des Industries Chimiques (UIC) is in stark contrast to the power and influence of the German Verband der Chemischen Industrie (VCI). French trade associations do provide a limited range of commercial services to member firms, but with many leading technology companies under full or partial state control, most look to the DREE and other government promotional institutions for support and guidance. Even most of the trade associations themselves are quick to defer to government authority and expertise on commercial issues.[44]

One notable exception that really proves the rule is the Franco-Arab Chamber of Commerce (FACC), formed by the Arab League to serve the same purposes and provide the same support to members as the Arab-British Chamber of Commerce in London. Like its British counterpart, it has grown rapidly because French firms view membership as a prerequisite for ensuring access to Arab markets, and for Arab countries in turn it has provided better links to information about small and medium-sized firms in France. The FACC undertakes an active program of seminars, conferences, and trade fairs, largely under Arab direction and unlike the level of activities of most French private trade associations.[45]

SUPPORTIVE POLICIES FOR TECHNOLOGY TRANSFER

The dominant role played by the government in advancing the transfer of technology is reaffirmed by the broad range of supportive services in finance, training, and government to government technical assistance. Such policies are designed both to enhance the attractiveness of French bids on large contracts and to acquaint foreign countries with the features of French life and culture. Perhaps more than any other European colonizer, the French leaders believed that the exposure of foreigners to the French way of life would not only be appealing to citizens in other countries, but it would also enhance French fortunes as a global power. As one government report put it:

> The spread of her language, her culture and her ideas, the attraction of her literature, science, technology and art, the merits of her ways of forming men, all these are for France essential means of action in her foreign policy through the influence she exercises because of them. Cultural action is closely linked with political and economic action, both of which it precedes. Cultural action therefore directly contributes to the power of our country in international affairs.[46]

Financing and Insurance

French technology exports are supported by an assortment of government-run insurance and financial services. While the DREE usually takes the central state role in negotiations leading to large export packages, the following financial and insurance institutions are often integrally involved: French commercial banks (most of which are now nationalized), the Banque de France, the Banque Française du Commerce Exterieur (BFCE), and the Compagnie Française d'Assurance pour le Commerce Exterieur (COFACE).[47] The two most important for purposes of technology trade, BFCE and COFACE, were established after World War II and now have almost four decades of experience.

Insurance for exporters is available through COFACE, which was organized as a quasi-public joint stock company.[48] To qualify, goods must have no more than 10 percent foreign content (except components manufactured within the EC, which may have up to 40 percent foreign content or 30 percent from countries with which France has a reciprocal agreement). COFACE insures against natural catastrophes, political risks and risks of nontransfer (where a government blocks or retards payment), commercial risks (insolvencies), inflation risks for contracts of one year or longer, exchange rate fluctuation (above 2.25 percent in certain currencies), and risks related to market development (start-up expenses and development of inventory abroad). Coverage is also available for contracts written in convertible currencies. The rate is 0.36 percent per annum for currencies within the European monetary system and 0.648 percent for others. COFACE offers a wide range of packages to buyers and suppliers, permitting coverage of 85 to 95 percent of contracts. About 27 percent of all French exports are insured, the vast majority of which are exports to developing countries and the Eastern bloc.

For short-term commercial risks (up to 6 months for consumer goods and raw materials and up to 2 years for some heavy capital goods), COFACE is empowered to make its own decisions up to defined amounts. In most other cases, decisions are made by the DREE in consultation with an interministerial committee, the Commission de Garanties et du Credit au Commerce Exterieur, made up of representatives of COFACE, Economic Affairs and Finance, Foreign Affairs, the relevant technical ministry, BFCE, the Banque de France, and the Credit National. Coverage is usually available for up to three years for light capital goods or up to five years in the case of very large contracts in such goods. For heavy capital equipment, the coverage varies by receiving country: 5 years for developed countries, 8.5 years for rapidly growing developing countries, and 10 years for poorer developing countries. These terms are compatible with the OECD agreements and change from time to time. The government's willingness to cover investment risks related to market development is also linked to export promotion, since such investors must demonstrate that investments will expand French exports. To date, this program has remained very small.[49]

Insurance premiums are calculated on a case-by-case basis. Part of the premium is calculated in a straightforward way: 0.25 percent per annum for insurance against political risks to private buyers; 0.50 percent per annum for political and commercial risk insurance if the buyer is a public firm guaranteed by its government or a private buyer approved by COFACE or has secured financing through a COFACE-approved bank; and 0.85 percent per annum for commercial and political risks to an unguaranteed private buyer. The remainder of the premium is determined by inspection of the individual contract. The French government also maintains a foreign investment insurance program as a vehicle for promoting exports, although it is dwarfed by the COFACE export insurance scheme. In order to qualify for investment insurance through COFACE, the investing firms must demonstrate that their projects will result in expanded French exports.

Insurance through COFACE is normally required to qualify for preferential export financing. Credit is available to both buyers and sellers for medium-term (2 to 7 years) and long-term (in excess of 7 years) export transactions, and goes overwhelmingly to support the export of capital goods.[50] The Banque de France and the BFCE coordinate these financing facilities. Commercial banks make available medium-term credits which, in turn, are refinanced by the Banque de France. The blended rate (5.5 percent in February 1981) is fixed by the BFCE, and since the commercial base rate varies over time, the proportion financed by the central bank varies accordingly. Long-term export credits are supported by a direct subsidy from the BFCE. The BFCE also provides for long-term "mixed" financing, which combines normal commercial loans with official development aid. Such packages are generally used to promote the export of capital goods to developing countries. There is no government program to subsidize short-term credits (less than 2 years), and these are generally financed at the "prime rate" (or base lending rate plus 1 percent for bank charges and the costs of insurance through COFACE).

Among a number of foreign competitors, the general perception has been that French financing is of great benefit to French exporters (often with the implication that French official policies give unfair advantage to their own firms). While comparisons are difficult, evidence suggests that this position is probably overstated. First, the French have regularly complied with the OECD consensus on interest rate subsidies and have adjusted their subsidies from time to time to keep them in line with the OECD agreement. Second, a U.S. State Department comparative study of export credit systems in the late 1970s found that only 8–10 percent of all French capital goods exports were financed at below market rates, compared to 6–8 percent in the United States and 15–20 percent in Britain.[51] That same study could detect no positive shifts in market shares for particular categories of French exports directly attributable to financing arrangements. Such changes were much more often tied to the quality or improvement of products and services.

However, the report does suggest that in particular large contract sales in the third world, notably in nuclear power plants, commercial aircraft, and steel-making facilities, the availability of financing may have played a role in winning contracts.[52] Indeed, the French themselves would like to think that such arrangements make a difference, given the attention they direct to "les Grands Contrats."[53] The actual amounts of credit extended have grown rapidly. In 1970, export credits of ff30 billion were made available; that figure reached ff120 billion in 1977, one-half of which went to developing countries.

Perhaps more important than either the precise terms or the amounts extended for both insurance and financing is the ease with which such support is mobilized. The close relations between BFCE, COFACE, the DREE, and the exporting firms permits the easy packaging of export offers, reducing the procedural obstacles for the importing nation. While state bureaucracies can be notoriously slow in handling such matters, the importance attached to "les Grands Contrats" appears to result in efficiency among French civil servants on these matters.

Training, Technical Assistance, and Foreign Aid

In the case of France, where training is viewed as an integral part of the government's policy of technical assistance and foreign aid, it makes sense to discuss the two together. Following from the notion that French cultural expansion is a useful vehicle of political influence, French foreign aid programs have long underwritten the costs of bringing in third world students to be educated in French universities and financed teaching the French language abroad. Scholarships awarded to foreign students numbered 600 in 1946 and approached 16,000 in the late 1960s. Some 108,000 foreign students were in French universities in 1981. Since 1920, the Service des Oeuvres has coordinated the teaching of French overseas, and its work greatly expanded after World War II. The number of French teachers abroad tripled in the 1960s, reaching almost 34,000 by the end of the decade and raising questions about the wisdom of focusing so much attention on foreign education at the expense of French students at home. The export of teachers was complemented by a steady flow of other cultural materials underwritten by the cultural fund of the Ministry of Foreign Affairs.

Technical assistance has also been an integral part of French foreign aid programs since World War II. Like cultural assistance, technical aid has always been closely tied to French political objectives. In the early postwar period, foreign aid was directed at countries under French rule or formerly under French rule as part of the strategy of creating an integrated French Union. After 1966, both the levels of aid and the number of recipients increased as de Gaulle attempted to expand French influence in the third world generally. During this time, the French devoted a larger percentage of gross national income to foreign assistance than any other country. In 1962, 2.5 percent of GNP was allocated, declining to 1.6 percent in 1967. Between 1970 and 1977 the absolute amount of French aid more than doubled; only the United States, with a much larger GNP, gave more. The French aid percentage of GNP dropped to 0.6, but it was still considerably larger than the British (0.38), the West Germans (0.31), the Japanese (0.25), and the Americans (0.22).[54]

The French also allocate more of this aid to technical assistance than any other country. Of the total technical personnel abroad, the French generally send one-third to one-half of the total, more than twice the number sent by the Americans. While educational programs use a significant proportion of these personnel, scientists, engineers, and technicians are also well represented. Much of this aid since 1962 has gone to former French colonies, with Algeria, Tunisia, and Morocco receiving the largest share in the Arab world. Algeria, in particular, has benefited from continuing French assistance. While France does contribute through multinational initiatives, most of the aid is distributed through bilateral channels, underlining the accompanying political objectives that Paris seeks to realize.

Technical assistance is also viewed as a way of creating future French export opportunities. The French, like the Germans, appear quite prepared to underwrite a long-term strategy. Typically, the French have entered into technical cooperation agreements of the sort pursued after the 1973–1974 oil crisis, through which technical assistance was swapped for assurances of oil supplies. Joint technical and commercial commissions are frequently established to facilitate such exchanges, and the French now have such arrangements with Iraq, Saudi Arabia, and Egypt, in addition to its former colonies in North Africa. An agreement of this sort was reached after long negotiations with Algeria in February 1982 in which the French contracted for Algerian gas (at 13.5 percent above the world market rate) in exchange for technical assistance. While the French admitted that they paid a high price for the improvement of political relations, they also signed a charter of economic cooperation in June 1982 that they hoped would open new opportunities to French exporters.[55]

The French program of nuclear power exports involves similar long-term commitments.[56] Typically, French scientists and technicians must first train local personnel in nuclear engineering and associated technologies. A small research reactor is then imported to provide hands-on experience before the large power plant is constructed. The acquisition of the necessary and accompanying capital equipment normally takes about ten years.

This pattern of cooperation in education, research activities, and eventual capital goods imports has been repeated in agriculture and a number of other industrial sectors. In infrastructural projects and contracts, the French have been especially attentive to Arab requests for more training and managerial assistance. Through the package to build the Cairo subway, for example, 300 Egyptian technicians were brought to Paris to get training assistance on the Paris Metro.[57] Similar training provisions are available in telecommunications, aviation, and electricity generation. Unlike in Britain, most of these provisions are negotiated with the participation of the government, although the actual training may be undertaken by private firms.

The Mitterrand government has indicated a strong commitment to improving French political and economic relations with the third world generally and with the Middle East in particular. The 1982 gas agreement with Algeria is often cited as proof of that determination. Yet, technical assistance that would eventually facilitate the growth in Arab countries of new industries whose exports would compete in French markets increases anxieties in a struggling French economy. Already the French have resorted to some protectionist measures against third world exports, drawing strong criticism from abroad. One cannot expect to find willing buyers of French goods in the Middle East if one is unwilling to purchase anything but Arab oil in return. The strength of the French commitment to foreign assistance and commercial exchange in the Middle East is likely to be measured, at least in part, by the strength of the French domestic economy.[58] The slow recovery of the French economy from global recession in the early 1980s has given rise to calls for protectionist relief and has directed the French government's primary efforts to resolving the economic crisis at home. With ample supplies and falling prices of petroleum, the economic bond between France and the Arab world is likely to weaken.

THE FRENCH STRATEGY ASSESSED

The French strategy for promoting technology trade and transfer to the Middle East provides a striking contrast to that pursued in Britain. While both played active political and economic roles in the region prior to World War II, the British have engaged in a steady official withdrawal, both politically and economically, while encouraging an active commercial relationship at the private level. The French, on the other hand, have attempted to maintain an active political and economic presence following the conclusion of the colonial wars in the early 1960s. In part, this divergence in official policy follows from different concepts of national interest, national roles in global politics, and relations with the United States. For Britain, the Middle East was a region from which it could withdraw gracefully, knowing that its interests were represented by the United States. For France, the Middle East provided an opportunity to exert its independence from the United States as part of its overall effort to regain its "rightful" place as a global power. In part, the British-French divergence follows from changing patterns of dependence on Middle East oil, growing British self-sufficiency, and continuing high levels of French imports. And finally, this divergence is encouraged by very different roles assigned to the state in the process of technology transfer.

As we have argued throughout this chapter, the heavy involvement of the French state in technology transfer grows logically from the state's participation in the domestic economy, and has been very helpful in "packaging" competitive bids and winning large contracts. The French have been most successful in arranging public works and infrastructural deals that draw on experience and know-how gathered at home, although they have also won their share of projects calling for industrial plants and capital equipment. From the highest political circles, the government has been attentive to the cultivation of strong political ties and the extension of foreign aid and technical assistance as necessary contributions to commercial discussion. State promotional institutions have also seen to it that the proper large firms are involved in early negotiations, that financing and insurance arrangements are in order, and that appropriate additional actors can be called on to meet the growing list of services required by most large management contracts. Superior coordination and organization may account for French successes at least as often as the superiority of French technology. Indeed, as in the case of the 1982 Algerian gas deal, when the French agreed to a price well above the market price, some argued that French political objectives outweighed the economic merits of landing some of these contracts. In other words, the French might, in some cases, win the contract but lose money in the process. The heavy political involvement of the state may be both an asset and a drawback in the transfer strategy. In cases where political objectives in foreign policy inform state behavior in commercial affairs, the French government's actions ironically resemble strategies frequently practiced in Washington.

We have also argued that the French approach has been less successful in the early and final phases of the transfer process, which are more conducive to private-sector initiative. French designers, engineers, and managers undoubtedly lose business from potential clients who view the close links between the private sector and the state in France as detrimental to the generation of rigorously independent advice. Similarly, small and medium-sized French firms, more accustomed to following the lead of the state rather than striking out on their own, are not likely to be well positioned to take advantage of the more specialized technology trade that results once large-scale projects are in place. French policies of long-term technical assistance may compensate somewhat for the lack of aggressiveness in the private sector, but where price and product quality are factors crucial in closing a deal, French firms are likely to have trouble meeting the terms of their industrial rivals. We are not suggesting that state-led initiatives cannot result in a vigorous and competitive private sector (for evidence would indicate otherwise in Japan), but rather that the particular form of state leadership in France has resulted in a less assertive group of private firms.

In sum, the French strategy grows logically from the country's political objectives in the Middle East and its patterns of economic organization and industrial development at home. Its strengths complement rather than compete directly with those of the British approach. Yet, over the years the French advantages may be more limited by time and circumstance. The French strategy is aimed at the era of the big project, a phase of economic development that has occupied Middle East nations over the past decade, but one that is already less dominant in development plans as large projects are completed and because the abundant flow of capital has been slowed by the glut in oil markets. This is not to imply that there is not a strong demand for such projects elsewhere in the third world, but debt problems and capital shortages in non-oil-producing developing countries are likely to limit severely the number of projects put out for bid.

5

WEST GERMANY: TECHNOLOGY, INDUSTRIAL DEVELOPMENT, AND THE DENIAL OF POLITICS

HISTORICAL CONTEXT

Germany does not share with France and Britain a long and intense history of political relations in the Middle East. As neither a Mediterranean power nor an early imperialist nation with global interests to protect, Germany had little interest in the Arab world until the late nineteenth century.[1] At that time, economic interests in Bismarck's Germany became increasingly active in the crumbling Ottoman Empire. German banks and businesses initially exported capital to Turkey, and the construction of German railways in the region soon extended interests to the Gulf. In 1899 the Germans won a concession to build the so-called Baghdad Railway, designed to connect Hamburg and Berlin with Baghdad and the Persian Gulf. This commercial artery was expanded to bring valuable raw materials to fuel German industrialization. Initially, Britain welcomed German interest in the region as a counter to Russian designs. But as Anglo-German rivalries grew prior to World War I, Berlin's involvement became a source of British uneasiness.

Germany's defeat in World War I, the collapse of the Ottoman empire, and the French and British agreement to share control in the Middle East resulted in a rapid decline of German interest and influence. The Weimar government directed most of its attention to Europe and to coping with the strictures of the Treaty of Versailles. German trade to the Middle East dropped sharply and remained low through the 1930s. The Nazi government did make some effort to align itself with those Arab nationalist sentiments directed against Britain and France, but the simultaneous opposition of those countries to German penetration limited what could be accomplished. While the Middle East was never central to Hitler's imperial designs, there was a growing German interest in Arab culture and societies in the 1930s.[2] Contacts were promoted by the German-Orient Society, which was the forerunner of the Nah und Mittlost Verein (Near and Middle East Association; discussed below). German banks and industrial firms also continued to show interest in expanded economic relations, but political constraints limited commercial and financial exchange.[3]

The Federal Republic of Germany was constructed after World War II with a moral debt and political commitment to the state of Israel that has limited and complicated its relations with the Arab world in the last four decades. Bonn has consistently defended Israel's right to exist and has encouraged the growth of political ties and economic relations between the two countries. As was the case after World War I, West Germany focused most of its attention in the early postwar years on problems at home—political and economic recovery, security issues, and relations with East Germany—leading some to complain that it had no Middle East policy at all.[4] The goal of reunification, which was pursued by attempting to limit East German contacts outside the Soviet bloc, required that Bonn enforce the so-called Hallstein Doctrine, under which the Federal Republic refused to engage in relations with any country that recognized East Germany. Roger Morgan argues that much of German diplomatic activity with Arab states in the 1950s and 1960s was informed by the Hallstein Doctrine, limiting the attention given to other political issues or to North–South relations in general.[5]

The promotion of economic contacts divorced from political affairs in the Middle East made particular sense for the West Germans, to the extent that it was possible. The conversion in Germany, as in the rest of the industrialized world, from a coal to an oil-based national economy in the 1950s and 1960s and the need to import virtually all of its petroleum needs, resulted in a growing dependence on the Middle East. The requirement that imports be financed by a steady increase in German exports, combined with the growing Arab interest in capital equipment and industrial technology, expanded the opportunities for economic relations. From the early 1950s, German politicians, particularly those representing the liberal business interests in the Free Democratic Party (FDP), cultivated ties with the Arab world that offered the promise of economic benefits.[6]

The advancement of economic interests in the Arab world required a delicate balance between political realities and Bonn's obligations to Israel.[7]German–Israeli relations were closest in the 1950s and 1960s, when memories of the Holocaust were most vivid, the forces of Arab nationalism were strongest, and the ability of the new Israeli state to defend itself against Arab threats was open to question. When the Federal

Republic established formal deplomatic relations with Israel in 1965, ten Arab states severed such relations with Germany. It was not until 1974, following extensive negotiations by the Brandt government and increased allocations of development aid, that they were reestablished.

The 1967 war prompted a discernable shift in Bonn's Middle East policy, although it was not nearly so marked as de Gaulle's decision in the same year to carve out a pro-Arab position. Since that time, German leaders have sought to achieve greater balance in their political relations between Israel and the Arabs, which is predictably viewed in Tel Aviv as an increasingly pro-Arab position. The Federal Republic has supported UN Resolution 242 calling for Israeli withdrawal from occupied territories, and has indicated its support for including the PLO in any negotiated settlement. During the 1973 war, Bonn refused to permit the United States to ship arms through West Germany to Israel. When OPEC announced the terms of the 1973 oil embargo, Germany was treated better than the United States, Japan, and the Netherlands, although less favorably than France and Britain.

Yet the ties to Israel are strong, and one must be careful not to overstate the tilt toward the Arabs. Through the 1960s and 1970s, Bonn held firm to its decision not to sell arms to Israel's Arab neighbors, thereby foregoing the lucrative market that was so profitable to other industrial powers. Growing pressure from German businesspeople and Arab customers put that policy in jeopardy in the early 1980s. Saudi Arabia has repeatedly sought to buy Leopard 2 tanks from Bonn, and German refusal has certainly not aided the prospects for German-Saudi trade in other areas.[8] While reiterating the country's refusal to supply offensive battle tanks in early 1984, Helmut Kohl announced a plan to sell Gepard anti-aircraft tanks and Marder personnel carriers to the Saudis.[9] In the face of strong Israeli objections, he argued that the weapons were for defensive purposes and were sold to a country that would not threaten Israel.[10] Whether this represents a concession to troubles in the German economy and a deeper shift in German–Middle Eastern relations remains to be seen.

As on other issues in foreign affairs, the Germans would like to downplay their political involvement in the Arab–Israel dispute, assume a position of political neutrality, and focus on their economic interests, which they view as of greater importance. This desire to separate diplomacy from commercial relations, a strategy quite different from that of the French and similar to that of the Japanese, makes good sense for the Germans but is less acceptable to the Middle East antagonists. Israel views unbridled economic relations between Germany and the Arabs as inevitably diminishing the former's commitment to the Jewish state. The Arabs, in turn, are eager to exploit growing economic ties with the West

Germans to gain support for Arab interests in a Mideast settlement. In other words, economic ties tend to spill over into political relations. Neither side wishes to permit Bonn the luxury of even-handedness for fear of giving advantage to the other. Nevertheless, greater West German political involvement in the Middle East is almost inevitable, given the evolution of its economic involvement, just as German economic might brought with it growing political influence in the European Community and the Atlantic Alliance.[11]

Efforts to expand economic relations with the region began in earnest in the 1960s. The Germans and Egyptians concluded an economic agreement in 1963 that funneled DM198 million in aid to Cairo as a vehicle for trade expansion. Trade continued to grow in the mid-1960s, even after the Arab states cut diplomatic relations in 1965. As Lily Feldman argues, West Germany was able to sustain reasonably intense commercial relations without formal diplomacy.[12]

Oil was the primary reason for Bonn's growing economic interest in the Arab world. By 1969, Germany depended on oil for 51 percent of its energy needs; 92 percent of this had to be imported; 89 percent of those imports came from the Middle East. The growing importance of Arab oil was also undoubtedly a major reason for efforts by the Brandt government to negotiate the reestablishment of diplomatic relations in the early 1970s. But the Arabs sought political objectives in these negotiations, most notably the call for Israeli withdrawal from occupied territories, which Bonn eventually accommodated. Germany's reluctance to help Israel during the 1973 war also appeared to be motivated by concern for petroleum supplies. The favorable treatment Germany received during the embargo could be interpreted as a reward for this political stance.

German dependence on Middle East oil continued through the 1970s and shows little likelihood of diminishing appreciably in the 1980s. Moreover, the increased revenues generated by higher oil prices has turned the Middle East into a vital market for German exports. Arab purchases comprised 3 percent of German exports in 1973, doubling to 6 percent by the end of the decade. For a country where exports constitute 30 percent of GNP and recession has plagued the economies of its traditional export markets for over a decade, the opportunities in Arab markets cannot be taken lightly. While German leaders continue to affirm their support for Israel, scholars such as Udo Steinbach see German foreign policy as increasingly caught between the constraints of moral obligation and the growing demands of *realpolitik*.[13] German diplomacy over the last decade has focused increasing attention on Arab states, with diplomatic visits and commercial missions scheduled routinely. Economic interdependence has steadily given rise to closer political ties.

In summary, German foreign policies toward the Arab world provide an interesting contrast to the policies of Britain and France. Britain began the postwar period with extensive political and economic commitments in the region, but has steadily reduced its involvement as it adjusted to the rank of middle power and began to draw on its supply of oil in the North Sea. Like Britain, France played an active role in the political and economic affairs of the Middle East after World War II, only to see its influence undermined by the forces of Arab nationalism. However, de Gaulle adopted a new strategy to reassert French political influence in the Mediterranean, which is limited by continuing French dependence on Arab oil and only modest success in exporting to Middle East markets. West Germany entered the Middle East with few political objectives other than those imposed on them by the postwar settlement. Germany's principal interests have remained economic, both to ensure access to oil and to sell goods in growing Arab economies. It has sought to pursue these goals in the marketplace and away from diplomatic entanglements. Ironically, economic successes have steadily pushed reluctant German leaders into a more prominent political role, one that may come to be the envy of the French.

For our purposes here, however, the priority assigned to economic relations by German policymakers and the appeal of Germany's industrial strength and technological prowess to the Arab nations suggest ideal conditions under which to promote technology transfer. The determination to divorce politics from economic exchange would seem to offer special advantages in several phases of the transfer process.

TRADE AND INVESTMENT POLICY

West Germany's strategy regarding technology trade and transfer, like those in Britain and France, is shaped in important ways by the history of relations between government and the private sector from the earliest days of the country's industrialization.[14] But unlike Britain and France, which have experienced relative continuity in those relations over the past century, the abrupt changes in government following World War I, during the 1930s, and again after World War II make generalizations about Germany more difficult. Periods of commitment to the principles of economic liberalism have been followed by heavy involvement of the state in industrial development, the most extensive of which was the experiment with National Socialism.

The economic system (*Soziale Marktwirtschaft*) adopted by the Federal Republic in 1949, under the watchful eye of the allied occupiers, was wedded fundamentally to liberal market principles, with periodic interventions permitted by the state as it advanced social welfare objectives.[15] This endorsement of the free play of market forces at home was complemented by a commitment to free trade abroad and a belief that German economic recovery and subsequent growth would be brought about by exports.[16] The success of the German liberal strategy is well known, bringing about not only an "economic miracle" within Germany, but creating a powerful export machine that readily penetrated international markets. Growing affluence, in turn, permitted German leadership on the left and the right to realize more and more of the objectives identified by advocates of the welfare state. And while the federal government has intervened to encourage social welfare programs and to ensure a favorable economic climate to German exporters, economic initiative has remained primarily in the hands of the private sector.

In some respects, the postwar division of Germany enhanced the prospects for industrial recovery and export expansion. As Michael Kreile argues:

> With almost two-thirds of prewar capacity in heavy industry and producer goods industries located in the Western zones, partition reinforced the concentration of basic and capital goods industries. This structure meshed almost perfectly with the postwar patterns of world demand. Reconstruction at home and abroad, the priority accorded to economic growth by the main partner countries and, subsequently, the industrialization drive of Eastern bloc and Third World countries resulted in a booming demand for capital equipment.[17]

The industrial sectors at the heart of this postwar recovery were mechanical engineering, the electrical industry, and chemicals, sectors that had been the backbone of German economic might prior to World War II. Allied plans for German postwar recovery were designed to prevent such industrial concentrations, which had been central to Hitler's war-making capabilities. But the attractions of cartelization and giantism as vehicles to international competitiveness are deeply rooted in German industrial history. Thus, by the 1970s, the German economy was once again dominated by a few industrial firms in each of these sectors. In chemicals, for example, Hoechst, BASF, and Bayer, three of four companies remaining after the allied dismantling of I.G. Farben, produced 85 percent of German chemicals, a concentration level far greater than that in the 1920s and 1930s.[18] Similar concentration and scale in firms producing electrical equipment and heavy machinery soon made German firms internationally competitive in the export of goods indispensable for the launching of any major program of industrialization. Export competitiveness was also enhanced by domestic economic policies designed to prevent the recurrence of inflation that plagued German recovery efforts after World War I. By holding down labor costs, limiting consumption, and undervaluing the German mark, the attractive prices of German goods permitted rapid penetration of foreign markets.

As in the early days of industrialization, the competitiveness of these sectors has been assisted by the close links between corporate leaders and German banks.[19] Unlike Britain, where banks are not permitted to mix deposit-taking and investment functions, German bankers are permitted, even expected, to take equity positions in large corporations. The three largest commercial banks, Dresdner Bank, Commerzbank, and Deutsche Bank, hold more than 25 percent of the stock in 28 of Germany's 100 largest corporations. Moreover, bankers regularly serve on the supervisory boards (*Aufsichtsrat*) of these corporations, participating actively in the firm's strategic planning and investment decisions. More importantly, bankers stand willing and able to provide the necessary financing for promising projects, the success of which will benefit them directly. Cooperation between the corporate and financial sectors of the economy is particularly advantageous in the negotiation of technology sales.

In some respects, British and German patterns of postwar economic organization are similar. Both espouse liberal economic principles at home and abroad, assigning to the private sector the primary role of initiating economic activities and making economic decisions. Both put the state in a secondary and supportive role, one responsible for creating an economic environment conducive to private-sector activities and for redistributing some of the benefits of economic growth through programs of social welfare. Yet, where the British economy was tied to old and declining industries and the trade in services, the German economy was rebuilt on more technologically advanced and innovation-driven industries that proved to be more adaptable and dynamic in the international marketplace. And while both counted heavily on exports for their well-being, British trade in goods and services was directed to familiar but declining former colonial markets, while German exporters were forced to be aggressive and to seek their fortunes in new and growing areas. Finally, the deeper roots of liberalism in Britain insist on a rigid separation between corporate activities and finance. They have conditioned British firms to be uncomfortable with excessive cooperation, and consortia arrangements with other firms can be contrasted with the German acceptance of close ties between banks and corporations and a tradition of greater industrial cooperation among leading firms. The successes enjoyed by the Federal Republic since the end of World War II have given rise to much less pressure for economic experimentation in planning of the sort that has been undertaken in both France and Britain.

West Germany's commitment to economic liberalism advocates the distinction between private and public activities. This complements the country's larger postwar foreign policy strategy, which has been to separate diplomatic affairs from commercial relations with priority given to the latter. Market criteria, not domestic or international politics, are seen as the desirable guides to choices both in the local economy and in foreign trade. However, as we concluded in the previous section, keeping politics out of economic affairs is more difficult as one's international economic influence grows; resisting political pressures may prove equally difficult at home as recession and unemployment replace prosperity and affluence.

While problems may loom on the horizon, the German strategy to downplay politics and diplomacy and to give attention to commercial relations by supporting the initiatives of the private sector have brought handsome returns in trade and investment. As was noted in Chapter 2, exports to OPEC countries increased from $4 billion in 1974 to $12.5 billion in 1980 and $15.7 billion in 1982, while imports grew from $9 billion in 1974 to $20.6 billion in 1980, declining to about one-half that amount in 1984. Exports to OPEC accounted for 4.5 percent of all German exports in 1974, a figure that doubled to 9 percent in 1977 before dropping to 6.5 percent in 1980. Imports dropped steadily from 13.0 percent of total German imports in 1974 to 7.8 percent in 1978, before the second round of oil price increases pushed the figure back to 11 percent in 1980. Most impressive has been the ability of German exporters to expand revenues to cover import costs after each major oil price increase. After absorbing the price increases of 1973–1974, which resulted in a $5 billion trade deficit with OPEC, it took only three years for exporters to increase export sales sufficiently to cover the rise in import costs. The Federal Republic ran export surpluses with OPEC in 1977 and 1978. The second round of price increases in 1979 resulted in deficits to OPEC of $4 billion in 1979 and $8 billion in 1980. By 1981 Germany had achieved a trade surplus with the Middle East and had recorded surpluses in 1982 and 1983 with OPEC as a whole. The predicted stability in oil prices over the next few years should ensure continuing German surpluses, but the decline in OPEC revenues and the Iran–Iraq War are likely to limit the rate of growth of German exports.

Country by country, the Germans exported most to Iran in the years prior to the 1979 revolution, reaching a high of $3.4 billion in 1978 before dropping back to the not inconsiderable sum of $1.6 billion in 1981, and then regaining the $3.0 billion level in 1983. The most rapid growth has come in exports to Saudi Arabia ($3.5 billion in 1982) and Iraq ($3.1 billion in 1982), which follow the distribution of German oil imports. The Germans have also boosted exports to Egypt ($1.1 billion in 1984) and Algeria ($1.4 billion in 1982), indicating an ability to penetrate markets formerly dominated by old colonial powers.

Even though the Germans have no restrictions on outward foreign direct investment, such investment in the Middle East has grown much more slowly than trade for reasons discussed below. While the annual flow of direct investment to the OPEC countries increased from DM675 million in 1970 to DM1.8 billion in 1979, this investment represented a declining share of total German foreign direct investment from 3.7 percent in 1970 to 2.7 percent in 1979. Inward direct investment from OPEC, on the other hand, increased from DM8 million in 1970 to DM6 billion in 1979, the latter figure representing 2.9 percent of all inward investment flows.[20]

This strong export record translates into a pattern of technology trade that is unlike either its British or French competitors. Of the four transfer phases, the weakest German performance has been in planning and consulting services. German consultants enjoy neither the long history of close relations with Arab clients that has been so advantageous to their British counterparts nor the state support and backing enjoyed by French firms such as Technip, Sofrerail, and Sofretes.[21] The Swedish government even underwrites feasibility studies if recipient countries are willing to commit themselves in advance to a Swedish consulting firm. Language is a further problem for German consultants since the facilitation of communication between the contractor and client is central to their role. A common response of German firms in the Middle East has been to hire an English representative to occupy this position, while at the same time insisting on English language training for all of its personnel. German firms have also resisted demands by importing countries for joint ventures with local firms, preferring to limit their commitments to the length of a single project.

In spite of these drawbacks, the consulting business has grown over the past decade. The value of Middle East contracts increased from $223 million in 1974 to $490 million four years later. Continuing expansion is expected through the 1980s. Among the factors accounting for this growth has been the German reputation for punctuality, reliablility, and quality of work. One firm that was successful in the field of telecommunications has been Detecon, which was formed in 1977 by Deutsche Bundespost (the German post office) and three commercial banks. The roots of the enterprise can be traced to the 1950s, when engineers from the Bundespost's telecommunications division were sent abroad to assist with development programs supported by the federal government and the United Nations. Those same specialists are now utilized by Detecon in its work in telecommunications planning all over the world. Detecon was responsible for designing the telecommunications system installed at Saudi Arabia's industrial complex at Yanbu, and the equipment recommended is more sophisticated than any that will be employed in the Federal Republic itself for another ten years. Dorsch Consult is another firm that has been active in the design of highway systems, particularly in Iran. V-Consult, a firm made up of architects, engineers, and scientists, was formed a decade ago to do consulting in the health sector, designing hospitals and medical facilities as well as pharmaceutical plants.

One reliable source of business has involved projects funded by German development aid that specify the retaining of German consultants as a condition for receiving aid. Business is also promoted by a trade association, the Union of Independent Consulting Engineers (VUBI), founded in 1945. This lists about 130 members, two-thirds of which do business in the Middle East. Another organization, German Consult AG, formed in 1970, boasts a membership of 500 small firms and aims to bring these firms into consortia with one another, such that together they are able to bid successfully against their American and British rivals. It succeeded in winning some 30 Middle East contracts by the late 1970s.

German companies have been relatively more successful in securing work on large infrastructural projects, both as lead firms and as subcontractors. Unlike those in Britain, German firms have benefited from their size and international competitiveness, which generate the confidence to bid aggressively for the biggest projects. The German economy's comparative advantage in heavy equipment and machinery as well as an earned reputation for reliablity in engineering are especially attractive to importing countries. Beginning with their involvement in railway construction in the early twentieth century, these firms have acquired considerable Middle East experience in the building of roads, dams, bridges, tunnels, and irrigation canals. But large German construction firms saw their business take off in the 1970s. Firms such as Phillipp Holzmann and Hochtief have devoted more and more attention to Middle East markets as business has slowed at home. The construction industry trade association estimated that member firms secured $3.9 billion in new contracts in 1981, $2.4 billion from Iraq alone. Indeed, recent German success in Iraq is of special interest. Prior to 1979, much of the attention of German contractors was directed to Iran. The uncertainties following the revolution caused attention to be directed to neighboring Iraq, and in only two short years German firms had penetrated this market, yielding handsome returns. Part of their success was attributed to a willingness to stay in the market and meet contractual obligations even as most of their competitors left with the outbreak of the Iran–Iraq War.[22] Insisting that trade and politics should remain separate, German businesspeople have frequently flourished when political entanglements have jeopardized the business of other international firms. This strategy has paid off not only in Iraq, but also in Algeria and in post-1979 Iran.

Siemens is another German firm that has been notably active in infrastructural projects. As a leading manufacturer of telecommunication equipment, it has won contracts throughout the Middle East and recently signed contracts to modernize and expand the Egyptian telecommunications network. A subsidiary of the Siemens group, Hospitalia International, has been a leading builder and supplier of Middle East hospitals and health facilities. It has built over 40 hospitals and 400 clinics in Saudi Arabia and is providing equipment to the King Khaled hospital in Riyadh. Another Siemens subsidiary, the power engineering firm Kraftwerk Union, did considerable work in Iran prior to 1979. Among its contracts was one to build a nuclear power plant, which was cancelled after the fall of the Shah. It has subsequently undertaken the construction of power plants and desalination facilities in Saudi Arabia.

Despite these successes, German firms argue that they compete under less than ideal conditions.[23] The most frequent complaint is that the Bonn government grants them insufficient support compared with the assistance provided to foreign rivals such as the French or the Japanese. The shortage of export credit, inadequate protection against exchange rate changes, limited insurance coverage, and little assistance in contract negotiations are among the inadequacies cited. Or, as a German contractor who worked on a Saudi construction project with a French firm put it, "While negotiations were going on, the French minister was there three times; no German officials showed up at all."[24]

High labor and materials costs have also hurt German contractors on construction projects. South Korean firms have captured a large share of the Middle East construction business by employing cheap Korean labor. One solution to this problem employed by Philipp Holzmann has been to form joint ventures with Korean firms, permitting them to undertake the basic construction while Holzmann provides the engineering technology. Even though they are well paid, it has been difficult to get German workers to work in foreign countries.

While comparisons are difficult, it is probably reasonable to say that the French and the Germans have enjoyed reasonably similar successes on the transfer of infrastructural technologies, with state assistance and remnants of colonial ties providing a slight advantage to the French. If we turn to large transfers of industrial plants and equipment, the Germans have a sizable lead, for it is in such projects that the Bonn strategy can draw on the strengths of the German domestic economy. Superiority in mechanical engineering and machinery manufacture makes a number of large German firms especially attractive to Middle East importers. As infrastructural demands decline, Arab states have sought suppliers of processing industries, particularly oil refineries and petrochemical plants. Oil refineries and aromatics plants have been built by Krupp-Koppers

GmbH, a division of Krupp, the giant German steel and munitions company. Uhde, an engineering subsidiary of the Germany chemical giant Hoechst, has built or won contracts to build petrochemical complexes in Morocco, Libya, Abu Dhabi, Egypt, Bahrain, and Saudi Arabia. Lurgi, a Frankfurt-based firm, has provided technology for metal and ore extraction and processing in both Saudi Arabia and Turkey. Mannesman Anlagenbau (MAB), a division of the Mannesman group, has been a major supplier of steel pipeline for long-distance movement of water and natural gas. Its best-known venture is a $910 million pipeline project to carry water from the Jubail desalination plant to Riyadh in Saudi Arabia.

The German preference has been to contract for turnkey facilities or management contracts that include training and maintenance services. In 1980 West German engineering firms signed turnkey contracts in the Middle East worth DM2.6 billion, compared to an overseas total of DM10.2 billion and a domestic total of only DM3 billion. However, countries such as Saudi Arabia have increasingly insisted on the establishment of joint ventures and, in some cases, the Germans have reluctantly agreed. A recent special report on German–Saudi economic relations reported 24 joint ventures involving prominent German companies such as Siemens, Korf, Daimler-Benz, Kraftwerk Union, and MAB.[25] Capital goods and services are the heart of the German–Saudi technology relationship, and the Saudis are seeking, through joint ventures and direct foreign investment, to sustain German interest in the kingdom. Continuing recession at home and a weak deutschmark make such investments particularly opportune for German firms.

While industrial plant and equipment transfers have generated the greatest returns for the largest German companies, attention has also been directed to more specialized transfer and the rewards that may accrue to small and medium-sized businesses. Vigorous and aggressive small firms are plentiful in Germany, but doing business abroad presents risks that are less easily absorbed by these companies. One must have reasonable assurance that there is an identifiable market for a specialized project before underwriting the costs of foreign marketing and sales. Such firms rarely have the luxury of balancing gains and losses from a diverse line of products. Fluctuations in exchange rates can unexpectedly narrow profit margins or eliminate profits altogether. With more limited resources and experience, these companies may have more difficulty locating prospective customers or negotiating acceptable terms. In their frequent role as subcontractors, they may have limited access to clients making it difficult to renegotiate terms or alter the products or services provided over the life of the contract.

In the face of these difficulties, a number of smaller German companies have shown great interest in cracking Arab markets. Private trade associations as well as the federal government have devised ways to assist them. One market that has generated considerable interest has been Tunisia. Attracted by their tourist experience in North Africa, Germans invested $23.4 million in Tunisia between 1972 and 1978, which helped to launch 83 projects and provided new employment opportunities for 9200 people.[26] Small firms have also been encouraged to seek opportunities in Saudi Arabia, where large projects are nearing completion and more specialized needs are becoming apparent. Again, continuing recession at home and a weak German currency make the advantages of foreign trade more attractive.

Both German and British suppliers appear capable of benefiting most from this last phase of technology transfer. British firms derive advantages from a longer British association in the Middle East; the Germans have demonstrated great determination. As one British engineer summed up the difference between the West German and other West European firms, "The Germans are more aggressive. Once they get their teeth into something they never let go. They will keep plugging away even if they never win anything."[27]

In sum, the lead given to the private sector after World War II and the pattern of export-led growth that has relied on the performance of industrial sectors that produce heavy capital equipment and machinery have yielded strong German performances in the second and third phases of technology transfer. Moreover, the strength and aggressiveness of specialized German firms would appear to hold promise for opportunities once the era of the big contract passes. Only in consulting, where the absence of colonial associations and the obstacle of language have limited German opportunities, has performance been mediocre.

The Germans, like the British and the French, have no explicit and articulated policy regarding technology transfer.[28] Following from its liberal economic philosophy, the Bonn government believes strongly that economic decisions should remain in private hands, but like the British government, it has developed institutions and policies to support and assist private entrepreneurs. By and large, the government looks favorably on all kinds of technology trade—turnkeys, licensing, and joint ventures—although it does monitor such outward flows by requiring all technology exports to gain clearance from the Federal Office of Commerce in Frankfurt-Eschborn. As a NATO member, the Federal Republic also monitors goods that appear on the COCOM list. In the case of Middle East trade, the policy has also been to prohibit the sales of arms to Israel's Arab neighbors.

The policies of three government ministries affect the strategy of technology transfer, and the division of labor among them reflects careful thought about the range of tasks to be undertaken in the complex process of developing and transferring technology from one society to another. Bundesministerium für Wirtschaft (the Federal Ministry of Economics), the head of which has for a long time been a member of the FDP, has acted as the lead ministry on issues of economic policy and has held most firmly to the liberal view that the initiation and negotiation of technology trade should be left to the private sector. Responsibility within the ministry is organized geographically, with the Middle East divided between those states in North Africa ("the poor states") and those east of the Red Sea ("the rich states").[29] In addition to collecting and disseminating information useful to German exporters, the ministry also engages in promotional activities to boost trade and investment opportunities. Among the most common is the organization of high-level commercial missions to the Middle East that bring together government officials, trade association leaders, and representatives of individual firms. In the case of Saudi Arabia, the German Foreign Office negotiated a Joint Economic Commission, which has provided a framework for promotional activities organized by the Economics Ministry.[30] The rapid expansion of German–Saudi trade is undoubtedly due in part to these supportive efforts.

By and large, the political and economic uncertainties in the volatile Middle East have resulted in a preference among German firms for turn-key or short-term management contracts rather than direct foreign investment and joint ventures. The belief that the Federal Republic has long-term economic interests in the region has led ministry officials to support measures designed to increase the attractiveness of investment commitments.[31] One example is formation of a Saudi–German joint venture company in which the German partner is Deutsche Entwicklungsgesellschaft (DEG), a specialized agency within the Ministry of Economic Cooperation, which is discussed below. The purpose of the company is to evaluate concrete projects and bring potential business partners together.

The Economics Ministry frequently hears complaints from German business leaders that it does too little to assist their foreign activities and that many of their competitors profit from state support at German expense. To date, the government's position has been that subsidies to less efficient foreign firms may make sense in the short term, but they undermine natural competitiveness in the long term.[32] German firms will be better served if they are forced to win business on their economic and technological merits. Economics, not politics, should be the basis for business decisions. This philosophy underpinned the government's decision to forego so-called technology-for-oil deals concluded by the French and others after the oil crisis, and to buy its oil on the world market. Officials argue that the 1980s demonstrate the merits of this strategy; the

French sit on high-priced oil contracts, and Arab states increasingly turn to the Germans as they become more sophisticated in evaluating the economic and technical merits of competitive bids.[33]

The Bundesministerium für Forschung und Technologie (DMFT; the Federal Ministry of Research and Technology) is the second government department directly involved in the transfer of technology. Since 1973, when the ministry was reconstituted to look after all basic research outside the universities and all applied research both in the universities and industry, the DMFT has been particularly concerned about the applications of research to industrial development and industrial policy in Germany. Among the German Social Democrats who provided its leadership through the 1970s, some conceived of the ministry as similar to the Ministry of International Trade and Industry (MITI) in Japan, intervening in the domestic economy with an eye to fostering new technology-intensive industries.[34] While the links to the Ministry of Economics were necessarily close, support for active intervention was not enthusiastically shared by the German FDP. Under Kohl and the Christian Democrats, the interventionist impulses in the DMFT became less prominent.

The ministry's participation in technology trade follows from a belief that successful transfer from country to country must begin with extensive research contacts between suppliers and recipients. Further, it is believed that such contacts will bring commercial opportunities for technologies developed in Germany. The typical pattern is first for Germany to conclude a scientific and technical cooperation agreement with a developing country. Such agreements may be defined broadly or they may target special industries such as nuclear power. Germany presently has such agreements in the Middle East with Egypt, Saudi Arabia, Iran, Iraq, and Kuwait. Following the agreement there is an exchange of technical personnel, and projects are assigned to the appropriate German and Middle East research institutes. The relatively small DMFT program (DM9 million in 1982) has focused on the promotion of future technologies likely to be viable in the Middle East, such as nuclear and solar power and desalination. After the completion of initial research and the development of pilot projects, viable ventures are sold to private commercial enterprises.[35] There is some indication that the approach of DMFT is changing under the CDU–FDP government. The Christian Democratic Union (CDU) has generally supported indirect assistance to industry such as tax breaks, rather than direct funding of special projects. The objectives are the same, but the new government prefers market incentives to direct subsidies.[36]

The third federal ministry with activities bearing on technology transfer is the Bundesministerium für Wirtschaftliche Zusammenarbeit (BMZ; the Ministry for Economic Cooperation). The ministry is charged with carrying out the Federal Republic's development policy, which is aimed at raising the living standards and social conditions of countries in the third world.[37] The policy is designed to enhance administrative efficiency, improve the functioning of market economies, and encourage better use of applied technologies. In addition to its work as the chief coordinator of all of West Germany's foreign aid programs, which are discussed in a following section, the ministry also has under its jurisdiction three semi-autonomous agencies whose work supports and complements other government activities relating to technology transfer. The first, Deutsche Entwicklungsgesellschaft (DEG; German Development Company), was established in Cologne in 1962 to promote cooperation between German companies and enterprises in developing countries by making equity investments or by granting loans. Wholly devoted to market principles and interested only in potentially profitable ventures, DEG also provides assistance in project design and planning.

The Gesellschaft für Technische Zusammenarbeit (GTZ; the Company for Technical Cooperation), located in Eschborn, provides technical aid and coordinates training in developing countries. Fully half of Germany's foreign aid is directed to technical assistance, giving GTZ a prominent place in foreign aid programs. The third organization under the wing of the BMZ is the Kreditanstalt für Wiederaufbau (KFW), which was established in Frankfurt in 1948 to assist in the financing of German economic recovery. The KFW is now responsible for disbursing capital assistance funds to developing countries and is the principal source of long-term export financing. The activities of each of these agencies are discussed more fully in the sections below on financing and foreign aid.

The German government, while relying heavily on the initiatives of private firms, gives considerable attention to policies designed to promote foreign trade and investment. The cooperation and coordination in the three ministries among civil servants looking after trade promotion and research and development assistance give evidence of a reasonably effective bureaucracy. At the root of the government strategy in the Middle East is a recognition of the increasing convergence of interests between the Federal Republic and the developing countries pursuing growth-oriented strategies such as Saudi Arabia, the Gulf States, Egypt, Iraq, and Algeria. The line between commercial opportunity and development assistance is more and more difficult to draw.

Private-sector organizations are also active in promoting German technology trade and investment. Three deserve special mention. The association of German Chambers of Industry and Commerce (DIHT) is a group of 69 local chambers that were created by public law and have compulsory membership for all businesses, with the exception of agriculture and handicrafts.[38] As well as providing the usual advisory services to members, the DIHT performs many of the services normally assigned to the commercial sections of embassies abroad. It has negotiated bilateral chambers of commerce agreements with most countries in the Middle East, and has opened offices in Tunis, Cairo, Teheran, and Riyadh. Negotiations have been initiated for an office in Algiers. Under public law, DIHT must also provide advice to government on various aspects of commercial policy; on the whole, its position reaffirms the liberal posture of the Ministry of Economics at home and abroad. German chambers of commerce also supervise vocational training in the Federal Republic.[39] Local chapters control three-year programs that not only train German workers but are open to foreign employees who might receive training as part of a management contract with a large German firm. There are opportunities for pre-contract training, on-the-job training, and retraining.

The many German trade associations organized by industry and coordinated through the Federation of German Industries (BDI) are also powerful tools of export promotion. In contrast to their French counterparts, most German trade associations are well organized and well financed and provide a wide range of services to would-be exporters. Perhaps the most important for the Middle East is the Verein Deutscher Maschinenbau-Anstalten (VDMA; German Mechanical Engineering Trade Association), which lists 3000 members and represents most all of German heavy and light industry. In chemicals, the VCI enjoys a similar reputation for strength and effectiveness. In consulting, the Union of Independent Consulting Engineers (VUBI), mentioned above, has also been reasonably successful in promoting the services of its members. In West Germany, leading industrial firms have been willing to invest considerable power in trade associations, perhaps because there are a limited number of large firms in each sector and all can expect to benefit.

A trade association directed specifically to the Arab world is the Nah und Mittlost Verein (NMV; Near and Middle East Association) founded first as the German–Persian Society in 1918 and renamed the German/Orient Society in 1934. Prior to World War II the association aimed to promote cultural relations, but since the end of the war its focus has shifted to economic affairs. It represents almost 80 percent of German exporting business to the region.[40] Like other trade associations, the NMV gathers information and attempts to uncover business opportunities for its members. A principal target of the future will be opportunities for small and medium-sized firms that logically follow the inroads made by large German firms over the last decade.[41] NMV also promoted the establishment of the Orient Institute in Hamburg, a small group of scholars outside the university system who do medium- and long-term studies on political, social, and legal developments in the Middle East, assessing their implications for German commerce. The institute is funded primarily by the state of Hamburg and receives additional support from German private foundations.[42]

Policies to promote trade and investment do not differ markedly in Britain and Germany. Both attempt to create an environment conducive to the conduct of business for private firms. Public institutes and private trade associations generate information helpful to businesses and have developed mechanics to put buyers and sellers together. In Germany, as in Britain, all of these efforts are likely to be of little help if individual firms fail to avail themselves of this assistance and seek out new business opportunities. The most telling difference between British and German economic performance in the Middle East has been the aggressiveness and confidence of German firms, compared to the reluctance of many British companies to enter the competitive fray.

SUPPORTIVE POLICIES FOR TECHNOLOGY TRANSFER

The Germans offer a full array of supportive measures for those engaged in technology transfer. For financing and insurance, exporters must rely more on private assistance than in either France or Britain, but the supportive role traditionally played by German banks compensates in part for the minimal government involvement. However, the Germans have probably gone furthest in trying to tie their foreign aid programs to commercial export opportunities. Both the efforts of the BMZ and the three semi-autonomous agencies under its jurisdiction indicate a desire to utilize German technical talents to the fullest in sustaining German exports and in providing the most valuable assistance to rapidly growing third world countries.

Financing and Insurance

West German exporters secure needed insurance and financing through a curious mix of private and government-authorized agencies and institutions. Insurance is supplied by a government-sanctioned consortium consisting of a private insurance company, Hermes, and a publicly held corporation, Treuarbeit.[43] In essence, the consortium works for the government; it evaluates the applications for insurance and issues policies. Premiums are paid to the government, which also bears the risk. The two companies specialize in capital risk. Hermes, the leading consortium partner, focuses on export and fabrication insurance, the latter covering losses sustained if orders are cancelled while goods are being produced. Treuarbeit specializes in capital investment coverage. Hermes is empowered to make its own decisions regarding what to insure if the value of the goods to be covered does not exceed DM2 million. For larger contracts, decisions are made by the Interministerial Committee for Export Guarantees, made up of representatives from Economics, Finance, Foreign Affairs, and Economic Cooperation, and advised by other financial officials. This interministerial committee also creates guidelines for determining political and commercial risks. The ceiling for insurance coverage is set annually by the Bundestag and in 1980 was DM150 billion.

In Germany a distinction is made between insurance for business conducted with foreign governments or public corporations and that undertaken with private enterprises.[44] An export guarantee for the former or "Bürgschaft" is offered at a rate of 0.5 to 1.0 percent of the value of the contract, depending on its size, plus a time premium of between 0.4 and 0.5 percent per month on the remaining amount after the first six months. The normal maximum coverage is 85 percent for commercial risks and 90 percent for political risks. Up to defined limits, the foreign contents of contracts may also be covered. If the foreign goods originate in the European Community, up to 40 percent of the value of the contract may be such goods; up to 30 percent if the goods are from Austria, Sweden, or Switzerland; no more than 10 percent if they come from any other country.[45] In addition to this supplier credit insurance, Hermes also offers buyer credit insurance for German banks that extend loans to foreign purchasers. Available at the same premium, banks may choose coverage for up to 95 percent against both commercial and political risks.

Insurance against exchange rate changes is available only for contracts longer than two years, and the large trade association of German industry, BDI, has lobbied hard for coverage for shorter periods.[46] As BDI officials argue, steady rises in the value of the mark, a common phenomenon over the past two decades, can erase profit margins altogether after German firms have struggled hard to do business in a foreign setting. Exchange rate risk is a big deterrent to small and medium-sized firms that the government would like to see more active in the Middle East. German insurance arrangements also offer no guarantees against cost escalation.[47] The slightly lower costs for insurance in France and the availability of both insurance and financing from the ECGD in Britain would appear to put German firms at some disadvantage.

The Federal Republic depends primarily on the banking system to extend credit at market rates for the financing of exports. The great bulk of short-term export financing to the Middle East is handled by private commercial banks. As discussed above, the significant equity positions held by German banks in large domestic firms make them keenly aware of the importance of being able to exploit export opportunities. The capital resources of the "big three" German banks are more than adequate to accommodate exporters' needs. While data is not readily available, German banks have clearly become extremely active in the Middle East over the past decade.[48] They have been reluctant to play a direct role by establishing subsidiaries and offices in the Arab world, but they have taken the more cautious route of consortium lending, short-term export financing, and permitting inward foreign direct investment by a number of Arab countries in the Federal Republic.

Long-term export financing to the Middle East is available via this route of consortium lending. The normal channel is Ausfuhrkredit-Gesellschaft (AKA), a private syndication of 56 commercial banks established in 1952.[49] AKA is not responsible to any government institution, but acts as a mechanism for pooling the credit resources of its members. Three lines of credit are offered for the refinancing of exporters' credits to foreign buyers. Line A provides long-term supplier credits for up to 90 percent of a given transaction at variable interest rates that average about 1 percent below the market rate. Line C provides buyer credits on the same terms. Resources come from individual bank contributions, and AKA members have set a ceiling of DM10 billion for these two lines of credit. Medium-term supplier credits (1–4 years) are available through Line B to developing countries at a preferential rate. Through Line B, AKA has access to rediscounting by the Bundesbank at preferential rates, 1.5 percent above the discount rate. As much as 70 percent of a contract's value may be financed through Line B or one may mix Line A and Line B financing in a single contract. A ceiling of DM5 billion has been placed on this cheaper source of refinancing.[50]

A second source of preferential financing is the KFW, the semi-autonomous agency of the Ministry of Economic Cooperation responsible for distributing development aid.[51] KFW offers credit for long-term loans (seven years or more) to suppliers or buyers who have arranged for insurance through Hermes. About DM800 million of credit is available each year and, due to high demands, KFW regularly mixes its loans with funds raised in capital markets at a 1:3 ratio, in order to assist more applicants. These rates have been consistently at or above the rate agreed on by OECD. Of the countries in the Middle East that trade actively with West Germany, probably only Egypt would qualify for this mixed financing.

Foreign Aid, Technical Assistance, and Training

In the Federal Republic, as in France, it makes sense to discuss foreign aid and training together, because as one analyst put it, "Foreign aid is so well organized in West Germany that it is almost an industry."[52] West German aid has grown steadily over the past decade, ranking behind the United States and France in total amount, and constituting 0.48 percent of GNP in 1982. Only about 15 percent of German aid is tied to the use of German goods and services, a figure well below that in the United States or France.

The philosophy of the government has been to allocate assistance that will improve the functioning of markets in developing countries, and consequently Bonn has generally been among the most adamant opponents of LDC demands for preferential treatment in the North–South dialogue. Therefore, its foreign aid programs have been designed to promote cooperation between the private sectors in Germany and developing countries, rather than granting aid outright to governments. As the Bonn cabinet recognized by resolution in 1979, the opportunities for cooperation grew rapidly after the increase in oil prices:

> Increased imports into the industrial countries from developing countries...can make a decisive contribution to enabling these countries to finance the capital goods necessary for their development. Expanding trade with the developing countries also has a positive effect on the German economy. The federal government emphasizes the importance of cooperation with the private sector for the economic, technological, and social progress of the developing countries. It supports this by further developing its instruments for promoting that cooperation. It emphasizes the need for lasting improvement in the investment climate in developing countries.[53]

Trade with and investment in developing countries are encouraged in a number of ways. A 1963 tax law aimed to assist investment by small and medium-sized German companies. Firms that invest in very poor developing countries are exempt from paying any tax on profits for the first six years, and then are taxed at a reduced rate thereafter. In addition to tax measures, the government in 1979 committed DM25 million to a fund to promote LDC investment to be used to arrange satisfactory credit terms.

The BMZ coordinates these trade and investment initiatives through its three autonomous agencies: the KFW, discussed above, which arranges financing; the DEG, the German Development Company, which organizes capital investment projects; and the GTZ, which arranges technical assistance and training. The DEG is administered by a supervisory board made up of government officials and representatives from industry, banking, and trade unions. The DEG solicits and approves project proposals from private German firms. Once approved, the DEG invests in the new enterprise (up to 50 percent) and helps to arrange additional financing. Once the enterprise begins to show a profit, the DEG is expected to sell its share of the operation to the private partner. In cooperation with the KFW, the DEG may also provide loans to the private firm for the purchase of fixed capital. New enterprises may also involve equity participation by companies in developing countries, encouraging long-term joint venture investments. In the late 1970s, for example, the Egyptian German Electrical Manufacturing Company (Egemac) was formed by the state-owned El-Nasr Transformers and Electrical Products Manufacturing Company (Elmaco) of Cairo and Siemens AG of Munich. DEG invested $2 million in the enterprise and loaned the partners another $1.1 million, bringing its share to 12 percent. Some 15 to 20 projects were under way in the Middle East in the early 1980s, with a number of others under active consideration. The charter of the DEG requires that it earn profits sufficient to cover its operating costs, so only projects with a reasonable chance of long-term profitability are considered. This requirement also encourages DEG to devote attention to so-called threshold countries in the third world, those that show reasonable promise of sustaining a pattern of growth and development.[54] Saudi Arabia, Algeria, and the Gulf States have been placed in this category. Iraq and Libya, with strict restrictions on the activities of foreigners in their economies, have forbidden the DEG from operating within their borders. As we have already noted, the DEG recently formed a joint venture company with a Saudi partner to promote the establishment of more long-term German investments within the kingdom.

Germany has long been known for excellence in scientific and technical education. The training of scientists and engineers has been given high priority in German universities since the late nineteenth century, and the resultant skills in the labor force were an important contribution to industrialization and modernization. Both the government and the private sector have viewed technical training as a valuable resource to be exported and a means to develop markets abroad for German technology exports. As already noted, the private sector has attempted to capitalize on the strengths of German technical education by linking training provisions in management contracts to the technical programs administered by local chapters of the DIHT. Individual German firms have been more responsive to the training needs of importing countries than either the British or the French.

The government in Bonn has also given attention to training. The bilateral scientific and technical agreements concluded with Arab countries and implemented by the Ministry for Research and Technology frequently begin cooperative research projects with educational opportunities for foreign scientists, engineers, and technicians. However, the most extensive commitment to training is made through the Gesellschaft für Technische Zusammenarbeit (GTZ), the BMZ's agency of technical cooperation.[55] Fully half of the Federal Republic's foreign aid (or $879 million in 1981) is devoted to technical assistance. GTZ, with a staff of 1200, sends its own experts and consultants to work on local development projects, particularly to assist with the training of local personnel. While the number of German technicians abroad does not approach those sent by France, the German commitment is growing rapidly. Most of this assistance is directed to the poorer countries of the third world, but the richer Middle Eastern countries are able to get the same assistance by purchasing it directly. GTZ works closely with the KFW and the DEG in deciding which projects are most worthy of support.

In 1984, 71,000 foreign students were studying in German universities, compared to 100,000 in France and 326,000 in the United States. Of this pool of foreign students, a small proportion came to Germany from the Middle East. Iranian students, numbering 7000 in 1982, are the largest group from the region, in keeping with German's extensive commercial relations with postrevolutionary Iran. Other Middle East countries are represented by smaller numbers, although at levels roughly comparable with those in Britain and France.

The German foreign aid program, through the coordinated activities of the KFW, DEG, and GTZ, is designed to support the efforts of private German firms to sell their goods and services in third world markets. Many of these have high-technology components. The foreign aid effort also seeks to ensure that such goods and services are absorbed effectively by third world economies. This dual approach has met resistance in developing countries not as enthusiastic as Germany about the benefits of a liberal economy, but it has, nevertheless, attracted a growing following in parts of the Middle East where German firms have won larger shares of the market.

THE GERMAN STRATEGY ASSESSED

The liberal character of postwar economic activity in the Federal Republic has limited the extent to which the state has become involved in promoting and financing technology trade and transfer. As in Britain, the government has generally played a supportive role, attempting to ensure "an even playing field" for all of the private players. However, the importance of exports to postwar recovery and continuing economic growth has made Bonn particularly attentive to the problems and opportunities of German exporters. Evidence of such attention can be found in the extent to which government ministries and agencies seek to consult and cooperate to ensure coordination among various promotional and financing schemes. Further, the German strategy has been to divorce diplomacy from economic affairs to the extent it is possible, with the intent of granting to the private sector the greatest room for economic maneuver. While we have suggested that the days of a low political profile may be coming to an end for the Federal Republic in the Middle East, to date Bonn has used this posture effectively, frequently enabling German firms to capitalize on others' political entanglements. Expansion of trade with Algeria and Iraq as well as continuing trade with Iran may be viewed as successful applications of this approach.

In the final analysis, however, it is the dynamism of the private sector in Germany that accounts for the successful penetration of Middle East markets, just as the weakness of private firms accounts for the more modest accomplishments of the British in the same region. In part, the needs of the Middle East over the past decade have played to German strength. Heavy capital equipment, machinery, transport equipment, and chemical and electrical engineering were the heart of the German economic miracle at home and the backbone of the successful German export performance. At a time when recession lingered in the domestic economy and in the economies of Germany's traditional trading partners, new markets in the Middle East were an ideal remedy. German firms quickly gained a reputation for supplying quality equipment and for efficiently and reliably fulfilling contract obligations.

The German strategy, which combines a vigorous and competitive private sector with government policies designed to create a climate conducive to foreign trade and investment, is well suited to each of the last three phases of the transfer process. The efforts of German firms to win large infrastructural contracts have yielded results that come close to matching the state-led strategy of the French. In securing large contracts for industrial plant and equipment, the Germans outdistance all of the Europeans. And the recent attention directed to assisting small and medium-sized companies in penetrating Middle East markets promises to give Bonn a large share of the more specialized technology market. Only in project design and consulting have German efforts produced modest returns.

The initiative taken by the private sector is likely to continue to pay dividends to the Germans in coming decades when Middle East countries complete much of their infrastructural investment and look for more specialized technological assistance. Already, private-sector organizations like the DIHT and the NMV, as well as research and investment programs sponsored by the Ministries for Research and Technology and Economic Cooperation, stress the importance of linking smaller German firms with their counterparts in the Middle East. While the opportunities are no doubt many and rapidly increasing, the uncertainties presented to smaller firms are bound to be more important barriers to business agreements than with large firms, and therefore the activities of trade associations and government support activities are likely to be correspondingly more important.

All in all, while the Germans have engaged in the competition for technology trade in the Middle East with important strikes against them—their links to the state of Israel, their lack of a colonial association to build upon, and considerable barriers of language and culture—the lesson of the 1970s is that such obstacles can be significantly reduced through a government strategy to diffuse political sensitivities and an active and aggressive posture assumed by a group of competitive industries in the private sector. While the fusion of politics and economics under state leadership made good sense for France, their separation and flexibility for the private sector are most appropriate for Germany.

6

JAPAN: MARKETING TECHNOLOGY UNENCUMBERED BY HISTORY

HISTORICAL CONTEXT

For a Western audience, perhaps the most important starting point in assessing Japan's involvement with the Middle East is the recognition that all of its ties are historically recent, culturally distant, and ideologically thin. Japan lacks any direct experience with anti-Semitism, Zionism, or the European pogroms, and does not have a substantial Jewish population. Similarly, this country has felt few direct influences from the Moslem religion or Arab culture. Nor have there been any long political connections between Japan and any country from the Middle East. No other industrial country, and certainly none of those investigated here, has such weak ties.

During the late nineteenth century, when Britain, France, the United States, and even Germany had already begun to establish footholds in the Middle East, Japan was barely emerging from two and a half centuries of self-imposed isolation. Virtually until the turn of the century, government and private sector concerns focused on protecting domestic sovereignty from Western encroachments and escaping the burdens of the harmful commercial treaties imposed on weak Japanese governments during the 1850s and 1860s. External connections were limited largely to young Japanese studying in the United States and Western Europe.[1]

When Japan did begin to expand territorially, it sought regional influence in Korea, north China, Southeast Asia, and the Pacific islands. Even the Greater East Asia Co-Prosperity Sphere, the grandiose zone of control proposed by Japan during the 1930s and 1940s, was not intended to extend beyond India. Hence, the Middle East was largely *terra incognita* in political terms.

It was not until the late 1920s that Japan began even minimal trade relations with the area, importing long-fiber Egyptian cotton. Various Japanese textile experts did business in the area, and the Yokohama Specie Bank opened a branch in Alexandria to assist with these transactions until Japan's entry into World War II in 1941. Limited involvement remained the pattern during the early postwar years. Defeat in World War II and subsequent military occupation by the United States pushed Japan to adopt foreign policy goals built around a close alliance with the United States and the very slow development of regional, and subsequently international, economic power. Overt foreign policy aspirations toward the Middle East remained far more circumscribed than those of Washington or the major European powers.[2]

For the most part, Japan's overseas activities remained limited to commercial ventures. By "separating politics from economics," the slogan of Prime Minister Ikeda, the country quietly, but effectively, began to achieve the domestic and international economic successes that have since become the object of such universal fascination.[3] Early economic ties to the Middle East began during this era with a trade agreement signed between Syria and Japan on June 8, 1953, an agreement that was followed by a succession of similar arrangements with other Middle Eastern countries.[4]

The most substantial stimulant to Japanese involvement with the Middle East came following changes in Japan's energy policy during the 1950s and 1960s. In the prewar and wartime periods, and continuing into the early 1950s, Japan relied for its energy primarily on coal, hydropower, firewood, and charcoal. It maintained near self-sufficiency by relying on these sources. However, as oil became cheaper and more readily available, Japanese political and business leaders shifted to petroleum as the principal source of commercial energy. Oil accounted for only 15 percent of Japan's energy use in 1951–1952; in 1963 it was 50 percent, and when the 1973 oil crisis hit the total was 70 percent. Almost 80 percent of that oil came to Japan from the Middle East, most of it delivered and marketed by the major oil companies.[5]

This shift in Japan's pattern of energy consumption made the country especially vulnerable to OPEC policies in the early 1970s and, as a consequence, Japan's foreign policy toward the Middle East was redefined following the quadrupling of oil prices.[6] Until that time, Japan had rather casually followed the United States' lead in the area, including that country's support for Israel. As Foreign Minister Okita stated in a press conference on January 10, 1980, few Japanese even realized where oil came from until 1973, and many assumed control over oil resources was in the hands of reliable oil companies. In the first few months after the embargo in late 1973, Vice-Premier Miki, MITI Minister Nakasone, and

Foreign Minister Kosaka all visited the Arab nations, each offering different packages of economic and technical aid in exchange for assurances of continuing supplies of oil. In addition, in what one scholar referred to as "the first open break with American foreign policy in postwar diplomatic history that Japan had dared to make," the country adopted a more staunchly pro-Arab position, supporting the OAPEC position on the Palestinians' right of self-determination, and calling for Israeli withdrawal from all Arab lands.[7]

Following the embargo, the Japanese Foreign Ministry expanded its presence, beefing up its Middle East and Africa bureaus and opening new embassies in the region. Tokyo also showed itself far more willing than Washington to accept PLO participation in Mideast peace talks. During a January 1976 Security Council session, for example, Japan's UN Ambassador Saito proposed a direct dialogue between the PLO and Israel. In 1980 both Anwar Sadat and Yasir Arafat were invited to Tokyo, and on December 13, 1980, Arafat met with Toshio Kimura, former foreign minister and president of the Japan Palestinian Friendship Committee. Four days later Sadat met with Foreign Minister Ito in Egypt. Sadat's planned trip to Tokyo was prevented only by his assassination.[8] While Japan's relationship with the United States remains the keystone of its foreign policy, oil dependency has made the country's leaders far less willing to follow the U.S. lead on Middle East issues than they were in the 1960s. Private actions in Japan have hewn to official policy lines. Numerous study groups on the Middle East were formed in the early 1970s, and in September 1974 the Economic Research Institute for the Middle East was established through the sponsorship of private groups.

Clearly, the primary thrust of Japan's technology and trade policies in the Middle East has been economic rather than political. Tokyo has been unwilling to participate in any arms buildup in the Persian Gulf, the Indian Ocean, or the Red Sea. As one observer concluded, "A reading of Japanese analyses of the Middle East in major newspapers and journals during [1979–1981] strikes the reader with its almost total lack of linkage between economic and political issues in Japan's foreign economic policy."[9] While the Japanese government has been inching toward a more positive role in world affairs during the past decade, including those in the Middle East, most efforts have been tentative and limited.

With the world's second largest gross national product and 15 percent of the world's manufacturing exports, Japan has a highly sophisticated economy, capable of playing an important role in the economic development of any country in the Middle East. Moreover, most countries in the region view Japan as a source of considerable potential assistance and welcome closer economic and political ties. The absence of unpleasant historical memories and political associations assists in the expansion of economic and technological exchange. Devoid of prior political entanglements, Japan is freer than most other industrialized countries to establish an economic presence in virtually all countries in the region, engaging in a substantial range of technology transfers. In some respects, the Japanese legacy of the past decade or so resembles the West German approach. Both countries count heavily on exports to fuel their domestic economic growth and are careful to ensure that politics does not unduly interfere with domestic economic well-being. The sophisticated economies of both Japan and Germany offer attractive technological opportunities for Middle East importers; at the same time, Middle East markets figure significantly in Japanese and German economic planning.

TRADE AND INVESTMENT

For most of its modern history, Japan has been a trading nation. Imports and exports as a percentage of GNP are actually far lower than for many European countries; however, there is a peculiar cast to Japanese trade, namely the high proportion of raw materials imported and the high proportion of manufacturing goods sent abroad.[10] The country's relative absence of raw materials and natural resources has been a major factor in this orientation. Japan imports nearly 100 percent of its oil, 89 percent of its natural gas, 99 percent of its iron ore, 96 percent of its copper, 82 percent of its lead, 69 percent of its zinc, 98 percent of its tin, all of its nickel, aluminum, cotton, wool, and maize, 79 percent of its coal, and 69 percent of its wood. In virtually all of these categories, Japan is at or near the top of the dependency list among the major industrialized countries.[11]

To earn the foreign reserves needed to pay for imported raw materials, Japan has traditionally relied on the export of manufactured products. This natural tendency is exacerbated by the fact that most national firms depend for their capital formation on the Japanese banking system and short-term loans. To pay the interest and roll-over costs of these loans, and to protect market shares, most of Japan's successful firms have, during periods of domestic slowdown, opted to increase exports rather than to cut employment or production. An ever-continuing search for new export markets has been the result. Obviously this has been widely beneficial to the national economy.

Eighty-five percent of Japan's exports are in the broad category of heavy industry and chemical goods, with the greatest concentration in transport equipment, autos, machinery, and metal goods. A scant 12 percent of the country's exports are of products from light industry; virtually none are in foodstuffs or minerals. Japan's world share of manufactured exports has become nearly equal to that of the United States (15–16 percent); only West Germany ranks higher with 18 percent. And while the U.S. share has been declining and that of West Germany has been stable, Japan's share has been growing rapidly.

Unlike Britain, and more like France and West Germany, government in Japan has traditionally been actively involved in foreign and domestic economic policy. This has been particularly true in trade and investment, where Japan has acted as a "developmental state," one in which the government (particularly since the 1960s) has taken a direct interest in promoting national economic growth and advancement.[12] At the same time, the country has benefited from a dynamic and creative private sector whose vitality is often overlooked and whose important role complements governmental activism.

Public policy has centered on the creation of market incentives designed to speed up, channel, or enhance private initiatives rather than to replace or contradict them. During the 1950s and early 1960s the focus was on manufacturing and heavy industry; since the mid-1970s government efforts have centered on long-range plans to shift the country away from reliance on manufacturing and into knowledge-intensive and high-technology sectors.[13] This new emphasis follows from growing energy shortages, ecological concerns, and high dependence on imported raw materials, which together make it difficult to sustain international competitiveness in heavy industry. In its place the government has sought to "promote creative technological innovation and . . . build a technology-advanced society by making the utmost use of its manpower—its most developed resource." Japan is seeking to become an information society with "computerization as the axis."[14]

It is of course an open question whether Japan will succeed in its efforts to facilitate technology-led development. However, in such key industries as steel, shipbuilding, microprocessing, autos, and machine tools, Japanese technology and productivity have already surpassed the West.

Many government agencies combine to assist Japanese technological advances and to provide access to world markets. The most important is the Ministry of International Trade and Industry (MITI; the postwar heir to the Ministry of Commerce and Industry), which is charged with promoting the nation's industrial development.[15] MITI's activities go far beyond technology transfer, but several bear directly on the process. First, the ministry long had responsibility for the formulation of the nation's industrial policy. During the 1950s and 1960s, MITI directed the reorganization, and in many cases the cartelization, of important segments of Japan's industries, both through the use of formal legal powers, and by employing informal administrative procedures. The ministry championed the development of technologically advanced industries and helped to structure or position specific industries to compete for world markets. MITI also still grants export licenses and arranges export insurance under the terms of the Amended Foreign Exchange and Foreign Trade Law of November 1980. MITI acts too as industry's voice in the Japanese cabinet and has pressed strongly for trade and direct investment as the appropriate means of technology transfer to the Middle East.

A second important government agency is the Japan External Trade Organization (JETRO; *Nihon Boeki Shinkokai*), which was established in 1958 under MITI's auspices to promote exports through overseas market research, trade centers, and advertising. By providing detailed information on foreign market conditions, product needs, tariff changes, and specifications for different products, JETRO serves as an international commercial intelligence service, providing focus and direction to Japanese trade.[16]

By mid-1980, JETRO had 79 fully staffed offices worldwide, including a number in the Middle East. In addition, the agency regularly publishes material providing timely marketing information for Japanese exporters. For example, one two-volume *White Paper on World Markets (Kaigai Shijo Hakusho)* provides detailed discussion of investment and trade regulations in Egypt, Saudi Arabia, and Turkey, as well as information on particularly promising investment opportunities in several Middle Eastern countries. The white paper also offers detailed outlines of recent political and economic developments country by country, as well as discussing their relationship to trends in Japanese foreign policy. By publishing information on Japan's overseas economic cooperation and foreign assistance, JETRO keeps private companies alert to the kinds of projects likely to gain official governmental support.

The Ministry of Finance (MOF) also plays an important role in assisting Japanese trade and investment, although its primary responsibilities bear only indirectly on technical cooperation and transfer. Through its oversight responsibilities for the Bank of Japan and for the Export-Import Bank, both of which are important to the financing of overseas projects, the MOF does exercise some influence on such decisions. As the ministry chiefly responsible for setting domestic tax policies, Finance also gives impetus to technology transfer through tax preferences offered to Japanese firms investing abroad and assurances of protection for overseas investments. Among the tax concessions are credits for foreign income tax and accelerated depreciation allowances for enterprises deriving income from overseas transactions or operations. The government has also negotiated arrangements to avoid double taxation with several Mideast countries. Technology exports are specifically encouraged by a tax exemption of 70 percent on total income received from the export of technology or property rights paid for in foreign currency.[17]

While these and other government institutions and policies are helpful, much of Japan's success in developing technological prowess at home and profitably exporting it to others has resulted from the efforts of a vigorous and dynamic private sector. For comparative purposes, three aspects of Japanese private industry deserve special attention. First, much of Japan's economy is dominated by large, competitive blocks of firms, tied together in groups known as *keiretsu*, or conglomerates. Mitsui, Mitsubishi, and Sumitomo are probably the most well known, but many other less well-known affiliations have been very successful. These groups have been particularly active in developing Japan's markets abroad, and competition among them has contributed immensely to the overall vitality of the economy.[18]

A second feature worth highlighting, and one closely tied to the growth of the *keiretsu*, is the national banking structure.[19] Japan's banks have made possible the financing of many of the mega-projects that have been initiated abroad and have been so profitable for Japanese companies in recent years. At the top of the banking hierarchy is the Bank of Japan, which is 55 percent government owned and which maintains close ties with the Ministry of Finance. During Japan's long period of rapid growth after World War II, the Bank of Japan was the primary source of capital for the transformation of Japanese industry. Recent moves to liberalize capital movements, combined with the internationalization of Japanese firms, have given Japanese companies access to credit from diverse sources, thereby diminishing the Bank of Japan's control over important industrial developments. Still, it remains the chief coordinator of Japan's financial market. Since Japanese firms rely heavily on borrowing rather than on the sale of stock to finance expansion, they maintain high debt-equity ratios by international standards. Consequently, banking influence over industrial decision-making remains more significant than in many other industrialized countries. It is also worth noting that all overseas activities by Japanese firms are reported to the Bank of Japan in accordance with the Foreign Exchange and Trade Laws as amended in November 1980.

The 13 so-called city or commercial banks rank somewhat below the Bank of Japan in size and prestige. Each of these services the needs of one or more of the *keiretsu* discussed above. Through their policies, the city banks play an important role in coordinating the domestic and overseas activities of the conglomerates. Such close financial-industrial linkages are frequently crucial to successful foreign activities in trade, direct investment, and technology transfer.[20]

Finally, mention should be made of Japanese trade companies (*sogo sosha*), institutions with no parallels in the other major industrialized states. While there are over 6,000 such organizations in Japan, nine trading companies dominate, with Mitsubishi, Marubeni, C. Itoh, Mitsui, Sumitomo, and Nissho Iwai among the most well known.[21] Because the term suggests little more than a brokering role, "trading company" is something of a misnomer, and the largest of Japan's trading companies offer a diversity of services including financing, resource development, construction, the organization of joint ventures, marketing, third-party trade, and information gathering.

The top ten trading companies handle some 50 percent of Japan's exports, 60 percent of its imports, and about 20 percent of domestic wholesale transactions. They manage operations valued at twice the size of the government's national budget or about 30 percent of the GNP. Trading companies have been particularly active in the Middle East, not only in facilitating direct trade but also in organizing most of Japan's big development projects in the region. In bidding for and successfully completing large project contracts, the trading companies have typically worked closely with the large Japanese banks. Together they can mobilize the necessary capital, secure the information required to operate in a foreign country, and facilitate the distribution and sale of products in international markets.[22]

Mechanisms also exist to facilitate close economic cooperation between the private and the public sectors in Japan, mechanisms which have been particularly useful to Japanese activities in the Middle East. One of the most important is an annual conference held in Vienna where both Japanese government officials and businesspeople concerned with the Middle East meet to exchange information and experiences. An annual report of this meeting summarizes developments in each of the major Middle Eastern and North African countries. It outlines official and private needs of the countries in the region, chronicles recent political and economic changes, and reviews Japanese business and governmental dealings with each country. Information for the report comes from the Japan Cooperation Center for the Middle East (*Chuto Kyoryoku Sentaa*), from MITI, and from private sources. The central point of this discussion of Japanese business and government economic activities is that both have generally complemented one another in the pursuit of common goals—advancing Japanese overseas trade through rapid adaptation to changing world market conditions and fostering changes that push Japan toward even greater technological sophistication. The results of this strategy of cooperation, as measured by the steep rise in Japan's exports to the Middle East, have been reviewed in Chapter 2.

Through the mid-1970s, Japan was largely a trader, both worldwide and in the Middle East; by the mid-1980s, the focus had shifted to direct overseas investment. Foreign investment throughout the world was dominated by U.S. and European firms into the 1970s; only in the last decade have Japanese firms undertaken significant investments abroad. Between 1951 and 1971, Japanese foreign investment totaled slightly over $4 billion. In the following decade, that total reached $32 billion.[23] By 1983, Japan ranked fourth in the total value of its overseas investments behind the United States, Britain, and West Germany. The average annual increase in the value of such expenditures has been about 10 percent over the past several years, and an aggressive program of capital investment is expected through the remainder of the decade. Projections by the Japan Economic Research Center put the total stake of Japanese multinationals overseas at nearly $80 billion by the end of 1985 and as high as $155 billion by 1990.[24]

In mid-1984, investments in the Middle East stood at about $2.7 billion, just over 5 percent of Japan's total overseas investment. Such investments have, however, gone through several stages.[25] Investment in oil development and extraction in the Middle East, primarily through the Arabian Oil Company (AOC), accounts for the fact that from 1951 to 1962 nearly 30 percent of Japan's investment went to the Middle East. Even though the average amount invested per year nearly tripled during the 1960s and into the early 1970s, as a proportion of total Japanese investment the figures showed a marked decline. Thus, only 1.2 percent of Japan's outflows for investment went to the Middle East for the 1972–1973 period. Following the first oil shock and the increased Japanese concern for the Middle East, average annual investment began to rise quickly in the next several years. This was due largely to private investment in several major complexes, including the Mitsui Group's gargantuan and ever problematic investment in the Bandar Khomeini oil refining plant in Iran (IJPC). This was Japan's largest overseas investment anywhere in the world. For several years, 1975–1978, the total proportion of Japanese investment going to the region grew to 6 percent, 8 percent and eventually a high of 10.7 percent in 1978.

During this period, Iran, pursuing the Shah's strategy of rapid modernization, was the major recipient of Japanese investment money. From 1976 to 1978 the country received 70 percent of Japan's Middle East investments, for a total of $706.5 million. Aside from continued investment in the neutral zone, only Saudi Arabia and the UAE benefited from any significant levels of Japanese investment during this period, Saudi Arabia getting $50 million in investments and the UAE getting some $72.4 million. Following the revolution in Iran, total Japanese investments in the Middle East fell sharply in proportion to its total investment outflows. In 1981, this meant that the Mideast accounted for only 1.1 percent of Japan's total investment. Yet the total volume invested in the region as of March 1982 still accounted for some $2.4 billion, representing some

5.2 percent of Japan's total overseas investments. $42 million of this was in agriculture, fishing, and mining; $24 million was in construction; $11 million was in commerce; banking and insurance accounted for $25 million; and the service sector totaled $80 million. In contrast to these relatively small sums, $1,078 million was in real estate and branch offices, while $1,094 million was in manufacturing, the vast bulk of which ($972 million) was in the chemical industry, again largely petrochemicals and oil-related investments, especially in the neutral zone. From these figures it is clear that Japanese investment was heavily weighted to promote general Japanese trade and services and to foster the sale of massive turnkey plants.[26]

Most of Japan's large trading companies have also established outposts in several Middle Eastern cities, in effect, buying, selling, bidding on contracts and engaging in turnkey plant exports, adapting strategies to changing climates or profit margins. The range and diversity of their activities, as well as their relative geographical and product strengths, are enormous. Mitsui, for example, has had longstanding links with Iran, and in spring 1973, established the above-mentioned Iran-Japan Petrochemical Company (IJPC), projected costs for which have been as high as $5 billion.[27] At the same time, Mitsui has been involved in much smaller projects, such as a $23 million contract for the construction of a power transmission network; in a $16.7 million venture with Fudo Construction Company of Japan for the construction of various administrative buildings and warehouses valued at $16.7 million in Iraq; and a pipeline and fuel storage facility in Kuwait that is being developed jointly with JGC Corporation. Typically Mitsui is credited with being strongly competitive in Iran, Kuwait, the UAE, and, along with Mitsubishi, in Egypt. Marubeni and Mitsubishi are among the strongest competitors in Saudi Arabia, while Nissho Iwai has a strong position in Kuwait. In contrast, C. Itoh, with 17 branches and a subsidiary in Bahrain, has operated most of its business out of Egypt, with Saudi Arabia as its major client. But as one recent report noted, the company has, like the other trading companies, a diversified portfolio that includes "televisions to Egypt; construction machinery to Iraq, Iran and Turkey; water and crude oil piping to Iraq and Saudi Arabia; car telephone systems to several Gulf countries; and telephone equipment to Kuwait, Saudi Arabia, Bahrain, the UAE and Qatar."[28] Ishikawajima-Harima Heavy Industries has had good performances in Algeria and North Yemen. It has constructed a liquified natural gas (LPG) plant in the former and a cement plant in the latter. Chiyoda Chemical and Engineering and Construction Company has major projects in at least nine Middle Eastern countries.

In addition to the trading companies, Japan is represented in the Middle East by outlets for major manufacturing companies, such as Toyota,

National Electric Company (NEC), Fujitsu, Hitachi, Seiko, Oki, Nissan Motors, and the like. Japan's banking and service sectors are also well represented in the area.

In short, the character of Japan's direct investment in the region is diverse. Turnkey operations, joint ventures with local partners, contract construction, and on-site sales from overseas subsidiaries are but some of the major techniques used by Japanese firms to garner a portion of the Middle Eastern market.

The most striking pattern emerging from an investigation of Japanese investment in the Middle East is that before the mid-1960s, natural resource development was a logical and important course of action for Japanese firms. But the overall scale of such investment was limited. As Japanese overseas investment began to increase, much of it went into a few limited countries, almost all of them outside the Middle East. The only major exception was Iran, particularly in the mid-1970s. Once Khoumeini's revolution took place, however, the most important Japanese investments in the Mideast were those in real estate and subsidiary development by the major Japanese manufacturing and trading companies. The presence of these latter in the region has, however, become quite substantial, and is intimately connected with the sales, marketing, and after-sales service of various products, ranging from small individual sales on such items as watches or automobiles to vastly more complex contracts involving complete turnkey plant development projects in areas such as desalination, petrochemicals, or cement.

Foreign investment is encouraged by government policies. For example, a liberal 1980 foreign exchange law facilitates overseas ventures. Rather than prohibiting all transactions unless authorized as an earlier law specified, the new legislation, with minor limitations, authorizes all transactions not specifically prohibited. Moreover, government investment guarantees and financing encourage such exports of capital. When projects are deemed to have "national significance," such as a $1.75 billion aluminum smelting complex in Indonesia, or the $4 billion coal liquification plant in Victoria, Australia, or the $2 billion petrochemical complex in Saudi Arabia, the government's Export-Import Bank provides loans on very favorable terms. In addition, the longstanding national policy of separating politics from economics has freed Japanese companies from government pressures to limit foreign investment as a result of boycott clauses or human rights violations in recipient countries. As Business Week recently noted, "If anything, the main source of government pressure on Japanese multinationals has come from the Ministry of International Trade and Industry's steady prodding to invest more abroad before foreign trade restraint or quotas are imposed."[29] The legacy of the last decade is that Japan is far more willing than it was in the past to transfer technology, either through direct sales and licensing, or else indirectly through investment, trade, and economic cooperation. Understandably, the most sophisticated technologies are protected. But as the Japanese economy has moved rapidly toward a more knowledge-based and technology-driven economy at home, there has been a growing willingness to pass on "last year's technologies" to others. Capital-rich countries in the Middle East have become natural partners in this expanding technology trade.

SUPPORTIVE POLICIES FOR TECHNOLOGY TRADE

Within this broad framework of supporting advancing industries and not protecting most of those in decline, the Japanese government has no explicitly stated policy on technology transfer, either generally or for the Middle East. Rather, sales or other transfers of technology are made largely at the discretion of individual firms. Where patents are held by the government, ad hoc deliberations determine recipient needs, and terms are negotiated between governments. In most cases, there is little opposition in principle to making such transfers, but the Japanese government often considers transfers of highly sophisticated technologies inappropriate for the level of development in most Middle East economies.

The explicit sale and licensing of technology represents one of the primary methods for the transfer of technology across national boundaries. Japan is becoming an increasingly important source of such transfers worldwide. Sales in 1980 accounted for approximately $125 million. However, technology transfers from Japan to the Middle East represent but a small part in Japan's total transfers worldwide. Thus, in the five years from 1976 to 1980, Japan conducted a total of 16,574 transfers, of which the Middle East accounted for only 480 cases (2.8 percent). However, the area has begun to gain an increasing share of the total value of Japan's expanding technology transfers. Thus in 1976, transfers to the Middle East were worth Y3.2 billion ($14.5 million); five years later that value had risen six times in nominal terms; as a proportion of Japan's total transfers, the share held by the Middle East rose from 3.8 to 15.2 percent.

The vast majority of these transfers were in areas related to the construction of manufacturing facilities. Thus, of the 480 total transfers, 80 (16.7 percent) were in construction and 370 (77.1 percent) were in manufacturing. For most of this period the predominant transfers were in the areas of synthetic and chemical fibers. By 1977 steel-related transfers also began to play an important role, and a year later machinery and transportation-related transfers also became significant. Receipts from precision instruments, pharmaceuticals, and telecommunications continue to account for a rather small proportion of total transfers to the Middle East.

One area where government policy on both sale of technology and direct exports is explicit and extremely restrictive concerns military armaments and equipment. The first articulation of this policy was in the mid-1950s by Prime Minister Sato, who outlined three central principles: Japan would not sell to countries engaged in conflicts; to countries on the United Nations' blacklist; or to countries in the Communist bloc. In 1976 Prime Minister Miki banned virtually all sales of military technology, including weapons, defense know-how, or weapons manufacturing equipment to any country, including the United States. Until recently, this ban has been strictly enforced by the Ministry of International Trade and Industry, through its control of export licenses, with MITI regularly taking a broad view of what it considers to be "military" equipment. Japanese policy on arms sales closely resembles that of West Germany, with the attendant costs and benefits. Tokyo is deprived of the lucrative arms business enjoyed by Britain, France, and the United States, but at the same time the ban frees the private sector from some of the political entanglements that often plague civilian companies within those latter countries.

Only during the administration of Prime Minister Nakasone did this policy begin to be questioned openly, and in January 1983 Japan officially agreed to allow the transfer of sophisticated military technologies to the United States.[30] It is too early to predict if future policy changes will affect Middle East transfers.

A second area where government policies directly impinge on trade and investment policies is Japan's energy policy. Japanese energy policy was at the heart of the warming of relations that occurred between Japan and the Middle East as outlined above. The composition of Japan's energy supplies made the country more vulnerable to oil cutoffs than any other industrial country. As a consequence of this high degree of dependency, Japan sought on the one hand to develop closer relations with the countries of the Middle East, particularly through trade, investment, and technology transfer. At the same time, it sought to reduce its long-term dependence on oil from the region.

Energy conservation has been one of the main targets of government policy. Favorable monetary and tax treatments have been promoted to encourage faster introduction of energy-saving equipment in industry. In 1979 a variety of legislation mandated drastic reductions in the energy consumption of specific consumer goods, including refrigerators, air conditioners, and automobiles. Public energy-saving efforts among individual consumers are also being fostered. As a result, Japan succeeded in steadily reducing its domestic oil consumption. Consequently, oil imports have been dropping for a decade.[31] A 1984 government survey predicts that oil will account for 52.5 percent of the nation's energy needs by 1990, compared to 60 percent in 1982.

The government has also sought to diversify Japan's dependency on Middle East oil. Hence, Canada, Mexico, China, and Indonesia have all been targeted by the Japanese government for favorable treatment due to the oil supplies these countries afford. Private industry is currently required to keep a 90-day reserve of oil, and the government maintains another 13-plus days of supply. By mid-1986 actual reserves were substantially greater.

Diversification of energy sources themselves is another aspect of national energy policy. Aside from efforts in geothermal, coal, and natural gas, the government has been particularly active in expanding nuclear energy production. By the end of 1984 there were 27 nuclear reactors nationwide. Diversification and conservation policies have significantly reduced Japanese dependence on Middle Eastern oil, particularly in the short run. Hence, government reaction to the 1973 oil embargo demonstrated almost total panic and a rush to embrace the Middle East as a matter of national life and death. Following the 1979 price increases, the government was unquestionably uneasy, but reacted with a greater sense of self-assurance. By the mid-1980s, the sense of short-term vulnerability had been reduced even more. As one observer noted in mid-1984, "The recent crisis in the Gulf, with bombing attacks on shipping threatening not just higher priced oil but a complete cut-off of oil supplies, evoked a very different response [in Tokyo]—one of almost complete equanimity."[32]

At the same time that diversification, conservation, and high reserves have reduced short-term vulnerability, long-term dependence on Middle Eastern oil remains an unassailable given in Japanese energy policy. A government survey conducted in August 1979 indicated that the country's total energy demand in 1995 will have risen by 136 percent over 1977 levels. Even with maximum conservation, the increase is likely to be 100 percent.[33] A 1983 report by the government advisory committee for energy noted that "Oil will continue to be the biggest supply source of energy in the medium and long-term and will play an important role to ensure flexibility in energy demand and supply patterns in Japan."[34] This fact is clearly appreciated by government policymakers; hence Japan has little alternative but to attempt to remain on good political and economic terms with the oil producers of the region.

By the middle of the 1980s, the consequences of this mixture could be characterized as twofold. On one hand, there was a tapering off of the frantic pursuit and rapid expansion of Japan's trade, investment, and technology transfer to the Middle East that characterized the mid- to late 1970s. Trade and investment to the Arab world have even fallen off somewhat as a proportion of Japan's total activities in these areas.

At the same time, the importance of Middle Eastern oil to Japan and the inevitability of some long-term dependency, combined with the general importance of the region as a market for Japanese goods, has led to an apparently permanent increase in both public and private commitments of resources to the region.

Finance and Insurance

As noted above, there are close links between many large private Japanese banks and the nation's biggest industries. Individually and in consortia, these banks provide much of the financing for Japanese overseas trade and more especially direct investment. Additional capital is available through the Japan Export-Import Bank (*Nihon Yushutsunyu Ginko*).[35] Established in the 1950s to promote exports, particularly sales of heavy machinery to developing countries on a deferred payments basis, the Bank expanded its activities in 1952 to include the financing of imports, particularly raw materials. Revisions in the Export-Import Bank Law have increased banking operations, permitting loans without commercial bank participation and credit to developing countries in arrears on their debts to Japan due to foreign exchange shortages.

The Ex-Im Bank provides both direct finance and guarantees. It finances activities through direct loans, largely in the form of suppliers credits, import financing, overseas investment financing, buyers' credits, and bank loans. It also guarantees similar projects financed commercially. Although the Bank may borrow from other institutions of the government and from foreign banks and other foreign institutions (Art. 39 of the Export-Import Bank Act), most of its resources come from the Fiscal Investment and Loan Program (FILP) which, in turn, is funded through postal savings and the reserve funds of pensions. During 1981 the Ex-Im Bank loan balance amounted to about Y5.5 billion (about $25 million); its capitalization was Y9.25 billion ($46 million); and its loan limit was Y1.2 trillion ($5.5 billion). The Bank is government owned and is overseen by the Ministry of Finance.[36] As of 1980, the Export-Import Bank had 13 overseas offices, including one in the Middle East.

The Export-Import Bank does not publish data on loans and credits by region and industrial sector. However, during the fiscal year ending in March 1982, the Bank made 19 loan commitments totaling Y104 billion to west Asia. While this figure was only 6 percent of that year's commitments, it was nearly triple the amount of the previous fiscal year. Investment credits totaled Y88 billion, which represented 26 percent of such loans. This amount was also up sharply, from Y18 billion the year before, even though it still represented only 8 percent of the Ex-Im Bank's total investment credits. Investment credits for plant exports to the region were even smaller, representing only 2 percent of the total figure.[37] Most investments were made in petrochemicals and chemicals.

While the Middle East receives no special attention or treatment according to sources within the Bank, Japanese business and government leaders have come to regard the Bank as the most important source for trade and investment projects in the region.

The Overseas Economic Cooperation Fund (OECF; discussed more fully below) also is involved in loans and investments to Japanese corporations as well as to foreign governments, in cases when projects include a substantial component of foreign assistance. As noted above, export insurance and licensing are the responsibility of MITI as part of its promotion of private-sector activities abroad.

Economic Cooperation

The Japanese government's economic cooperation activities or foreign economic assistance contribute significantly to technology transfer in the Middle East. Much that is labeled "economic cooperation" in Japan more closely resembles strictly commercial ventures and is undertaken in partnership with the private sector. Some activities, however, are independent of such commerical ventures, and it is these undertakings and their influence on technology transfer that are the subject of this section.

The Ministry of Foreign Affairs is primarily responsible for official economic cooperation. MITI, the Economic Planning Agency, and the MOF all play somewhat less important roles, along with several specific agencies under their jurisdiction. In addition to providing import and export credits to Japanese corporations, the Export-Import Bank of Japan also extends loans to foreign governments with a grant element of less than 25 percent. Assistance provided by the Ex-Im Bank is not limited to less developed countries. Another public corporation, the OECF (established in 1961), also assists Japanese corporations in trade and investment as well as making loans to foreign governments with a grant element of more than 25 percent.[38] OECF finances programs and projects that the Export-Import Bank is unable to finance, particularly politically important projects that are of questionable commercial viability.

The third relevant agency is the Japan International Cooperation Agency (JICA), established in 1974 by combining the Overseas Technical Cooperation Agency (OTCA) with the Japanese Emigration Service (JEMIS).[39] At present JICA performs a variety of functions related to Japan's overseas economic cooperation. In conjunction with the Ministry of Foreign Affairs, it oversees government-sponsored technical cooperation, training and dispatching Japanese volunteers overseas. The agency also arranges the investment and financing for riskier development projects, and recruits and trains Japanese experts to provide technical assistance in those projects. Finally, JICA also sends out Japanese experts to do surveys of potential development projects. The results of these technical assessments often provide the basis for government decisions in developing countries. Because Japanese firms are frequently the recipients of contract awards, such early Japanese involvement is particularly important as a vehicle for technology trade.

Japanese economic cooperation falls into one of four categories. The first is Official Development Assistance (ODA), bilateral assistance provided by the Japanese government to developing countries for economic development or improvements in welfare. ODA always includes a grant element of at least 25 percent. "Other Official Flows" include export credits, direct investment financing, and transactions with multilateral agencies on market terms. Grants by other voluntary agencies make up the third category, and the fourth is composed of "private flows," such as direct foreign investment, export credits, and funds from multilateral private organizations.

Bilateral ODA from Japan takes the form of grant assistance, technical cooperation, or development lending and capital. In 1982 Japan ranked fourth among the OECD countries in ODA. Its total of $3.0 billion was well below the U.S. total of $8.3 billion, but close to that of France ($4.0 billion) and West Germany ($3.2 billion). Because much of Japan's aid is mixed with commercial lending, some argue that it is less generous than might first appear. Tokyo ranks near the bottom of the OECD countries in the purely grant element of its aid, and in the amount of aid given as a percentage of GNP (0.35 percent).[40]

Japan has been sensitive to such judgments and in 1977 announced that by 1980 the total amount of its ODA would be doubled. During the North–South conference in Cancun, Mexico in October 1981, Prime Minister Suzuki pledged a similar doubling of the 1975–1980 amounts for the following five years. Japan has also untied many of its foreign aid loans, permitting firms from both developed and developing countries to bid on the associated contracts, a policy that contrasts sharply with the tied aid policies of the United States and other governments that limit bidding to their own firms or those from certain limited numbers of developing countries.

Until the late 1970s the Middle East was not a primary recipient of bilateral Japanese assistance. During the 1960s virtually all of Japan's ODA was concentrated in Asia, particularly Southeast Asia. As late as 1970 the Asian region still received more than 98 percent of Japan's ODA.

Indonesia (33.6 percent), South Korea (23.3 percent), Pakistan (10.6 percent), India (8.2 percent), the Philippines (5.2 percent), and Thailand (4.6 percent) were the primary beneficiaries. Following the oil shock, Japanese assistance to the Middle East grew rapidly. After receiving 10 percent and 7.8 percent of Japan's ODA in 1975 and 1976, the region attracted 24.5 percent and 22.7 percent in 1977 and 1978, with large projects in Iran accounting for much of the increase. In subsequent years the level stabilized around 10 percent, reflecting a Ministry of Foreign Affairs desire to maintain a regional aid distribution that would see approximately 70 percent going to Asia, and 10 percent each to the Middle East, Africa, and Latin America.[41]

Japan tries to tailor the mix of financial and technical cooperation to the requirements and resources of each Middle East nation. By and large, non-oil-producing countries receive both financial and technical cooperation, while oil producers receive only the latter. Saudi Arabia, Kuwait, Oman, Qatar, and the UAE have ample capital to finance their import needs, and by and large, Japan provides them with only technical assistance. However, where extensive development programs require even more capital than oil revenues provide, as in Iran, Iraq, and Algeria, Japan has also helped with financial assistance.

Generally, the government extends yen credits only to countries with an annual per capita income below $1,500. In certain politically sensitive cases, officials in the Ministry of Foreign Affairs have made exceptions. Because of its crucial role in the Middle East peace process and its perpetual financial difficulties, Egypt, for example, has regularly received Japanese credits. Such credits are usually extended for infrastructural projects such as railways, irrigation, and agricultural development. In 1981 Egypt received approximately twice as much Japanese ODA as any other recipient in the Middle East, but the amount extended was a very modest $4.6 million.[42]

Much of Japanese aid is closely tied to commercial ventures by private firms. The trading companies, in particular, have negotiated both with Middle East governments and with Japanese aid officials to gain support for potentially lucrative projects. Speaking "off the record," one major trading company official indicated that his company frequently submitted a list of seven to ten project proposals to the recipient government. These proposals would be drawn up based on information provided by the trading company's offices in the region. The recipient government, in turn, would use these proposals as the basis for an official request for aid filed with the local Japanese embassy. The embassy would then transfer such requests to the relevant government agencies and offices in Tokyo, which in turn would be lobbied heavily by Japan-based trading company officials. With the request for aid approved, the recipient government would in turn award most of the project's work to the initiating trading company.

In addition to financial aid, Japan considers the provision of technical know-how "a very fundamental element in economic cooperation, in that the acquisition of such skills serves to disseminate technical knowledge and thus promotes a recipient country's development."[43] Several programs exist for the provision of technical know-how, including the acceptance of trainees from less developed countries, the dispatch of experts and development survey teams from Japan, and in limited instances, the provision of technical equipment to promote training. Many of these are under the supervision of JICA.

One noteworthy program for public–private sector cooperation in the acceptance of foreign trainees is the Association for Overseas Technical Scholarship (AOTS), an essentially private agency whose operational expenses are covered in part by the government. To assist private companies in securing trainees from foreign countries, AOTS may provide as much as 75 percent of the associated costs. If training manuals or texts are required, MITI helps to defray expenses. The purpose of the program is to provide general and generic training. Hence, AOTS avoids assistance to company-specific commercial ventures or for on-the-job training in any ongoing commercial venture within the Middle East. Ideally, trainees study in Japan. Such generalized training programs are seen to be of increased importance in improving Japan's relations with the Middle East by developing the human resources in the region. As one recent assessment put it:

> It is important for Japan to develop friendlier relations with such oil-producing countries as Saudi Arabia, the UAE, Iraq, and Kuwait in the Middle East, regardless of its oil purchase from these countries. Economic and technical cooperation is considered instrumental in cementing these relations. As oil-producing states have abundant capital available for development, it is necessary to step up technical cooperation based on technology transfer through such cooperation programs as formulation of economic and social development plans, expert assignment, and acceptance of trainees.[44]

Despite such optimistic statements, the actual numbers of individuals sent to or received from the Middle East through all programs remain comparatively small. As recently as 1981, for example, although the Middle and Near East accounted for 10.8 percent of all trainees accepted by Japan through these programs, the actual number involved was only 47. Japanese experts dispatched to the region both as individuals and as members of survey teams totaled only 501, and overseas volunteers sent to the region numbered only 102. The Japanese language is a major impediment to expanded numbers. Further, a very limited number of trainees are accepted, and few experts are sent in fields such as atomic energy, chemical industries, and telecommunications. The vast majority are in agriculture and fisheries, transport, construction, management, and medical care and welfare.

THE JAPANESE STRATEGY ASSESSED

Japanese economic efforts in the Middle East have rested, as have its overall domestic and foreign economic policies, on a close and cooperative relationship between government and the private sector. Such coordination has been easier in Japan than in any of the other three countries we have examined because Japan has been ruled by a single conservative, pro-business political party since 1955. Absent the pendular swings in policy that often follow elections in the other countries, and with little serious debate either inside or outside government in Japan about the "correct" relationship between business and the state, Japan has consistently pursued policies aimed at advancing trade, investment, and technological superiority in all global markets and has, since 1973, devoted considerable attention to the Middle East.

As this chapter has shown, the Japanese efforts in the region have been particularly successful as measured by increased exports, turnkey plant sales, and direct investment. Such success is even more notable given the recent development of Japanese interests in the Arab world and the historical, cultural, geographical, and ideological distances that separate the two areas.

Measured simply in terms of technology transfer, the Japanese strategy has succeeded on many fronts. There have been major increases in the export of physical technologies and capital assets in the form of plants and goods. Japanese managers, technicians, and government officials have transferred scientific and technical knowledge designed to facilitate indigenous production, including the training of local managers and technicians. The forms of this transfer have also been widely diverse. Direct sales have included telecommunications and textiles, desalination plants and dirt bikes, jet aircraft and jacuzzis. Direct investment has ranged from massive projects, such as the 13-unit Bandhar Khoumeni complex in Iran or the Al-Jubail complex in Saudi Arabia, to much smaller investments in plants making forklifts, watches, and cassette recorders. In some instances, Japanese firms have undertaken projects individually; in others, several Japanese firms have collaborated through consortia; in still others, one or more Japanese firms have worked with those of other countries from Switzerland, South Korea, or Yugoslavia, sometimes as the principal and sometimes as subcontractor. Some investments have been of the turnkey variety; others have been joint ventures with domestic participation. The apparent willingness of Japanese firms to consider a wide variety in their forms of involvement with Middle East projects has undoubtedly contributed to the cumulative success Japan has enjoyed in the region. So too has the willingness of the Japanese government to provide support services to the private sector. These range from information gathering, such as that provided by JETRO, to direct financial assistance provided through the Export-Import Bank or through government-to-government collaboration in its foreign economic assistance projects. Sensitivity to the range of needs expressed by recipients of technology has undoubtedly been among the most critical factors in Japanese success.

The entire Japanese economy has been built around high levels of private competition in sales and services, combined with government efforts to induce the private sector to become ever more technologically sophisticated and more attuned to world market opportunities. Consequently, Japanese businesspeople have long had the reputation of being willing, if not required, to shift and adapt their strategies and proposals to changing market conditions. The prevailing Japanese attitude seems to be, "Tell us what you need and we'll provide it, in whatever color or shape you prefer," conscious that if they do not, someone else will. And because of the dynamism and continued sophistication of Japanese operations, there has been a general willingness on the part of government officials and private-sector businesspeople to pass on most technologies to the Middle East without serious fears of creating potential competitors.

The Middle East became relevant at an opportune time for Japan. As the Japanese economy continued to expand, but as Japanese products began to face barriers developed in response to the world recession and domestic protectionism, the Middle East emerged as a virtually untouched market for most Japanese firms. The sudden wealth and developmental aspirations of many Middle Eastern countries blended well with Japanese abilities and desires to expand their own markets and overseas investments. The particular form of the ties between the two will undoubtedly change as Japan seeks to reduce its dependency on Middle East oil, and as many Middle East countries move away from heavy investments in massive infrastructural projects to narrower, more sophisticated, and more diversified needs. But the Japanese strategy of the past decade and a half seems admirably suited to adjusting to such changes and to reacting to them in ways that will deepen, rather than weaken, Japanese technology transfers to the region.

7

THE EUROPEAN COMMUNITY AND
THE EURO-ARAB DIALOGUE

In the four preceding chapters we have assumed that technology flows from the industrialized countries to the developing countries in the Middle East, primarily through bilateral channels, whether initiated by the public or the private sector. Both political and economic reasons have played important roles in the decisions of European and Japanese governments to promote actively the sale of technologies to the region. Moreover, in countries where initiative has been left to the private sector, competitive and aggressive national firms have used technology sales to offset the prolonged downturn in economic activity at home, and at the same time to penetrate rapidly growing economies that most likely will outperform traditional markets to the end of the century.

Our view has been that these bilateral flows of technology, driven as they are by careful calculations of self-interest, are much more likely to expand steadily than transfers channeled through multilateral regional or international institutions and agencies. Such multilateral efforts are too often constrained by the failure to achieve a workable political consensus among states of varying interests and objectives, and absent the political will such organizations can seldom mobilize the economic resources to foster technology trade.

Nevertheless, as was discussed in Chapter 2, Western Europe and the Middle East as geographical regions have shared a long history, although seldom as political or economic equals, often characterized by conflict and conquest. However, the independence of the Arab states and the growing European dependence on oil in the 1950s and 1960s laid the foundation for relations based on greater equality and a wider range of mutual interests. The birth and development of the European Community in the

1950s and 1960s and the creation of the Arab League, which was founded with successful European integration as an admired example, provided the institutional means to deepen ties between the two regions. The quadrupling of oil prices in 1973–1974 not only demonstrated Arab political power vis-à-vis Europe and others, but it also made clear the economic ties between the two regions that could be given concrete expression by these multilateral fora. In other words, the special circumstances of the early 1970s and the common interests that emerge from them give us reason to expect more from region-to-region negotiations than might normally be the case, particularly when they were given form as the so-called Euro–Arab dialogue.

Ideally, one might expect that a region-to-region strategy of technology trade might offer much both to the Europeans and to the Arabs. Building on the different advantages of the three principal European states as indicated by the different stages of the generic transfer process, this strategy could provide benefits to all, in effect creating a mutually advantageous division of labor. Britain's strength in consulting and design could work well with French superiority in large public works projects, which in turn could pave the way for German prowess in industrial development. With strengths thus identified, the common approach could foster complementarity rather than exacerbate competition. From the Arab side, a group of countries, each with individual strengths, could be seen as providing an attractive package of technology requirements that would meet the changing needs of the generic transfer process. If unrelated political squabbles could be isolated from this dialogue and sufficient leadership from both the EC and the Arab League was forthcoming, a deal of sorts that fostered technology exchange would seem to be possible. Geographical proximity and a long history of political association and cultural exchange would seem to enhance the prospects further. Such a regional partnership would offer Europe significant advantages over either the United States or Japan. It is not surprising therefore that technology transfer was identified by both sides early in the so-called Euro–Arab dialogue as an issue with obvious payoffs for all.

This chapter treats this somewhat unique case of multilateral negotiations between the European Community and the Middle East to assess its impact on the course of technology trade over the past decade. First, we treat briefly the historical context of relations between the two regions and discuss more fully the political and economic changes that took place in the early 1970s. Second, we trace the twists and turns in European–Arab relations after 1973 by examining a series of bilateral agreements that the EC concluded with individual Arab states on the Mediterranean rim and then by following the fortunes of the so-called Euro–Arab dialogue, which caught the imagination of the European community and the Arab League after the oil crisis.

EUROPE AND THE MIDDLE EAST
IN HISTORICAL PERSPECTIVE

In the words of Claude Cheysson, the European Commissioner for Development, "The peoples of the southern Mediterranean and Europe have lived together for centuries, getting to know each other and conquering each other. We have spent centuries following each other around the Mediterranean. . . . it is hardly an accident that so much of our life has been shared from the time of Alexander the Great to the Euro–Arab dialogue."[1] Both regions made major contributions to the foundations of Western civilization and shared benefits of the earliest networks of trade and commerce both on the Mediterranean and on the land routes to the Far East. The gap in economic performance and political legitimacy widened markedly in the eighteenth and nineteenth centuries when the modern European nation-state took on its now familiar form and industrialization accompanied political change. However, during the same period old empires clung to power in the Arab world and the industrial revolution passed it by. The failure of the Arab world to develop economically can be tied to the failures of political administration as well as a number of social and economic factors—the lack of a vigorous merchant class, the weakness of local demand, the scarcity of natural resources, and the inadequacy of domestic systems of transport. Growing European political and economic strength was followed by global penetration in the Maghreb, and the British drive into the eastern Mediterranean established colonial administrations that further retarded political and economic modernization in Arab states.

It was not until after World War II that the major changes were set in motion that would push Euro–Arab relations into greater balance. As we have seen, the crumbling of European empires and the evolution of European powers into nations of middle rank diminished European influence in the Middle East through the steady process of decolonization. The European departure was pushed along by the flowering of Arab nationalism, which became the instrument of political modernization and nation-building in newly independent countries from Algeria and Tunisia to Syria and Iraq. Similarly, economic relationships changed as oil fueled economic recovery and subsequent prosperity in Europe, and petroleum revenues increasingly accrued to Arab states. Moreover, having long been without the coal that powered the early industrial revolution, the Arab states now had ample energy supplies of their own to boost their economic fortunes. And the growing reliance of industrialized states on Arab oil so vital to their economic progress gave Arab states leverage useful in the advancement of their own economic objectives.

The 1973–1974 quadrupling of oil prices and embargo dramatized just how much the balance of political and economic power had shifted between Western Europe and the Arab Middle East. The Europeans could no longer set the political agenda for Arab states as they had during the colonial period, nor could they advance unconditional support of Israel as they had for a decade after the war. More and more, the Arabs took the political initiative on issues like the conditions for a Middle East settlement or the treatment of Palestinian claims for a homeland. The European states were forced to seek ways to accommodate them. While individually some European countries have gone farther to achieve this accommodation than others, all have moved much closer to the Arab view through joint positions taken in the European Community. One demonstration of support that the Arabs have demanded of the Europeans is in the willingness to grant military assistance and sell arms. With the exception of the West Germans, whose opposition to arms sales appears to be weakening, the major European states became willing, even eager, suppliers of an arms race that threatens to destabilize the region even further but offers lucrative gains for Western providers.

However, it is ironic that European support, long sought by Arab leaders, is of less service to Arab interests in a day when European influence is on the decline in the region and the United States, with its continuing support of Israel, is a much more crucial actor. Indeed, some have argued that the American presence in the Arab–Israel dispute permits Europeans to take a stronger pro-Arab stand, knowing that the United States will protect Israeli interests. Similar flexibility has for some time been exercised by both the French and more recently by the West Germans in their relations with Eastern Europe and the Soviet Union, where Washington has taken the firmer stand. In short, while European political support for Arab interests and designs may be welcome, it may do little subtantively to advance such interests.[2]

The oil crisis and its subsequent commercial and financial ramifications also demonstrated a convergence of economic interests between the two regions that holds promise for a lasting partnership. The dependence of Europe on Middle Eastern oil in the early 1970s is well known. At the time of the price hikes, 71 percent of crude imported by the EC came from Arab states. While that figure declined to 67 percent in 1975 and 58 percent in 1981, Europe will continue to be highly dependent on Arab sources for the foreseeable future. Moreover, the two rounds of price increases in 1973–1974 and again in 1979 created major trade imbalances between the two regions and gave Europeans great incentive to try to cover their deficits by expanding exports to the Middle East. By 1980, the Arab League nations replaced the United States as the EC's largest trading partner, taking 15.5 percent of total European exports. In a decade of slack demand at home, export sales in the Middle East have become vital to the continuing health of a large number of European firms.

European financial institutions also became an attractive home for Arab capital when oil revenues exceeded the spending capabilities of many OPEC nations. Such capital was particularly welcome to Western banks suffering under credit squeezes at home and hopeful of being able to sustain a moderate pace of lending. As time has passed, the European economies have come to rely on the Arabs almost as much for their consumption of EC goods and services as for their production and export of petroleum. It is this rapid expansion of two-way trade that offers the greatest potential for economic partnership, not the one-way European dependence on oil.

For their part the Arab states have viewed expanded trade with Europe as a means of narrowing the gap in industrial development between the two regions that grew so rapidly in the nineteenth century. In other words, technology trade has figured prominently in Arab imports from Europe over the past decade. In 1978, 30.4 percent of EC exports to the Arab League were manufactures and 48.1 percent were machinery. And while Europe only maintained and did not increase its percentage share of goods and services exported to Arab states in the years after the oil crisis (the Japanese doubled their share from 6 to 12 percent and the Americans increased theirs from 10 to 12 percent), they remained far and away the leading supplier at 44 percent. For reasons of geography, habit, and the current complementarity of their economic needs, it makes good sense for Arab countries to continue to look to Europe as the most logical economic partner and principal mentor in their thrust toward modernization. While there are potential conflicts in economic strategy, particularly as Arab economies diversify away from crude oil exports and seek to move downstream into refined products and petrochemicals where European firms have established strength, the overall picture appears to offer far more opportunities for exchange than potential for protectionism.[3]

The Arab attraction for Europe has also been deepened by the model of the European Economic Community and the advantages of economic integration. As one EC report put it, "The Arabs and the Europeans have found only one way both to achieve security and peace in their respective regions and at the same time promote economic development: to unite. This is the reason for the birth of a pan-Arab organization, the

League of Arab States, as well as of the European Communities."[4] The Arabs watched with envy as Europe made steady progress toward the goal of a common market for goods and services in the 1950s and 1960s. The seven independent Arab nations that had established the League of Arab states in 1945 had similar goals in mind. Unfortunately, the League's steady expansion (there were 22 members in 1977, following the independence of Djibouti) has made it an increasingly unwieldy body politically, even though the common commitment to economic development and integration remains strong. Radical regimes in Iraq, Algeria, and Libya are required to find common ground with more moderate governments in Egypt and Tunisia for any common action. Thus, the prospects for progress have diminished steadily. The difficulty of forging unity has been tough enough in the expanded EC where political orientation and economic circumstances are far less diverse. The fragility of the political consensus holding the Arab League together was indicated by the decision to expel the Egyptians from the League in 1979 following the conclusion of the Camp David accords and to move League headquarters from Cairo to Tunis.

Frustrations with progress of the Arab League to date was one reason why a group of six Gulf States (Saudi Arabia, Kuwait, Oman, Qatar, Bahrain, and the United Arab Emirates) recently formed the Gulf Cooperation Council (GCC) to promote cooperation across a spectrum of social and economic matters.[5] Organized and dominated by Saudi Arabia, the GCC has also given attention to the growing security problems in the Gulf region, particularly as the hostilities of the Iran–Iraq War spill into the waterway that is so vital to these oil exporters.

As economic interdependence between the two regions has grown, the European Community has, for its part, also looked for institutional mechanisms to tie these Mediterranean partners together, following the pattern established with other former colonies in Africa and the Far East. The requirement that both the EC and the Arab League speak with one voice rather than the 30 voices of their individual member states generally facilitates negotiations between the two sides. It is to the efforts of the European Community to give form and substance to relations with Middle East countries individually and with the Arab League as a whole over the past decade that we now turn.

THE BILATERAL COOPERATION AGREEMENTS

EC interest in cooperation with the Middle East has followed two separate and parallel paths. The first predates the oil crisis and must be seen as part of the EC's re-evaluation of its policy toward the third world, following the 1969 decision to admit Britain with its continuing Commonwealth obligations. The second, which has come to be called the Euro-Arab dialogue, is a direct result of the 1973–1974 embargo and petroleum price hikes. Both address technology trade and transfer as central to the respective sets of negotiations.

When the European Economic Community was launched among the six initial members in the late 1950s, efforts were made to accommodate the colonies or former colonies of the six founding members. Many of these colonies had enjoyed a history of active trade relations with Europe, but were likely to be denied liberal access to European markets as the six moved toward the esablishment of a common market with a common external tariff. The decision was to grant to these countries (most of which were former French colonies) associate membership in the EEC, thereby giving them preferential access to European markets. The entry of Britain in 1973 and pressure to grant access to Commonwealth states resulted in a package of preferential trade arrangements agreed upon in 1975. The Lome Agreement formalized EC trade relations with 44 countries in Africa, the Caribbean, and the Pacific (ACP).

Accompanying these initiatives was the development of an EC Mediterranean policy aimed at linking community members with countries on the eastern and southern Mediterranean rim.[6] While there was a longer-standing European interest in having accords with the Arab states complementary to those evolving with the ACP countries, there was also the recognition of growing European petroleum imports and the economic and political security ramifications that dependence on these Arab states would have in coming decades. For their part, the Arab states were increasingly receptive to EC overtures, particularly after the October 1973 War as Arab leaders began a more active campaign to secure Western political support for recovery of the occupied territories and for the legitimacy of Palestinian claims.

In November 1973, the foreign ministers of the nine states issued the so-called Brussels Declaration urging negotiation of bilateral cooperation agreements between the EC and individual Mediterranean states. In that same document, the Europeans stated their opposition to Israeli occupation of territories held since 1967 and their belief that any Middle East settlement must take account of the rights of Palestinians. At the Arab summit conference in Algiers in late November, the Arab leaders responded to the EC declaration by stressing the common interests of the two regions and the need for mutual cooperation. When the European heads of state met in Copenhagen in December, four uninvited Arab foreign ministers came to indicate their interest in long-term economic, technical, and cultural cooperation. Their request produced an EC declaration that stressed the need for "negotiations with oil-producing countries on comprehensive arrangements comprising cooperation on a wide scale for the economic and industrial development of these countries, industrial investments and stable energy supplies to the member countries at reasonable prices."[7]

The first consequence of the Copenhagen Declaration was the initiation by the EC of negotiations for separate cooperation agreements with each of the states bordering on the Mediterranean, including Israel. The EC strategy was to conclude identical bilateral agreements of unlimited duration with each nation. There was ample precedent for such bilateral agreements from the 1960s. The Community negotiated a trade agreement with Lebanon in 1965 which was subsequently renewed. Talks with Iran in the early 1960s produced a commercial agreement in 1963, and discussions with Egypt yielded a trade agreement in 1972, which was superseded by a more comprehensive pact in 1976.[8] Bilateral negotiations, which were begun in late 1973, produced a 1975 agreement with Israel followed by agreements with the three Maghreb countries (Algeria, Tunisia, Morocco) in March and April 1976 and with three of the Mashraq countries (Syria, Jordan, Egypt) in October of the same year. An agreement with Lebanon was delayed by events in that country in 1976 but was eventually concluded in May 1977.[9] Mauritania, Somalia, Sudan, and Djibouti are signatories of the Lome convention and enjoy preferential access to European markets. Altogether, 11 of the 22 Arab League states are now linked to the EC through one form of cooperation agreement or another. Libya is the only country bordering on the Mediterranean not party to such an agreement, and the Qaddafi regime has shown no interest in undertaking the necessary negotiations.

The EC has also not moved to conclude agreements with the Gulf States, although the newly formed Gulf Cooperation Council might provide the proper framework for future talks.[10] By and large, the bilateral agreements have been aimed at the poorer members of the Arab League, those in need of technical and financial assistance and with chronic trade deficits with the community. Preferential trade arrangements and financial assistance are difficult to justify for the wealthy Gulf States, although the current conditions of glut on world oil markets could alter that situation.

The seven Arab bilateral agreements are identical to each other in outline and coverage. Each permits tariff-free entry of Arab manufactured goods into European markets, although Arab states have very few industrial goods to sell. Moreover, some of those that they have begun to produce for export, such as refined petroleum products and textiles, are excluded from preferential treatment. The list of exceptions may well grow steadily as Arab states produce more competitive industrial exports. Arab agricultural exports are also highly restricted, and they are likely to become even more so with the recent entry of Greece, Spain, and Portugal into the EC.

In addition to trade preferences, the agreements also commit the EC to economic, financial, and technical assistance for the seven countries. This assistance, which is allocated for five-year periods, totaled 639 million ECU between 1976 and 1981, and 957 million ECU have been allocated for the years 1981–1986. Funding includes grants and soft loans from the EC budget and World Bank–type loans from the European Investment Bank (EIB).[11] The absolute amount of assistance is low, but coupled with other investment funds it indicates a kind of moral guarantee for particular projects. For example, in late 1981, the EC had participated in projects on new and renewable energy resources in Algeria, Egypt, Jordan, and Syria. All involved research projects staffed by European and Arab scientists.

The bilateral agreements also promote other types of economic cooperation with a direct bearing on technology transfer. The Tunisian agreement, for example, specifies greater contacts between industrial policymakers, promoters, and businesspeople in Tunisia and the Community; access to patents and other industrial property on favorable terms; cooperation in science, technology, and environmental protection; EEC assistance in energy research programs; and encouragement of private investment through political and economic guarantees.[12] Among the more pertinent objectives identified are the development of basic infrastructure, expansion of vocational training, and support for local research programs. While requirements differ marginally from country to country, the individual agreements address similar development concerns in all seven countries.

A Cooperation Council, composed of representatives of the Council of the European Communities and the Commission and members of the Arab government, administers the agreement. The council meets annually to make decisions regarding ways to meet the objectives of the agreement, and it is assisted between meetings by specialized committees that carry out assigned tasks.

Together, the bilateral agreements of the mid-1970s provide a framework for enhancing economic and technical cooperation between the two regions. To date, the commitments made in the name of these agreements have remained modest, but they do represent a contract between the two regions to increase the levels of cooperation and provide the institutional machinery to do so. Moreover, the bilateral character of the agreements permits the EC to maintain good relations with individual states should larger political disagreements between the regions develop or divisions appear within the Arab League. Such flexibility was helpful in 1979 following the Egyptian ouster; continuing European cooperation with Egypt did not have to await an improvement in relations between the Arab League and Cairo.

THE EURO–ARAB DIALOGUE

The second, and in some ways more interesting, series of negotiations to grow out of the Copenhagen Declaration was a more formal and comprehensive dialogue between Europe and the Arab world that sought high-level agreements among political leaders in both regions. Much more a specific product of the political and economic events of 1973–1974 than the bilateral agreements, the Euro–Arab dialogue (EAD) reflected the Arab League's desire to secure Europe's support for its political objectives following the 1973 War and the EC's effort to gain assurances regarding the price and availability of oil.[13] The European determination to separate politics from economics and to focus on the latter was fundamentally at odds with the Arab strategy to use economic leverage for political purposes. The clash of these two approaches prevented any meaningful movement in the early days of the dialogue.[14] With time, the Europeans agreed to pay homage to Arab political demands, while the Arabs began to view the dialogue as having greater value for their emerging pursuit of economic objectives.

Representatives of the two sides met first in March 1974 to devise institutional procedures. At this and a subsequent July meeting in Paris, it was agreed that various expert working groups would convene first to identify possible areas of cooperation. A general committee would then be formed to define the procedures by which negotiations would proceed. Following sufficient progress in negotiations, a high-level meeting of foreign ministers would finalize specific decisions and implement the substance of the agreements. Work was delayed, however, by a number of political difficulties. The first issue centered on the question of Palestinian participation in the Arab delegation. The Europeans opposed a Palestinian representative, and the Arabs insisted on a PLO presence. It took until February 1975 to reach an acceptable compromise, the so-called Dublin formula, which recommended that delegations be "homogeneous," that is, members would not serve as representatives of particular countries or groups. Under the formula, Palestinians could participate without raising the issue of representation.

The second obstacle was the U.S. opposition to any independent initiatives pursued with the Arabs by oil-consuming countries. Washington tried to orchestrate unity among consuming states as a means to counter the producers' cartel and some Europeans were reluctant to oppose the U.S. strategy openly.[15] On the Arab side, the Saudis too were reluctant to antagonize the Americans, on whom they were increasingly relying for military support and for leadership in the negotiation of a Middle East settlement. Third, EC credibility with the Arabs was challenged when the community concluded and signed the first bilateral cooperation agreement with Israel. Only when steady progress was made with parallel Arab bilateral agreements did the issue of the Israeli accord begin to diminish in importance.

The first deliberative session of the dialogue at the expert level was held in Cairo in June 1975. The meeting produced a joint memorandum recognizing the dialogue as "a product of joint political will that emerged at the highest level with a view to establishing a special relationship between the two groups."[16] More specifically, it called for "the development of the Arab world in its entirety and of lessening the technological gap separating Arab and European countries."[17] Working committees of experts were formed to address seven areas of possible cooperation: agriculture and rural development; financial cooperation; cultural, social, and labor questions; industrialization; infrastructure; scientific and technical cooperation; and trade. The seven expert groups met in Rome in July and in Abu Dhabi in November to complete much of their preliminary work.

The General Committee of the EAD was convened in May 1976 in Luxembourg to advance the work of the expert groups through political negotiation. In addition to reviewing the progress of the seven working committees, the General Committee became a forum for airing different political positions on the Middle East conflict. The Europeans did consent at Luxembourg to treat political issues as a legitimate part of the EAD, but constant political maneuvering detracted from economic and technical negotiations where progress was more likely. The General Committee met again in February 1977 in Tunis, at the end of October 1977 in Brussels, and in December 1978 in Damascus.

Arab insistence on the discussion of political issues gradually narrowed the differences between the Arab and the European positions on the Middle East conflict.[18] In the Brussels Declaration of November 1973, the Europeans had stated their belief that the recognition of Palestinian rights and PLO participation were central to any durable peace in the Middle East, and this stance was reaffirmed at the Tunis meeting. Prior to the 1977 Brussels meeting, the European Council of Ministers in a separate declaration indicated its support for a homeland for the Palestinian people. The Brussels joint statement also cited a UN resolution supported by all nine EC members indicating opposition to Israeli policies in occupied territories. But the Community stopped short of conceding to Arab demands concerning the recognition of the PLO and the discontinuance of economic aid to Israel until occupied lands were returned.

The progress of the seven working groups of the EAD was slow between 1975 and 1978, but important projects bearing on the transfer of technology were initiated. The industrialization group worked first on the development of technical standards that could be followed by Arab countries in their industrialization projects. It also undertook the complex issue of defining acceptable contract conditions for Arab countries negotiating with large international suppliers. A third project was the initiation of market studies in industrial sectors such as refining, petrochemicals, fertilizers, and iron and steel. The sectoral studies were designed to test market demand for new Arab products and to identify potential disturbances in markets where European firms were major producers. As we discuss below, European chemical firms were particularly uneasy about the prospect of new Middle Eastern petrochemical plants coming onstream and exporting products into markets already plagued by slack demand and surplus capacity. Here, the Arabs took an increasing interest in the economic benefits of Euro–Arab cooperation while the Europeans were inclined to drag their feet.

The working groups on scientific and technological cooperation explored the feasibility of projects in solar energy, radiological protection, and oceanography. Plans were also laid for the establishment of an "Arab Institute for Water Desalination and Resources" and for the creation of an Arab Polytechnic Institute.

A joint group composed of experts from industrialization and scientific and technological cooperation took up the issue of technology directly, proposing the establishment of a Euro–Arab center for technology transfer. In Tunis, the General Committee accepted the proposal in principle, and in Damascus it was decided to locate the center in an Arab city.[19]

The infrastructural working group focused on ways to improve air and sea transportation facilities in Arab countries. At the Brussels meeting, the General Committee agreed to fund a study of training requirements in the sea transport sector and a project to harmonize Arab maritime statistics. It also approved studies for new ports in Tantous, Syria and Basra, Iraq.

In agriculture, feasibility studies were funded for an irrigation scheme in Somalia, a cattle project in the Sudan, and a seed potato research project in Iraq. Altogether the General Committee funded 19 projects in Brussels and Damascus, with initial contributions of $15 million from the Arabs and $3.5 million from the EC.[20]

All of this preliminary work was suspended in April 1979, following the signing of the Camp David agreements between Egypt and Israel.[21] The removal of Egypt from the Arab League and the relocation of its headquarters from Cairo to Tunis further clouded the future of the EAD. The bureaucratic confusion caused by the departure of Egyptian officials and the loss of League records was at least as damaging as the political decision to suspend discussions.[22]

While the Europeans publicly supported the Israeli–Egyptian peace treaty, they maneuvered privately to reaffirm their commitments to the large group of Arab states and to the Palestinians. As one analyst documents, the call for Palestinian self-determination and full involvement in the peace process was mentioned on several occasions by prominent European statesmen in the months following the Camp David accords.[23] The divergence between U.S. and European Middle East policies also resulted in strained relations between some of the Atlantic allies.[24]

European heads of state voiced their strongest support for Arab claims at the June 1980 Venice summit. A joint statement called both for Palestinian self-determination and for the PLO to be a part of any peace settlement. It also suggested that the EC would take an active part in assuring that such objectives were met. Tied to this political stance was a call for resumption of the Euro–Arab dialogue which, it was argued, should also advance these political objectives.

The European efforts to re-launch the EAD paid off in November, when the two sides met in Luxembourg to discuss the guidelines for resuming the dialogue at all levels. It was agreed that an ad hoc group should be formed to prepare for a high-level ministers' meeting before the summer of 1981. This group met four times in 1981 to determine the issues that would be taken up by the ministers. Those that received primary attention were the Euro–Arab center for the transfer of technology, the status of contracts, the promotion and protection of investment, and a Euro–Arab center for trade cooperation. The ministers' meeting was twice postponed in that summer, first because of political divisions within the Arab League after the Saudi Arabians presented their own plan for a Middle East settlement, and then again following the Israeli attack on an Iraqi nuclear reactor. It was delayed again in 1982 first because of the Arab disapproval of European participation in the Sinai peacekeeping force and then because of the war in Lebanon in the summer. Continuing uncertainties in Lebanon and the threatened expansion of the Iran–Iraq War once again disrupted the plans for resumed negotiations in 1983 and 1984.

Most EC officials are increasingly skeptical that the EAD has a viable future.[25] Not only do political circumstances repeatedly interfere, but the economic and technical discussions require continuity if projects are to be completed and personal relations are to develop. Progress had been achieved between 1975 and 1978, but the lapse of five years required re-negotiated agreements, new personnel, and new funding. One EC official even went so far as to argue that the EAD now effectively discourages EC–Arab League cooperation.[26] By always linking political and economic issues in the framework of the dialogue, cooperation that would otherwise be possible at the economic and technical level is prevented. Hence, the benefits of the bilateral accords between the EC and individual Arab countries are apparent as are the initiatives of European states acting on their own.

In spite of the political difficulties, the Euro–Arab dialogue is likely to remain a feature of relations between the two regions.[27] The common economic interests that both sides identified in the early 1970s have not changed and, if anything, have become even more important. The Europeans are less dependent on Arab petroleum than they were, particularly in a time of excess supply and falling prices. Yet all except Britain would suffer serious economic hardships if Arab oil was again embargoed. Moreover, they have come to rely significantly on Arab civilian and military markets to sustain their exports. For their part, the Arabs continue to press Europe for political support in the Middle East, but as it has become clear that Washington and not Brussels holds the key to an acceptable settlement, Arab economic interests in Europe have been reshaping Arab objectives in the dialogue. In the wealthier Gulf States, where massive industrialization projects undertaken in the 1970s are being completed in the 1980s, there is a growing need to identify markets for the new products turned out by these projects. Given the limited domestic demand, production is targeted for export; for historical and geographical reasons, European markets are the first to be explored.[28] In a growing competition for market share, political intervention may more often come from the European side as governments are pressed by domestic firms and whole industries to take protective action against Arab exports. Should this pattern become a prominent feature of commercial relations, the EAD could play a useful role in mediating between importing and exporting countries to avoid a rapid retreat into protectionism.

This scenario has already been played out in a part of the dialogue that has been promoted by the Arabs even in the face of the political difficulties of the late 1970s and early 1980s. The issue is the sectoral work on petrochemicals and refining undertaken first by the industrialization working group in 1975.[29] Simply put, Arab producers wanted outlet guarantees for their base petrochemicals and refinery products once their plants came on line in the 1980s. At the time, European chemical companies were still reeling from the consequences of the oil price hikes and were dubious about the viability of Arab petrochemical projects. Consequently, they refused to participate in any negotiations. The EC recommendation was to commission a single market survey of 12 or 13 petroleum products as a way to get the Arabs to think about the difficulties of selling their products in highly competitive northern markets. The study was completed prior to the 1979 suspension of the dialogue. The departure of Egyptian personnel and the loss of records in Cairo required the reorganization of the working group and repetition of much of the sectoral research. When parts of the dialogue were resumed in May 1981, petrochemicals and refining was one of three areas (standardization and contracts were the other two) in which work was begun. Propelled by strong Arab interests, the work of these groups continued through the political difficulties in 1981 and 1982, and in January 1983 $330,000 was committed to update and computerize the marketing study. The European chemical industry has remained skeptical about the whole process, but as the Arab plants are readied for production the appeal of some kind of negotiated settlement grows. Already there are rumors that protectionism will be sought when Arab chemicals hit European markets, just as textile manufacturers have won relief from Arab exports. The European Commission's position and that of officials of the Federation of European Chemical Trade Association (CEFIC) is that dialogue is needed to prevent disruptions in trade and ill will that could jeopardize a very important partnership for both sides.[30] A discussion about a sensible division of labor in chemicals and appropriate policies to bring about the necessary market adjustments ought to have appeal in each region. The EC Commission has already taken the lead in Europe, and it is not yet clear whether the European chemical companies can be brought along.

The effective transfer of technology to the Middle East and progress with industrialization should raise other economic issues reflecting shifts in the division of labor between the two regions. Those issues too might more logically be addressed by the institutions of the EAD than by the narrower framework of bilateral relations. To date, the most apparent obstacles to dialogue have been the repeated interventions by Arab states seeking political objectives in the Middle East conflict. The diffusion or resolution of these political issues would likely result in the Arabs using the EAD more directly for economic purposes. And while there may be strong political interests in Europe that would resist using the EAD to foster economic adjustments, most EC governments are likely to see the merits of such deliberations over the long term.

CONCLUSION

This chapter has traced the legacy of region-to-region negotiations over the past decade. Unlike the record in many arenas of multilateral diplomacy, there was good reason to expect rapid progress in these discussions. On the issues of technology transfer, the generic process, as applied in the European country's discussions (Chapters 3–5) used in this analysis, identified a strong complementarity in supplier country strategies that could easily result in raidly expanding technology trade facilitated by the European Community. These varied strengths of EC suppliers and the financial resources of the League's member states following the increase in oil prices offered fertile ground for region-to-region transfers. However, in spite of such compelling economic factors, the political agenda in the Middle East regularly interfered with multilateral progress on commercial matters. Political disputes resulted in the rapid suspension of all multilateral negotiations and became the most salient feature of the EAD in its first decade. Whether compelling economic problems and opportunities provide greater incentives to get on with the work that has begun, or whether they will remain subservient to political interests, are questions likely to be answered in the next decade. Our expectation is that multilateral negotiations of this sort, even where common interests continue to be very strong, will produce only modest results; the temptation to manipulate such procedures for political purposes will prove irresistible. Bilateral negotiations, while often lacking the broader perspective that could result in much more substantial interregional trade, can regularly achieve more modest economic grains, since they target the interests of only two countries and seldom require regional political consensus. In short, while the potential for technology trade orchestrated at the regional level is substantial and the generic process readily reveals the benefits for both suppliers and recipients, political realities make bilateral strategies a more viable route to expanded exchange.

8

CONCLUSIONS

Much has been written in the 1970s and 1980s about the decline of U.S. postwar economic hegemony in world markets and the rise of other industrial competitors such as Japan, West Germany, France, and Italy. Fierce competition for existing markets in the industrialized countries and elaborate strategies to capture new markets in developing countries have become everyday features of international economics. This battle for markets is being waged not only among industrialized countries; a growing number of developing countries have also begun elbowing their way into the international marketplace. Commercial and financial affairs now regularly capture the attention of statesmen and policymakers, long attuned to security and political-diplomatic relations. Between industrialized and developing nations, issues of energy and commerce have replaced debates over empire, alliance, and formal colonial rule. International economics has moved from the business page to the front page.

In the 1980s the search for national advantage in international affairs has focused on rapid change in global markets and shifting national advantage in particular industrial sectors—what has been called "the evolving international division of labor." Industrialized nations, long comfortable with adequate markets at home and abroad for their textile, steel, and chemical products, have been shaken by new foreign competitors and have scrambled to find new ways to compete in old markets. Alternatively, they have abandoned old industries in favor of establishing markets for new ones.

New foreign competitors are found not only in other industrialized countries but also in third world economies, where competitiveness has been enhanced by the rapid acquisition of new technologies through direct purchase or through foreign direct investment by multinational firms.

Easy access to technology by the South has put added pressures on industrialized countries to accelerate technological change in their own economies so as to capture the benefits of the product cycle as soon as possible.

As a consequence of such changes, both the strategies for technology development and the processes by which it is diffused or transferred have become important in understanding and explaining the shifting fortunes of the economies of individual nations and the evolving structure of the international political economy as a whole. Properly managed, the transfer of existing technologies to have-not nations, coupled with the promotion of new technological developments at home, can be extremely rewarding to industrialized countries. Similarly, the acquisition of appropriate know-how and hardware from abroad can serve as an effective vehicle in the service of third world development, providing a means by which to carve out one's own niche in international trade.

Knowledge about technology diffusion spreads rapidly among potential recipients. As third world nations both collaborate and compete with one another in their desire to move forward with development, the impact of technology transfers in other countries and the conditions under which new technologies have been made available soon become common knowledge. Such new knowledge among potential recipients enhances their ability to choose among competing technologies, and to bargain more effectively over the conditions of their transfer. This would seem to be particularly true in countries within a common region sharing linguistic and cultural attributes, as is the case with the Middle East.

Despite such potential advantages, the export and purchase of technology also raises potential problems that observers of the transfer process have repeatedly noted. Suppliers, particularly multinational firms, may too quickly export the advantages of their technological breakthrough to economies where other factor costs such as labor or raw materials are lower, thereby depriving the initial developer of the rewards of R&D investment. Technology sales may be lucrative for suppliers in the short term, but in the long term they may erode the advantages of technological development. In the very active technology market that we have examined in the Middle East, where suppliers compete vigorously for business, the longer-term welfare of the supplier countries' economies may be more difficult to protect. Indeed, any reluctance to sell high-technology items for fear of eroding one's own competitive position in world markets may quickly translate into an attractive sale for another provider.

Similarly, the ready availability of new technologies at competitive prices may entice recipient countries into purchasing know-how and hardware that are unsuitable for their particular development needs. Unwise purchases may distort and frustrate development objectives, as discussions of the need for "appropriate" technology have rightfully pointed out.

Our view in the preceding chapters has been that common ground can be found and common interests of technology suppliers and recipients can be served through a carefully negotiated process of technology transfer and trade. This final chapter offers three general conclusions that derive from the experiences in the Middle East over the decade following the oil shock of 1973. We believe these may be instructive in locating such common ground and serving such common interests.

First, common ground between supplier and recipient can best be identified by sorting out the wide range of needs that acquiring nations have and the range of products and skills available from potential donor nations. We have deliberately defined technology broadly to include not only the purchase of physical hardware, but also the acquisition of the knowledge necessary to make technological choices, to utilize hardware productively, and to maintain it effectively. We have argued that the complexity of technology transfer can best be captured by conceiving of a loosely defined generic process through which successful acquiring nations pass. Such countries need to engage in a comprehensive exercise of planning and design to know what technologies to import, how to adapt those technologies to their particular needs, and how to bargain successfully with a range of potential suppliers. Only by doing so can they assure themselves of the highest quality at the best price. Early purchases should focus primarily on infrastructural projects. Acquisitions for such projects provide the foundation for subsequent successful expansion of both industrial and agricultural development. With time, we have argued, more attention will be directed to the start-up of new industries, which often will require the purchase of considerable heavy capital equipment readily available in the international marketplace. If and when such industries are successfully brought on line, the emphasis on imported technology will shift to smaller and more specialized needs. Only in this way can industrial processes be refined and updated in such a way as to keep new industries competitive, while simultaneously providing a broadening range of supportive services. As we noted in Chapter 1, this final stage reflects the complex character of a modern industrialized economy. The kinds of technological exchanges that take place increasingly come to resemble those that occur regularly among advanced Western economies. Successive moves through the generic process most likely signal the increasing maturation of the developing country's economy. A growing number of countries in the Pacific Basin region (Hong Kong, Taiwan, South Korea) are rapidly approaching this level of technological sophistication. One might also expect the beginnings of indigenous technological development and a reduced reliance on imported know-how.

Although the potential benefits of technology transfer may seem un-questionable to many, we have made no such assumptions concerning whether third world states should utilize technology imports as part of their broader development strategies. A country's economic circum-stances and its political environment are likely to figure importantly in the prominence given to foreign technologies. Thus, where national leaders equate technology imports with economic and political depen-dence on the industrialized North, stringent controls on imports are likely to be imposed. Even in the capital-rich Middle East region, where large-scale imports have been easily financed, some national leaders have chosen to circumscribe carefully the levels and kinds of technology im-ported. For example, the national leadership in Iraq has, for a long time, insisted on turnkey packages in an effort to minimize the time and ex-tent of contact with foreign providers. And there is little doubt that the appeal of the revolutionary movement in Iran was built in part on a re-jection of the Shah's determination to transform Iran into a modern in-dustrialized country through the wholesale introduction of foreign tech-nologies.

Thus for legitimate political and economic reasons, technology trans-fer will not be utilized by all developing states. Moreover, development in those countries may well proceed successfully without foreign as-sistance. However, we do believe that technology transfer, properly un-derstood and effectively managed, offers much to recipient states. The growing determination over the past decade to gain access to Western technologies in both second and third world nations is testimony to this position. Moreover, the growing sophistication that has been demon-strated by certain acquiring nations in the Middle East reaffirms our be-lief in the attractiveness of technology imports and our conviction that well-informed third world buyers can regularly serve their development objectives through such purchases. The expanded use of sophisticated medium- and long-term management contracts, specifying not only hard-ware but a wide range of training, retraining, and maintenance services, and drawn up in complex legal language, are evidence of careful and well-informed purchasing. The Saudi insistence on an expanded list of joint ventures and the willingness of the Germans and Japanese, among others, to accommodate such preferences, further suggest a mutual recog-nition of the need for long-term economic relationships that will broaden and deepen the Saudi modernization process.

The growing economic competition among potential suppliers for third world markets provides a particularly attractive environment for technology recipients. Increased options and better bargaining power reduce some of the political dilemmas and economic inequalities that might have characterized the exchange process when a more limited number of potential suppliers could be identified.

Our second and more important conclusion grows from the primary attention that we have given to the interests of the technology suppliers. Namely, exporting countries differ in the emphases they put on trade in technology, and by building on their unique strengths each of the supplier countries can enjoy lucrative returns from their activities in technology trade. The Japanese share of technology trade grew most rapidly in the period examined, although this rapid growth must be explained in part by the relatively low levels of Japanese trade with the region in the early 1970s. One might expect sales to level off in the coming decade. The French position weakened somewhat in the years in question, a surprising outcome given the view that performance should have been enhanced by the strong role taken by the French state.

In elaborating the generic process of technology transfer, we identified different kinds of tasks to be performed by technology suppliers. Alternative strategies permit those suppliers to develop their particular strengths and create a suitable niche in the technology marketplace. In essence, we are suggesting that social and political institutions in supplier countries, combined with the presence or absence of historical associations with the recipient countries, create different opportunities and obstacles to technology providers. Economic calculations of comparative advantage are rarely the sole determinant of the strategies chosen. Because of the length and complexity of the technology transfer process, there are many opportunities for suppliers, and these are not limited to those countries normally expected to capture most of the rewards of international competition.

The policy lesson that seems to follow is that supplier countries should do a better job of assessing their own strengths and weaknesses in the business of technology trade. They should then concentrate their resources in regions and areas of strength. While our analysis has not focused on the United States, this conclusion, in light of the West European and Japanese experience, has important consequences for U.S. policy.

In assessing the relative strengths of supplier countries in technology trade, three sets of factors have been particularly important in the Middle East. First, there are the length, character, and peculiar features of the historical and political relationship between the supplier country and the Middle East as a whole and with individual countries within the region. As we have discussed at some length in the preceding chapters, each of the four supplier countries has a unique historical relationship with the countries of the Middle East, each one of which simultaneously offers unique opportunities for technology trade as well as barriers and obstacles to such commercial exchange. Britain's long association with the Gulf region, permitting the development of close personal relations, is undoubtedly an important reason for the success of British consultants, architects, and engineers in landing lucrative contracts in the region. At the same time, the inability of British firms to penetrate former French colonies in North Africa suggests the suspicion with which former colonial powers are regarded by those countries. The British, too, have generally considered it inappropriate to use political relationships in the service of trade objectives. From time to time this has resulted in loss of business to others. The hard line of the Thatcher government on PLO recognition has probably cost British firms some business where French, Italian, German, and Japanese governments have been more willing to offer political flexibility in the service of economic interests.

France has most consciously sought to build strong political ties to Arab states in the Middle East, both in the interest of increasing French influence in the region and to lay the foundation for strong economic ties. The technology-for-oil swaps were a natural outcome of the vulnerable French energy position in the early 1970s and the desire to find markets for sophisticated French technologies in nuclear power, telecommunications, and military hardware. Military sales probably have been the single most lucrative payoff from this strategy of building close political ties. These sales have been aided by policies in West Germany and Japan that hamper selling such hardware. A review of such policies in Bonn and Tokyo could lead to a rapid change in the French position. While the French strategy of tying political and economic relations closely together has been successful in some areas, it has not been without costs. A big danger has been that if political relations sour for any reason, economic fortunes are likely to suffer as well. Uneasy relations with Algeria over the past decade are a case in point. When relations between the two countries deteriorated in the late 1970s, trade dropped off sharply, permitting West Germany, Japan, and the United States to gain larger shares of the market. Moreover, French contracts with Middle East nations, negotiated with considerable government participation, often reflect a political price for goods and services, enabling France to win the business, but sometimes with little or no margin for profit. French willingness to sign contracts for high-priced petroleum and natural gas in the late 1970s has been particularly costly in the years of oil abundance that have followed.

West Germany and Japan have historical associations with the Middle East that are both shorter and less developed. Moreover, the postwar West German connections with Israel have made delicate the management of all relations with Arab states. Yet, both Germany and Japan have made concerted efforts to depoliticize their relations with Middle East states to permit continued economic associations, regardless of the vagaries of Middle East politics. Both have insisted that the economic and technical merits of a particular deal should motivate the parties and that politics should not be permitted to intrude. Where importing countries have encountered difficult political relations with earlier colonial suppliers, such a strategy has been particularly successful in allowing new suppliers to penetrate new markets. Firms from both Germany and Japan have been quick to build business in politically volatile countries like Algeria, Iran, and Iraq. However, while business has been brisk in such areas, it has not come without risks as, for example, Japanese petrochemical companies have learned in Iran.

A conscious effort by supplier countries to divorce politics from economics does not remove the roots of political instability in recipient countries, nor does it prevent such countries from seeking to extract political concessions in return. The growing pressure on suppliers to sell arms is only one example of Arab efforts to erode the separation of politics and economics. The recent entry of Germany and Japan into the Middle East market also highlights other barriers to trade. Language differences, the lack of longstanding personal business relationships, and unfamiliarity with Arab life and culture undoubtedly make deals more difficult to negotiate, although businesspeople from both countries have worked hard to overcome these disadvantages.

In sum, the state of relations between the technology-providing state and the recipient state, as shaped both by history and contemporary politics, is important in understanding the policy of technology trade adopted by each supplier country. If the evidence provided by these four countries is instructive, and we believe it is, each supplier is encouraged and constrained by history and politics in different ways; each circumstance offers particular opportunities, but each also creates special obstacles. The adept policymaker is the one who seeks to make the most of opportunities while being simultaneously cognizant of potential difficulties.

The second set of factors affecting the supplier country's strategy is the manner and extent of state intervention in economic activities at home and abroad. As students of industrial policy have argued, foreign economic policies or the strategies that industrialized countries have employed to meet the challenges of an interdependent world, have varied widely country by country. Some have proven far more successful than others in ensuring the required adaptations. The lesson of this research is that the effective coordination of economic activities in the public and private sectors is the key to making the necessary changes to remain competitive in the global marketplace. Our view is that the different tasks of technology transfer required of supplier countries, as revealed by the complex generic process that we have described, may best be served by different industrial policies in exporting states. It follows, therefore, that by virtue of the character of public/private relations in supplier country economies, policymakers should think in terms of specializing and servicing particular needs of the transfer process.

Put baldly, some parts of the transfer process are likely to be facilitated by state coordination and intervention, while some are better left to the initiatives of the private sector. Those supplier states (such as France and to a lesser extent Japan) that grant public officials a large role in the management of national firms and in the negotiation of contracts with technology importers are particularly well suited to large-scale ventures, such as infrastructural projects or the construction of large industrial plants where national industry has maintained a competitive position. Contracts for nuclear power plants, mass transit systems, the building of dams and airports, and the preparation of harbors as well as the establishment of educational and training facilities and programs are often provided by exporters where state presence in these activities has been pronounced.

State presence and/or assistance may also be useful in facilitating large-scale industrial transfers as recipient countries launch new industries and make substantial investments in capital equipment and machinery. As we have seen, the supportive activities of MITI and the coordinating functions of the Japanese trading companies give that country's suppliers the position to compete effectively in such markets. Similarly, large German firms, whose strength is in heavy engineering and construction and whose efforts are facilitated by supportive government policies (if not by direct government participation), are also competitive in ventures of this kind. Both infrastructural transfer and transfers of large-scale heavy capital equipment are complex, often requiring multiple providers and the sale of a wide range of services from physical hardware to training and maintenance know-how. They are what the French call "les grand contrats," and they have commanded the most attention in the capital-rich Middle East over the past decade. Such deals are likely to be negotiated and managed successfully either by very large firms with access to wide-ranging resources and suppliers or by effective state leadership where public authorities are able to coordinate such suppliers and services. Of the countries we have examined, Japan (with its trading companies plus indirect assistance from the state) and France (with direct government intervention) provide two examples of success in these kinds of transfer. Large German firms have also enjoyed considerable success in large-scale industrial transfers, while coordination of such large contracts has been most difficult to achieve in Britain.

Both the early planning stages of technology transfer and the smaller-scale, more specialized transfers of products, know-how, and services that follow the introduction of new industries are better served by suppliers who have developed close personal relations with importers and who know well the needs of those purchasers. Large-scale management and coordination become less important than personalized attention and specialized service. As the chapter on Britain has argued, detailed attention accompanied by a strong sense of trust among the parties has been the foundation of the lucrative designing and consulting business built by British architects and engineers in the Middle East. Such trusting relationships are often long in the making. In such cases particular national economic strengths support and reinforce historical relations and associations. A strict separation between the private sector and public authority is often an advantage in the consulting business, as architects and engineers seek to assure clients of objective advice regarding proposed projects, attempting to avoid identification as advocates for their own national firms. French consultants have had a more difficult time establishing such objectivity, for they seldom recommend non-French firms for projects they have designed. Japanese trading firms would seem to be in a similar situation, although both German and Japanese consultants have worked hard for a larger share of the market. All three countries lag behind the British, with their long historical association and reputation for fair play.

The final stage of the transfer process, what we have called "specialized technology trade," is also likely to be best served by suppliers where the state plays at most a modest role in the economy, and small and medium-sized firms are given considerable freedom of maneuver. Here, where the value of individual sales is modest by contrast to multimillion or billion dollar infrastructural or industrial contracts, small and medium-sized firms are often likely to be more interested and appropriate for such transactions. Completing such deals requires an interested and active group of firms eager to line up foreign business, and channels that put sellers and buyers together. The Germans, the British, and the Japanese have taken steps to ensure themselves a growing share of this specialized trade. In both Germany and Britain, the work of private or quasi-public trade associations has focused on providing services for the medium and small-sized firm to position it to take advantage of sales opportunities in the Middle East. Admitting their weakness in landing large contracts, the British Committee on Middle East Trade (COMET) has concentrated its efforts on improving Britain's role as supplier to larger contractors and ensuring more specialized trade. The commercial offices of British embassies abroad are also geared to provide such services. Similarly, the Near and Middle East Association in Germany gives considerable attention to small and middle-sized suppliers. Moreover, the local and foreign offices of the German Chambers of Commerce (DIHT) provide many of the same services supplied by British embassies.

While their approach is somewhat different, the Japanese too give considerable attention to specialized technology sales. Japanese trading companies offer many tools for seeking out new opportunities, large and small, and an array of marketing techniques that permit Japanese firms to penetrate new markets successfully. Government bodies such as JETRO also provide market access services to smaller Japanese firms. The tenacity of Japanese firms of all sizes in the Middle East and elsewhere is well known, while the determination to service effectively all new markets they enter is undoubtedly a reason for their success in high-technology trade.

French policy and the large state presence in the French economy are least suited to this specialized technology trade. The tendency of French firms to look to the state for guidance and direction in foreign sales, which was an asset for the state in facilitating large package transfers, becomes a liability where initiative in the private sector is valuable. The tendency for private sector trade associations and organizations such as the French Chamber of Commerce to defer to state officials on all issues of technology trade is just one indication of this lack of initiative.

Arab states, recognizing that the era of the large contract may be nearing an end, have also initiated activities to ensure a steady flow of processes and services. Perhaps the most notable are the various Chambers of Commerce established by the Arab League in most industrialized countries. These have taken over some of the commercial activities of Arab embassies in order to expedite commercial exchange as well as to moniter provisions of the Arab boycott of firms doing business with Israel. A major emphasis in each of these offices is to devise ways to put small buyers and sellers together and facilitate such business transactions.

In sum, the variation in the roles played by the public and private sectors in the economies of the four industrialized countries suggests different strengths and weaknesses that each brings to technology trade and transfer. Most simply put, where the state plays an effective role, either directly or indirectly, in managing and coordinating large-scale economic ventures, the exporting country is likely to benefit from the sale of infrastructural and large industrial transfers; where vigorous private-sector activity dominates performance in the economy and small and medium-sized firms flourish, benefits are likely to be found both in consulting work and in specialized smaller-scale technology trade. However, it should be noted that large-scale transfers may also be successfully organized by multinational firms or trading companies, particularly when such firms operate with the indirect support and cooperation of their home governments. Of the four countries we have studied, France best fits the model of state-led transfer, while Britain most closely resembles the model of transfer orchestrated by the private sector with only indirect government support and assistance. West Germany and Japan can be positioned somewhere between, with the capability to compete both for large-scale industrial transfers and smaller-scale specialized transfers. Both are blessed with very vigorous large and small private firms driven by strong interests in foreign markets. Both are also blessed with governments sympathetic to the need for ensuring the long-term export competitiveness of their domestically based firms. With the exception of the consulting business won primarily by British architects, engineers, and planners, German and Japanese firms have shown considerable strength in all parts of the technology transfer process. In comparative perspective, the public/private sector mix probably offers more to Germany and Japan than to Britain and France. However, this conclusion should not overshadow the particular advantages enjoyed by Britain and France. Rather, it shows that all supplier states can share, if not equally, the rewards of technology sales. Furthermore, playing to one's strengths and specializing allows one to avoid much of the damage of head-to-head competition with one's rivals.

A final cluster of differences that distinguish the various strengths of supplier countries centers on the character and features of the domestic economies of these countries, particularly as they relate to technological prowess. Such features follow the historical evolution of those economies and most notably the path and direction taken since World War II. Britain's identified difficulties and strengths in technology trade follow the course of its national economy over the past three decades. Although it was the first of Western economies to industrialize, Britain has seen others pass her by in key industries and much of the British effort of the postwar years has been devoted to reversing this legacy of industrial decline. With few exceptions, aggressive export performance has not been the characteristic of British firms, and much of the success in the third world has been limited to the old colonial areas or the present British Commonwealth. Among high-technology industries, the British have long done well in telecommunications, medical services, and aircraft supplies, although they have struggled to maintain market shares over the past decades. Blessed with a large group of highly trained scientists, engineers, and other technical professionals, the British economy has long been on the leading edge of technological change. Innovative, small and medium-sized firms in Britain have long produced a more than respectable share of new products and ideas, although the country's record in penetrating and dominating foreign markets has been less than sterling in the postwar years. The discovery of North Sea oil and the diminished dependence on Middle East supplies of petroleum have also made the regular expansion of British exports less imperative for maintaining a balance of trade with the region.

The strength in British external accounts has long been in services (financial services in particular), but a wider range of professional services as well. The success we have identified in architectural, engineering, and other consulting services in the Middle East generally, and in the Gulf region in particular, is certainly compatible with this longstanding British orientation.

With the activities of the state permeating most of the French economy, one might expect strength where government efforts to promote technological change and industrial development have been concentrated. One barometer of government efforts can be found in the priorities identified in France's five-year planning exercise at home. Among the industries singled out for attention over the years have been nuclear power supervised by Electricité de France, telecommunications, and aerospace, often with military applications. While such efforts were often initially designed to serve domestic purposes, they frequently create export opportunities, which in turn encourage officials to seek markets for such new products. Nuclear power and telecommunications have been two French industries that have prospered in the Middle East, as have the well-publicized French sales of military equipment and technology.

The backbone of the German economic recovery, the so-called German economic miracle that occurred after World War II, was concentrated in electrical equipment and engineering, machinery, and chemicals. The names of the successful German firms in these industries are well known: Siemens, Kraftwork Union, Hoechst, BASF, and Lurgi. Their size and dominance within their respective industries are as commanding as they were in the years between the two world wars. While largely privately owned and operated, such firms have benefited from supportive government policies. Following a strategy of export-led growth after the war, such firms put a premium on penetrating foreign markets as well as serving domestic economic needs. The Middle East has been a natural locus for such industrial giants, able as they are to meet the heavy engineering and construction needs of countries embarking on a path of rapid industrialization. In many respects, German national economic strength has matched most closely the needs of Middle East nations as the latter have initiated large infrastructural projects or have contemplated the building of new and more diverse industries. Large German firms have been most comfortable providing large turnkey ventures. They have been uneasy with longer-term economic associations. Such preferences explain the attractiveness of contract work in Iraq and Iran over the last decade, where other national firms have steadily retreated.

Japanese strengths also can be traced to the country's postwar pattern of national economic development. As the Japanese economy has undergone dramatic technological changes in a wide range of indusries over the past three decades, individual Japanese firms have sought to capitalize on these changes through exports to the Arab countries. In direct sales, Japanese automobiles and other vehicles have made important inroads into the Middle East, just as they have in almost every other global market. But perhaps the most striking gains in high technology have been in telecommunications, semiconductors, and microprocessors. The electronics industry, which has produced such steady gains for Japanese exporters in other overseas markets, holds great promise for the Middle East as well. Those industries that have been designated for R&D support by MITI, large Japanese firms and trading companies, have repeatedly performed well in the capital-rich Middle East.

And as Japan's domestic economy begins its transition to more technology and knowledge-intensive industries, there is likely to be a greater willingness to transfer older industrial technologies and possibly even entire manufacturing operations to the region. Similarly, Japanese firms should be increasingly well positioned for business in services, process technology, and smaller-scale transfers.

This quick review of the sectoral strengths of the various industrialized suppliers suggests one lesson that appears compatible with the argument regarding the different mixes of public/private-sector strategies in technology trade. While there is considerable overlap and competition among supplier countries as one examines economies industry by industry, it is also possible to identify particular strengths held by each country. Maximizing such national advantages would seem to be one way that suppliers could ensure themselves a continuing share of the lucrative Middle East technology market.

Our discussion of supplier strategies to promote technology trade has assumed that such trade is best managed bilaterally rather than trusting such exchange to international or regional institutions. This stance appears justified on both political and economic grounds. Our confidence in its merits is supported by the experience of the Euro–Arab dialogue and other attempts at European–Middle East cooperation discussed in Chapter 7. From an economic and technical standpoint, the process of technology transfer is highly complex and diverse. Suppliers' success in promoting technology trade follows first and foremost from an understanding of this complexity, and then from an ability to recognize how best to match their own economic and technical strengths to servicing the various needs of recipient countries. As we have argued, this not only requires an ability to provide needed hardware, but also to "service" that hardware and to develop other indigenous human resources. In some stages of the process, these "matches" can be provided by government management and assistance; at other stages, government facilitation of the negotiation among private buyers and sellers may be all that is needed. At all stages, the development of trusting and sensitive relationships among the parties is extremely important. Meeting such diverse needs in an environment conducive to solid business relationships is tough enough to accomplish between two nation-states. The multilateral setting rarely permits either sufficiently specific or trusting negotiations. As the Euro–Arab dialogue has shown time and again, economic exchange too easily becomes the political pawn of one group or another, thereby discouraging and delaying serious economic and technical deliberations. Moreover, discussions must necessarily follow from a shaky consensus about technology trade among suppliers and recipients and rarely can meet the specific interests of any participant in a very satisfactory way. Neither side is thus willing to invest much in subsequent negotiations, and little of much value is the likely result. However, multilateral discussions can serve to promote information exchange, as a Center of Technology Transfer could do through the Euro–Arab dialogue.

The third conclusion is more tentative and speculative and follows from data only beginning to emerge for the Middle East. This is that there is a discernible evolution in the *form* of technology transfer, which, if successfully sustained, offers encouraging prospects, both economic and political, for recipients and suppliers. A heavy reliance on turnkeys and short-term transfers in the early 1970s has given way to the increasing use of medium- and longer-term management contracts. Under such arrangements, buyer and seller agree to work together to ensure effective transfer over a period of five to ten years. As we have noted throughout, technical and economic benefits can result for both from this longer-term commitment. The recipient gains assured access to improvements in process technology and makes sure that the technological skills of indigenous workers keep pace with hardware purchases. The supplier sells from a broader range of parts and services and increases the likelihood of developing a longer-term economic relationship with his customer. Such contracts, if effectively negotiated and administered, may lead to more stable economic and political relationships between providing and purchasing countries. In some Arab countries there is mounting evidence that the era of the big contract is coming to a close, that infrastructural projects and preliminary industrial plant capacity are soon to be completed, and that more attention will be devoted to smaller and more specialized technology trade. As this transition begins, it is interesting to note that there is growing interest in a number of recipient countries (Saudi Arabia being the most vocal example) in expanding the number of joint ventures with potential technology providers as well as making attractive the conditions for foreign direct investment. The German government, among suppliers, has encouraged reluctant German firms to consider joint ventures and has developed institutional mechanisms to foster such ventures. Japan has shown growing interest in foreign direct investment throughout the region, although the experience with petrochemicals in Iran has surely moderated earlier enthusiasm.

Joint ventures and FDI suggest a further maturing of the economic relationship between technology providers and recipients. They also more nearly resemble the pattern of technology exchange among industrialized states. Both reflect confidence on the part of suppliers that economies in recipient states offer long-term commercial benefits and that domestic political circumstances and foreign policy relationships are showing greater stability. While there is some evidence that these forms of technology transfer are becoming more attractive, conditions over the past few years in the Middle East remind us that such an evolution is far from inevitable. Two sets of developments may work to undo much of what has been achieved in technology trade since the increase in oil prices in the early 1970s. First, the glut in oil markets and declining revenues have required that producing states rethink their development plans and slow the import of new technologies. The diminished Middle Eastern capacity to finance imports and the reduced vigor in domestic markets also make investors wary of longer-term commitments. Moreover, the declining leverage of Arab states over oil-consuming countries in an era of petroleum abundance makes it more difficult for producing states to strike technology-for-oil deals. Second, the revolution in Iran, the Iran–Iraq War, the collapse of political order in Lebanon, and the ever widening threat of terrorism have combined to underline once again the volatility of Middle East politics. Such an environment hardly instills the confidence necessary to support stable economic relationships. The cumulative result of all these trends has been to induce a drop-off in exports and investments by the supplier countries in the Middle East, a tendency that was pointed out clearly in the quantitative data in Chapter 2.

If, as was suggested through the earlier chapters, successful technology transfer requires a two-way mix of need and capability, the recent decline in such transfers only underlines the point. As the Middle East countries have smaller oil-generated sums to spend, their technological options are narrowed. They also lose attractiveness to industrialized countries as markets for trade and investments. Moreover, as the pressures to offset the costs of oil purchases are reduced, governments in the industrialized countries are less anxious to support national firms in their efforts to penetrate new markets with new technologies.

In sum, the decade after the rise in oil prices gave us a glimpse of how the form of technology transfer might evolve under the best of circumstances—where purchasers were flush with funds and suppliers had attractive technologies and strong motives to promote technology sales. The last few years have indicated how fragile and perhaps how unique this environment may have been. They thus raise troublesome questions about the prospects for maintaining the trajectory of mutually beneficial technology trade and transfer over a meaningful period of time. While we do not despair at the task of fostering such an environment, recent developments reemphasize the difficulties.

LESSONS FOR OTHER SUPPLIERS

The virtue of comparative policy analysis is that it allows us to examine how different political and economic systems tackle similar policy problems and to evaluate how various features of those systems contribute to particular outcomes. Much of the conventional wisdom about foreign economic policy in industrialized states would lead us to predict that countries with particular institutional relationships, especially those where the state and public officials are given a prominent role, would be more successful at promoting technology trade than those where the state plays a smaller role and the private sector is left to manage economic tasks. By highlighting the complexities of technology transfer through what we have called a generic process, we have tried to suggest that very different policies to promote technology trade can be rewarding to a range of industrialized suppliers. By building on one's peculiar and unique national strengths, any supplier country with attractive technologies can enjoy good fortune in a region of eager buyers. What is even more interesting is that a country with a large state presence in technology trade promotion (such as France) enjoys advantages only in a narrow part of the generic process, namely where infrastructural and early industrial projects are undertaken. Alternatively, countries with innovative and aggressive private sectors enjoy a wider range of opportunities, and these increase steadily as transfer unfolds and the receiving country's economy becomes steadily more modern and complex. In countries such as Germany and Japan, where a vigorous private sector is supported in numerous ways by governments eager to see such firms succeed, the opportunities for lucrative sales are even greater. The strength of the private sector in the United States would place the U.S. approach in this latter category, although the lack of indirect support generally provided by government policy would position U.S. firms less favorably than their Japanese or German rivals. So, too, would the predominance given to political rather than economic factors in U.S. government support mechanisms. This is seen clearly in U.S. links to Israel on strategic grounds that in turn hurt U.S. commerce in the region as a whole. Nevertheless, our fundamental point is that national strategies regarding technology trade are seldom the simple product of design and conscious policy, but rather follow from the unique historical relations the supplier country has with recipient countries, the pattern of public/private sector cooperation in foreign economic affairs, and the peculiar sectoral strengths of the national economy in technology-driven areas. Every supplier country, which would include all OECD countries as well as a number of the newly industrializing countries (NICs), is capable of capturing significant shares of technology trade it if builds on such historical relationships and targets parts of the transfer process that match its domestic economic strengths. At the same time, no supplier is completely the victim of history. As the example of Japan most strikingly suggests, a country with few historical links to a region can, with sufficient motivation and quality goods to sell, make rapid economic inroads into suddenly recognized markets. New strategies can be adapted, and new structures of support can be created, with an eye toward taking increased advantage of changing markets and of differing positions along the generic path of technology transfer.

Common interests among suppliers and recipients of technology can form the basis for a lasting commercial relationship, yet, as the experience in the Middle East reveals, the uneven terrain of political relations can easily obscure these common interests and frustrate technology exchange, particularly in the early stages of transfer. German and Japanese efforts to separate political and economic affairs and to forego lucrative military sales are cases where political interference has been minimal, but it is unclear how long such divisions can be maintained. In the United States and Britain, public officials are much more likely to sacrifice economic objectives for political purposes, raising the question of whether one can even talk of continuity in the pattern of technology trade, and whether the character of the technology transferred will ever reach the complexity we outline in the final stages of generic process.

Finally, while we chose to focus on the Middle East because of the rapidity with which transfers were taking place in the mid- and late 1970s, and the evolutionary trends that might be revealed as a result, the return to relative capital scarcity in the region and the diminished bargaining position of the Arab states further underline the difficulties of moving beyond the preliminary large-scale infrastructural and industrial transfers of the past decade. The true success of the technology transfer process is apparent only when exchanges begin to occur with considerable regularity among medium and small-sized buyers and sellers in the private sector. Without a congenial political climate and steady infusions of capital, the promise of technology exchange is likely to remain largely unfulfilled for all parties.

NOTES

Chapter 1: Technology Transfer and the International Political Economy

1. For example, Folker Frobel, Jhurgen Heinrichs, and Otto Krege, *The New International Division of Labour* (New York: Cambridge University Press, 1980); OECD, *Facing the Future* (Paris: OECD, 1979); Bela Belassa, *The Changing International Division of Labour in Manufactured Goods* (World Bank, May 1979), mimeo; *La Division Internationale du Travail*, études de politique industrielle, 2 vols. (La Documentation Françaises: Paris, 1976); OECD, *The Case for Positive Adjustment Policies* (Paris: OECD, 1979), see especially, "Science, Technology and Innovation in Positive Adjustment Policies," pp. 42-50. See also Daniel Bell, *The Coming of Post-Industrial Society* (New York: Basic Books, 1973) for a discussion of the role of technology in advanced economies and the importance it would play in their continued prosperity.

2. The Brandt Commission Report, *North–South: A Program for Survival* (Cambridge, MA: MIT Press, 1980), pp. 187-200, stresses the importance of technology transfer. See also OECD, *North–South Technology Transfer: The Adjustments Ahead* (Paris: OECD, 1981). For a good historical treatment of technology transfer, particularly from Britain to Europe and the United States, see N. Rosenberg, "The International Transfer of Industrial Technology: Past and Present" in OECD, *North/South* (Analytical Studies), pp. 25-54.

3. UNCTAD has long examined the negative consequences of technology transfer and has drafted codes of conduct to attempt to regulate such flows. See UNCTAD, *Transfer of Technology: Technological Dependence, Its Nature, Consequences and Policy Implications*, report by the UNCTAD Secretariat, June 6, 1974. See also Dieter Ernst, "A Code of Conduct for the Transfer of Technology: Establishing New Rules or Codifying the Status Quo?" in *The New International Economic Order*, edited by Karl P. Sauvant and Jajo Hasenpflug (Boulder, CO: Westview Press, 1977), pp. 297-314; Helge Hveem, "Selective Dissociation in The Technology Sector," in *The Antinomies of Interdependence*, edited by John G. Ruggie (New York: Columbia, 1983), pp. 273-316; Gunnar Myrdal, "The Transfer of Technology to Underdeveloped Countries," *Scientific American* (September 1974): 173-82.

4. See, for example, David Yoffie, *Power and Protectionism* (New York: Columbia University Press, 1983).

5. For a good review of international efforts to regulate technology transfer in the third world (with a focus on Latin America), see E. M. Graham, "The Terms of Transfer of Technology to the Developing Nations: A Survey of the Major Issues," in OCED, *North/South Technology Transfer* (Analytical Studies), pp. 55-87.

6. See Raymond Vernon, "International Investment and International Trade in the Product Cycle," *Quarterly Journal of Economics* 80 (May 1966): 190-204; and Raymond Vernon, *Sovereignty at Bay* (New York: Basic Books, 1971).

7. Robert Gilpin, *U.S. Power and the Multinational Corporation* (New York: Basic Books, 1975).

8. It is worth remembering that in the 1950s and 1960s there was considerable concern about the technological gap between the United States and Europe and pressure to devise ways to promote technology transfer from the former to the latter. See especially J. J. Servan Schreiber, *The American Challenge* (New York: Atheneum, 1968). The French, in particular, complained of the dominance of the U.S. technological position and expressed fears of perpetual dependence, language not unlike what one hears today from the South.

9. The notion of a technological imperative is certainly not new. See, for example, Jacques Ellul, *The Technological Society* (New York: Knopf, 1964).

10. See David Landes, *The Unbound Prometheus* (Cambridge: Cambridge University Press, 1969).

11. Much of industrial policy debate focuses on the ability of countries to adapt to changes in the international marketplace. See Peter J. Katzenstein, *Between Power and Plenty: Foreign Economic Policies of Advanced Industrialized States* (Madison WI: University of Wisconsin Press, 1977); John Zysman and Laura Tyson, *American Industry in International Competition* (Ithaca, NY: Cornell University Press, 1983); William Diebold, *Industrial Policy as an International Issue* (New York: McGraw-Hill, 1980); John Pinder, ed., *National Industrial Strategies and the World Economy* (Totowa, NJ: Allanheld, Osmus, 1982); Robert Reich, *The Next American Frontier* (New York: Times Books, 1983); OECD, *The Case for Positive Adjustment Policies* (Paris: OECD, 1979).

12. Ezra F. Vogel, *Japan as Number 1* (Cambridge, MA: Harvard University Press, 1979); Yoffie, *Power and Protectionism*; Kent Calder and Roy Hofheinz, *The East Asia Edge* (New York: Basic Books, 1982).

13. John G. Ruggie, "Introduction: International Interdependence and National Welfare," in *The Antinomies of Interdependence* (New York: Columbia University Press, 1983), pp. 1–39.

14. Yoffie, *Power and Protectionism*.

15. How to avoid the negative ramifications of technology transfer is the theme of OECD, *North–South/Technology Transfer* and OECD, *The Case for Positive Adjustment Policies*. See also Gilpin, *U.S. Power* and D. J. Teece, *The Multinational Corporation and the Resource Cost of International Resources Transfer* (Cambridge, MA: Ballinger, 1977).

16. UNCTAD, *Transfer of Technology*; Hveem, "Selective Dissociation."

17. F. R. Root, "The Role of International Business in the Diffusion of Technological Innovation," *Economics and Business Bulletin*, 20, no. 4 (Summer 1968), pp. 17–25.

18. B. Jones, "The Role of Technology in the Theory of International Trade," in *The Technology Factor in International Trade*, edited by R. Vernon (New York: Columbia University Press, 1970). This discussion draws heavily from a good review of their definitional conceptual issues by J. H. Dunning, "Toward a Taxonomy of Technology Transfer and Possible Impacts on OECD Countries," in OECD, *North/South Technology Transfer* (Analytical Studies), pp. 8–24.

19. See, for example, John V. Granger, *Technology and International Relations* (San Francisco, CA: W. H. Freeman, 1979), pp. 10–12; D. J. Teece, *The Multinational Corporation*, and H. G. Johnson, "The State of Theory in Relation to Empirical Analysis," in Vernon, *The Technology Factor*.

20. Johnson, "The State of Theory."

21. For a historical perspective on the process of technology transfer, see N. Rosenberg, "The International Transfer."

22. Much of the theory underlying the Brandt Commission Report, *North/South: A Program for Survival*, and that underlying the position of many of those who seek benefits from the dialogue between developed and developing countries, is premised on the belief that for the North to take such discussion seriously, there must be identifiable mutual benefits in any proposed changes. Our view too is that for the flow of technology from North to South to increase, suppliers as well as recipients must see it in their interests to support such flows.

23. See Peter Evans, *Dependent Development* (Princeton, NJ: Princeton University Press, 1979), and Oswaldo Sunkel, "Transnational Capitalism and National Disintegration in Latin America," *Social and Economic Studies* 22 (1973): 132–76.

24. Hveem, "Selective Dissociation."

25. India is one developing country that has invested heavily in human capital, and has a pool of scientists and technicians that rival many industrialized countries. See, for example, "Science in India," *Nature* 308 (April 1984): 581-600.

26. See Joseph M. Grieco, "Between Dependency and Autonomy: India's Experience with the International Computer Industry," *International Organization* 36 (Summer 1982): 609-32; David Jodice, "Sources of Change in Third World Regimes for Foreign Direct Investment, 1968-1976," *International Organization* 34 (Spring 1980): 177-206; and Robert L. Curry and Donald Rothchild, "On Economic Bargaining between African Governments and Multinational Companies," *Journal of Modern African Companies* 12 (February 1974): 173-89.

27. For a good summary of these intergovernmental agreements, see J. Delorme, "The Changing Legal Framework for Technology Transfer," in OECD, *North/South* (Analytical Studies), Annex III, pp. 146-67.

28. Ibid., p. 155.

29. Ibid., P. 149.

30. Ibid., p. 151.

31. Ibid.

32. See, for example, Jack N. Behrman, *National Interests and the Multinational Enterprise: Tensions Among the North Atlantic Countries* (Englewood Cliffs, NJ: Prentice-Hall, 1970), Chapter 4.

33. E. M. Graham, "The Terms of Transfer of Technology to the Developing Nations: A Survey of the Major Issues," in OECD *North/South* (Analytical Studies), pp. 68-83.

34. See Devora Grunspan, "Technology Transfer Patterns and Industrialization: A Study of Licensing in Costa Rica," *International Organization* 36 (Autumn 1982): 795-806; and Constantine Vaitsos, "Power, Knowledge, and Development Policy: Relations Between Transnational Enterprises and Developing Countries," in *A World Divided*, edited by G. K. Helleiner (Cambridge: Cambridge University Press, 1976).

35. See, for example, Wolfgang Friedmann and Jean-Pierre Beguin, *Joint International Business Ventures in Developing Countries* (Paris: Columbia University Press, 1971).

36. Ernst F. Schumacher, *Small is Beautiful* (London: Blond and Briggs, 1973); OECD, *Appropriate Technology: Problems and Promises* (Paris: OECD, 1977); Harvey Brooks, "Critique of the Concept of Appropriate Technology," in *Appropriate Technology and Social Values—A Critical Appraisal*, edited by F. Long and A. Oleson (Cambridge, MA: Ballinger, 1980).

37. The best reputation for independence and objectivity in the consulting business is probably enjoyed by British architects and engineers. Consequently, British consulting firms do a booming business in developing countries. To get some sense of the range of services and clients, see Association of Consulting Engineers, *Overseas Work Entrusted to Members During 1983* (London, 1984).

38. See Office of Technology Assessment, *Technology Trade and Transfer to the Middle East*.

39. See Katzenstein, *Between Power and Plenty*.

Chapter 2: Trade and Technology Transfer: The Major Trends

1. Office of Technology Assessment, *Technology Transfer to the Middle East* (Washington, D.C.: OTA, 1984), p. 22.

2. Ibid., p. 101.

3. *Middle East Economic Digest*, September 7, 1984, p. 6.

4. OTA, *Technology Transfer*, p. 105.

Chapter 3: Britain: Trading Technology in the Postcolonial Era

1. We use the concept of strategy following from the way it has been used by Peter J. Katzenstein, "Conclusion: Domestic Structures and Strategies of Foreign Economic Policy," in *Between Power and Plenty: Foreign Economic Policies of Advanced Industralized States*, edited by Peter J. Katzenstein (Madison, WI: University of Wisconsin Press, 1977), pp. 295-336.

2. See *The Export Credit Financing Systems in OECD Member Countries* (Paris: OECD, 1982), pp. 7-12.

3. Ibid.

4. Elizabeth Monroe, *Britain's Moment in the Middle East* (Baltimore, MD: Johns Hopkins University Press, 1981).

5. Ibid., pp. 11-13; John Gallagher and Ronald Robinson, *Africa and the Victorians* (New York: St. Martin's, 1961); Jacob Abadi, *Britain's Withdrawal from the Middle East, 1947-1971* (Princeton, NJ: Kingston Press, 1982); Sir Reader Bullard, *Britain and the Middle East* (London: Hutchinson, Unity Library, 1964).

6. Royal Institute of International Affairs, *British Interests in the Mediterranean and the Middle East* (London: Oxford, 1958), pp. 2-3.

7. For a thorough treatment of this process of withdrawal see Abadi, *Britain's Withdrawal.*

8. There are a number of good studies of British foreign policy after World War II and the adjustments to medium-power status. See David Calleo, *Britain's Future* (New York: Horizon Press, 1968); Richard Rosecrance, *Defense of the Realm: British Strategy in the Nuclear Epoch* (New York: Columbia University Press, 1968); Max Beloff, *The Future of British Foreign Policy* (New York: Tadlinger, 1969); F. S. Northedge, *British Foreign Policy* (New York: Praeger, 1962); Joseph Frankel, *British Foreign Policy, 1945-1973* (London: Oxford University Press, 1975).

9. Among the best accounts of the same crisis and its impact on British policy are Leon D. Epstein, *British Politics in the Suez Crisis* (Urbana: University of Illinois Press, 1964); Selwyn Lloyd, *Suez, 1956: A Personal Account* (New York: Mayflower Books, 1978); and Hugh Thomas, *The Suez Affair* (London: Weidenfeld and Nicolson, 1967).

10. Elizabeth Monroe, *The Changing Balance of Power in the Persian Gulf* (New York: 1972).

11. Ibid., p. 115.

12. The report of a study group in the late 1950s pointed out the need for increased British economic penetration of the Middle East as oil dependence grew and political influence declined: "But in any case we now have reason to know that Britain is no longer nearly so powerful in the Middle East as formerly, neither is there a unique position there. There are merely mutual needs, ours for oil, theirs for markets, technical help and understanding." Royal Institute of International Affairs, *British Interests*, p. 123.

13. Dominique Moisi suggests one policy consequence as a result of this similar energy position in comparing Britain with Germany: "The British, even more than the Germans, are largely motivated in their policy in the area by their link to the USA, free as they are because of a crucial new factor, their near total independence from Arab oil." See Moisi, "Europe and the Middle East," in *The Middle East and the Western Alliance*, edited by Steven L. Speigel (London: Allen and Unwin, 1982), pp. 18-32.

14. "Thatcher Sets Her Sights on the Gulf," *The Middle East* (October 1982): 24-26.

15. Monroe, *Britain's Moment*, p. 161.

16. Sari J. Nasir, *The Arabs and the English*, 2nd ed. (London: Longman, 1979).

17. Ibid., p. 172.

18. There is a rich literature on British industrial development. See, for example, Andrew Shonfield, *Modern Capitalism: The Changing Balance of Public and Private Power* (New

York: Oxford University Press, 1965), Chapter 6; Stephen Blank, *Industry and Government in Britain: The Federation of British Industries in Politics, 1945–1965* (Lexington, MA: Lexington Books, 1973); Trevor Smith, "Industrial Planning in Britain," in *Politics, Planning and Public Policy,* edited by Jack Hayward and Michael Waston (Cambridge: Cambridge University Press, 1975); Stephen Young, *Intervention in the Mixed Economy: The Evolution of British Industrial Policy, 1964–1972* (London: Croon Helm, 1974).

19. Accounts of the British system of free trade and its consequences are many. See J. B. Condliffe, *The Commerce of Nations* (New York: W. W. Norton, 1950); E. J. Hobsbawm, *Industry and Empire* (London: Penguin, 1969); and John Seely, *Expansion of England* (London: Macmillan, 1925). On British foreign investment see Susan Strange, *Sterling and British Power* (London: Oxford University Press, 1971); Robert Gilpin, *U.S. Power and the Multinational Corporation* (New York: Basic Books, 1975), Chapter 3.

20. See Trevor Smith, "Industrial Planning in Britain," in *Planning and Politics: the British Experience, 1960–1976,* edited by Michael Shanks (London: George Allen and Unwin, 1977); Samuel Brittan, *Steering the Economy: The Role of the Treasury* (London: Secker and Warburg, 1969).

21. "Security Export Control," *British Business* (supplement), March 28, 1980. Goods listed in this publication require a license before they can be exported.

22. OECD, *International Investment and Multinational Enterprises: Recent International Direct Investment Trends* (Paris: OECD, 1981).

23. "The UK and the Gulf, 1971–1981," *Middle East Economic Digest* (MEED) (December 1981): 36–37.

24. Ibid., p. 37.

25. Ibid., pp. 48–49.

26. Ibid., p. 56.

27. Ibid., p. 10.

28. Interview at COMET, January 1983.

29. Ibid. On the role of British finance and banks and their role in industrial development more generally, see Vivian Authony, *Banks and Markets,* 3rd ed. (London: Heineman, 1979); John Zysman, *Governments, Markets and Growth: Financial Systems and the Politics of Industrial Change* (Ithaca, NY: Cornell University Press, 1983).

30. "UK and the Gulf," p. 10.

31. Ibid.

32. Interview with John Biffen (Secretary of State for Trade), "The UK and the Gulf," p. 33.

33. British Overseas Trade Board, "BOTB's Service" (September 1982).

34. Interview, Department of Trade, London, January 1983.

35. Ibid.

36. Ibid.

37. Interview at COMET, London, January 1983.

38. The Joint Arab-British Chamber of Commerce (ABCC), "Memorandum and Articles of Association" (1975). The ABCC also regularly publishes a *Trade Information Bulletin* for its members.

39. OECD, *The Export Credit,* pp. 236–40.

40. Ibid., p. 236.

41. *ECGD Services* (London: HMSO, 1982).

42. OECD, *The Export Credit,* p. 230.

43. *ECGD Services,* pp. 9–10.

44. All of these programs are discussed in greater detail in *ECGD Services.*

45. "Telecommunications, Electronics, and the Middle East" *MEED* (Special Report, January 1981): 22–23.

46. OECD, *Development Co-operation* (1982 Review) (Paris: OECD, 1982).

47. World Bank, *World Development Report 1983* (Oxford: Oxford University Press, 1983), p. 104.

48. OECD, *Development Co-operation*, p. 154.

Chapter 4: France: Technology Trade, Politics, and the State

1. The long-term importance of Algeria to France is traced by William B. Cohen, "Legacy of Empire: The Algerian Connection," *Journal of Contemporary History* 15 (January 1980): 113–14.

2. For good discussions of the various ramifications of the Algerian struggle for independence, see Tony Smith, *The French Stake in Algeria* (Ithaca, NY: Cornell University Press, 1978); William G. Andrews, *French Politics and Algeria* (New York: Appleton-Century-Crofts, 1962); Edward Kolodziej, *French International Policy under DeGaulle and Pompidou* (Ithaca, NY: Cornell University Press, 1974).

3. See, particularly, Smith, *The French Stake*.

4. Kolodziej, *French International Policy*, p. 448.

5. Ibid., pp. 478–80.

6. Among the many books on deGaulle's foreign policy, see Kolodziej, *French International Policy*; Alfred Grosser, *French Foreign Policy under DeGaulle* (Boston, MA: Little, Brown, and Co. 1965); Herbet Tint, *French Foreign Policy Since the Second World War* (New York: St. Martins, 1972); Wolfram F. Henrieder and Graeme P. Auton, *The Foreign Policies of West Germany, France and Britain* (Englewood Cliffs, NJ: Prentice Hall, 1980); Edward Morse, *Foreign Policy and Interdependence in Gaullist France* (Princeton, NJ: Princeton University Press, 1973).

7. Kolodziej, *French International Policy*, pp. 478–80.

8. This theme is advanced by F. Roy Willis, *The French Paradox: Understanding Contemporary France* (Stanford, CA: Hoover Institution Press, 1982). See also Thankman Fuhr. von Munchhausen, "France's Relations with the Arab World," *Aussenpolitik* (1981).

9. See Kolodziej, *French International Policy*, Chapter 10. See also Paul Balta and Claudine Bulleaux, *La politique arabe de la France de Gaulle à Pompidou* (Paris, 1973).

10. Charles Saint-Prot, *La France et le renouveau arabe de Charles de Gaulle à Valery Giscard d'Estaing* (Paris, 1980).

11. Algeria, Iraq, and Saudi Arabia.

12. Saint-Prot, *La France et le renouveau arabe*.

13. Cohen, "Legacy of Empire," p. 120.

14. "France and the Middle East," *MEED* (May 1982): 6.

15. "Giscard the Baptist Preaches in the Desert," *The Economist*, March 8, 1980, pp. 51–52.

16. See, for example, von Munchhausen, "France's Relations"; Frederick Seager, "New Directions in French Middle East Policy," *Middle East Review* (Spring/Summer 1982): 49–54; Thomas Carothers, "Mitterrand and the Middle East," *The World Today*, 38 (October 1982): 381–86; Marie-Claude Smouts, "External Policy of François Mitterand," *International Affairs* 59 (Spring 1983): 155–67.

17. Interview at the Commissariat à l'Energie Atomique (CEA), Paris, July 1983.

18. Interview at the Ministry of Research and Industry, Paris, January 1983.

19. Carothers, "Mitterrand and the Middle East."

20. Smouts, "External Policy," p. 167.

21. Ibid., p. 164.

22. See "Mitterrand Puts the Profit Motive First," *The Middle East* (October 1982): 23–26; "Anglo-French Dogfight in Gulf Skies," *The Middle East* (August 1981): 52–54; and von Munchhausen, "France's Relations."

23. Edward A. Kolodziej, "France and the Arms Trade," *International Affairs*, 56, No. 1 (January 1980): 54–72.

24. Smouts, "External Policy," p. 163.

25. On early French industrial development, see Andrew Schonfield, *Modern Capitalism* (London: Oxford University Press, 1970), Chapter 5; H. Milward and S. B. Saul, *The Development of the Economies of Continental Europe* (Cambridge, MA: Harvard University Press, 1977); Rondo E. Cameron, *France and the Economic Development of Europe, 1800–1914* (Princeton, NJ: Princeton University Press, 1961).

26. Charles P. Kindleberger, "The Postwar Resurgence of the French Economy," in *In Search of France*, edited by Stanley Hoffmann (New York: Harper & Row, 1963), pp. 118–58.

27. John Zysman, "The French State in the International Economy," in *Between Power and Plenty: Foreign Economic Policies of Advanced Industrialized States*, edited by Peter J. Katzenstein (Madison, WI: University of Wisconsin Press, 1977), p. 269.

28. On the changing role of the state in the economy in the postwar years, see Charles-Albert Michalet, "France," in Vernon, *Big Business and the State*, pp. 105–25; Jean-Jacques Bonnaud, "Planning and Industry in France," in Hayward and Watson, *Politics, Planning and Public Policy*, pp. 93–110; Stephen Cohen, *Modern Capitalist Planning* (Cambridge, MA: Harvard University Press, 1969); John H. McArthur and Bruce R. Scott, *Industrial Planning in France* (Boston, MA: Harvard Division of Research, Graduate School of Business Administration, 1969); John Zysman, *Political Strategies for Industrial Order* (Berkeley, CA: University of California Press, 1977).

29. The rationalization process in the chemical industry is treated in Thomas L. Ilgen, "Better Living Through Chemistry: The Chemical Industry in the World Economy," *International Organization* 37, no. 4 (Autumn 1983): 647–80.

30. Kindleberger, "The Postwar Resurgence," pp. 148–58.

31. On the recruitment of French elites, see Henry Ehrman, *Organized Business in France* (Princeton, NJ: Princeton University Press, 1957); Ezra N. Suleiman, *Politics, Power and Bureaucracy in France: The Administrative Elite* (Princeton, NJ: Princeton University Press, 1974); Ezra N. Suleiman, *Elites in French Society: The Politics of Survival* (Princeton, NJ: Princeton University Press, 1978).

32. See Jean Fourastie, *Les Trente glorieuses ou la revolution invisible de 1946 à 1975* (Paris: Fayard, 1979). The state did not enjoy success in all economic sectors, however. On the difficulties in electronics, see Zysman, *Political Strategies*.

33. Charles de Gaulle, *Memoirs d'espoir Le Renouveau, 1958–1962* (Paris: Plon, 1970), p. 139.

34. Interview at the Ministry of Research and Industry, Paris, January 1983.

35. Interview at CEA, Paris, January 1983. Officials were insistent that France had fulfilled all of the international safety requirements for nuclear exports in the case of the sale to Iraq.

36. OECD, *International Investment and Multinational Enterprises: Recent International Direct Investment Trade* (Paris: OECD, 1981).

37. *Moniteur du Commerce International* (December 1978).

38. "France and the Middle East," *The Middle East* (May 1979), p. 120.

39. "Les Grands Contrats," *Moniteur du Commerce International*, April 26, 1982.

40. Untangling the intricacies and interrelationships of the French bureaucracy is a difficult task for any researcher. A helpful, if somewhat dated, guide in the foreign policy realm is Jean du Boisberranger, *Domaine et instruments de la politique etrangere de la France* (Paris: La Documentation Française, January 15, 1976).

41. CFCE publishes an annual issue of *LeMoci* entitled "Les Grands Contrats," which gives a good accounting of the large French export deals organized by geographical region.

42. One way to get a feeling for this connection between internal planning and export promotion is to read some of the many publications of the Commissariat General du Plan detailing the reasons for planning choices. On the current period, see, for example, *Demain la france dans le monde, preparation du huitieme plan, 1981–1985* (Paris: La Documentation Française, 1980).

43. Lawrence G. Franko and Sherry Stephenson, "French Export Behavior in Third World Markets," in *World Trade Competition: Western Countries in Third World Markets*, edited by Center for Strategic and International Studies (New York: Praeger, 1981), pp. 183–229.

44. Interview with the French Chamber of Commerce, Paris, January 1983.

45. The Franco-Arab Chamber of Commerce has given special attention to the technology issues by convening several French-Arab conferences to discuss the development and transfer of technology. The results of these meetings are summarized in two reports, *Colloque sur la formation professionelle et le transfer de technologie* (Amman, May 27–30, 1979) and *Colloque sur les energies nouvelles* (Sousse, Tunisia, October 27–30, 1980). On the role of French banking and finance more generally see John Zysman, *Governments, Markets and Growth: Financial Systems and the Politics of Industrial Change*, (Ithaca, NY: Cornell University Press, 1983), Chapter 3.

46. Quoted in Tint, *French Foreign Policy*, p. 166.

47. OECD, *The Export Credit*, pp. 91–99. See also Franko and Stephenson, "French Export Behavior," pp. 183–93.

48. OECD, *The Export Credit*, pp. 92–96; Franko and Stephenson. "French Export Behavior," pp. 187–89.

49. Ibid., p. 189.

50. Ibid., pp. 189–94, OECD, *The Export Credit*, pp. 96–99.

51. U.S. Department of State, *Export Credit Systems of the Major Powers and their Role in Export of Capital Goods* (Washington, D.C., 1977), p. 2.

52. Ibid., p. 8.

53. Marc Bouteiller, "Les grands contrats conclu avec le Tiers Monde," in *Impact des relations avec le Tiers Monde sur l'economie française*, edited by Yves Berthelot and Jacque DeBendt (Paris: La Documentation Française, 1982), pp. 179–210.

54. Franko and Stephenson, "French Export Behavior," p. 197.

55. Interview at the Ministry of Research and Industry, Paris, January 1983.

56. This process was described by officials at CEA, Paris, January 1983.

57. Interview at the Ministry of Research and Industry, Paris, January 1983.

58. This concern is also raised by Smouts, "External Policy."

Chapter 5: West Germany: Technology, Industrial Development, and the Denial of Politics

1. See Lukasz Herszowicz, *The Third Reich and the Middle East* (London: Routledge & Kegan Paul, 1966), Chapter 1.

2. Ibid., Chapter 2. See also Jehuda L. Wallach, ed., *Germany and the Middle East, 1835–1939* (Tel Aviv: Israel Press, 1975).

3. Herszowicz, *The Third Reich*, pp. 40–41.

4. Accounts of postwar German foreign policy in the 1950s and 1960s seldom treat German third world policy at all. See, for example, Wolfram F. Hanrieder, *The Stable Cri-*

sis: Two Decades of German Foreign Policy (New York: Harper & Row, 1970); Karl Kaiser, *German Foreign Policy in Transition: Bonn Between East and West* (London: Oxford University Press, 1968); Alfred Grosser, *Germany in our Time: A Political History of the Postwar Years* (New York: Praeger, 1971); Peter H. Merkl, *German Foreign Policies West and East: On the Threshold of a New European Era* (Santa Barbara, CA: ABC Clio, 1970).

5. Roger Morgan, "West Germany's Foreign Policy Agenda," *The Washington Papers*, no. 54 (Beverly Hills, CA: Sage, 1978), pp. 58-69.

6. Lily Gardner Feldman, *The Special Relationship Between West Germany and Israel* (London: George Allen & Unwin, 1984), Chapter 8.

7. Bonn's foreign policy in the region is traced by Udo Steinbach, "German Policy on the Middle East and the Gulf," *Aussenpolitik*, 32, no. 4 (1981): 315-31.

8. Interview at the Ministry of Economics, Bonn, January 1983.

9. *The New York Times*, January 22, 1984, p. 9.

10. Ibid., March 7, 1984, p. 9.

11. Steinbach, "Germany Policy," and Wolfram Hanrieder, "Germany as Number Two?" *International Studies Quarterly* 27 (March 1982): 57-86.

12. Feldman, *The Special Relationship*, Chapter 8.

13. Steinbach, "German Policy."

14. For background in German industrial development see K. Borchardt, "The Industrial Revolution in Germany, 1700-1914," in *Fontana Economic History of Europe*, vol. 4 (London 1971); Alexander Gerschenkron, *Bread and Democracy in Germany* (New York: Fertig, 1966); Karl Hardach, *The Political Economy of Germany in the Twentieth Century* (Berkeley, CA: University of California Press, 1976); Fritz Stern, *Gold and Iron: Bismarck, Bleichroder and the Building of the German Empire* (New York: Knopf, 1977).

15. For a discussion of German economic development after World War II, see Henry Wallich, *Mainsprings of the German Revival* (New Haven, CT: Yale University Press, 1955); Edwin Hartrich, *The Fourth and Richest Reich* (New York: Macmillan, 1980); George Kuster, "Germany," in *Big Business and the State*, edited by Raymond Vernon (Cambridge, MA: Harvard University Press, 1974).

16. On the Federal Republic's foreign economic policy, see Michael Kreile, "West Germany: The Dynamics of Expansion," in Katzenstein, *Between Power and Plenty*, pp. 191-224.

17. Ibid., pp. 192-93.

18. See Thomas L. Ilgen, "Better Living Through Chemistry: The Chemical Industry in the World Economy," *International Organization* 37, no. 4 (Autumn 1983): 670-75.

19. The importance of German banks has been noted by many. See, for example, Alexander Gerschenkron, *Economic Backwardness in Historical Perspective* (Cambridge, MA: Belknap, 1963); Herbert Feis, *Europe: The World's Banker, 1870-1914* (New Haven, CT: Yale University Press, 1930); John Zysman, *Governments, Markets and Growth: Financial Systems and the Politics of Industrial Change* (Ithaca, NY: Cornell University Press, 1983); Andrew Spindler, *The Politics of International Credit: Private Finance and Foreign Policy in Germany and Japan* (Washington, D.C.: Brookings Institute, 1984), Chapter 2.

20. OECD, *International Investment and Multinational Enterprises: Recent International Direct Investment Trends* (Paris: OECD, 1981), pp. 75-78.

21. For a good discussion of German consulting fortunes in the Middle East, see "West Germany and the Middle East," *Middle East Economic Digest* (MEED) (February 1982): 34-44.

22. German-Iraqi trade is treated in "Iraq: A MEED Special Report," *MEED* (October 1982): pp. 24-29.

23. Interview at the Ministry of Economics, Bonn, January 1983.

24. *MEED* (February 1982): 26.

25. "Saudi Arabia: Special Report," *MEED*, p. 66.

26. "West Germany and the Middle East," *MEED*, p. 24.

27. "Saudi Arabia," *MEED*, p. 30.

28. For an unofficial review of German policies regarding technology trade, see H. Theirl, "Technologies for Developing Countries," Bundesministeriam für Wirtschaffliche Zusamorenarbeit (Ministry for Economic Cooperation BMZ), (mimeo). Theirl indicates that the Germans have given considerable attention to the question of appropriate technologies for developing countries, following the work of E. F. Schumacher.

29. Interview at the Ministry of Economics, Bonn, January 1983.

30. "Saudi Arabia," *MEED*, p. 30.

31. Interview at the Mininstry of Economics, Bonn, January 1983.

32. Ibid.

33. Ibid.

34. Ibid.

35. Ibid.

36. Ibid.

37. Interview at BMZ, Bonn, January 1983. See also Theirl, "Technologies."

38. Interview at German Chamber of Commerce DIHT, Bonn, January 1983.

39. Ibid.

40. Interview at Nah und Mittlost Verein (Near and Middle East Association; NMV) Bonn, January 1983.

41. Ibid.

42. Ibid. See also, "Islam and Orientalism," *The Middle East* (June 1980): 98.

43. See OECD, *The Export Credit Financing Systems in OECD Member Countries* (Paris: OECD, 1982), pp. 102–106; "West Germany," *MEED* (November 1979): 17–18.

44. Ibid.

45. OECD, *The Export Credit*, p. 103.

46. "West Germany," *MEED*, p. 17.

47. Ibid., p. 18. The *MEED* article cites a study published by Fritz Paetzolt and Dietmar Petersen, "Political Investment Risks in Developing Countries" (Cologne: DEC, 1978), which indicates government's interest in assessing the risks of ensuring German investments abroad, with an eye to more assistance for small and medium-sized firms.

48. Ibid., pp. 21–22.

49. OECD, *The Export Credit*, p. 107–16.

50. Ibid.

51. Ibid. Kreditanstaff fur Wiederaufbau (KFW) also has a loan program specially designed for the development of new technologies in the third world. See KFW "Technology Program," mimeo, 1981.

52. "West Germany," *MEED*, p. 12. For background on West German foreign aid programs, see Karel Holbik and Henry Myers, *West German Foreign Aid, 1956–1966: Its Economic and Political Aspects* (Boston, MA: Boston University Press, 1968); Jack L. Knusel, *West German Aid to Developing Nations* (New York: Praeger, 1968).

53. Ibid.

54. This notion of "threshold" countries is discussed in "West Germany and the Middle East," *Middle East* (June 1980): 90–91.

55. "West Germany," *MEED*, p. 13. Interview at BMZ, Bonn, January 1983.

Chapter 6: Japan: Marketing Technology Unencumbered by History

1. See, for example, W. G. Beasley, *The Meiji Restoration* (Stanford, CA: Stanford University Press, 1972), pp. 366–78.

2. Tomita Nobuo and Sone Yasunori, eds., *Sekai Seiji no naka no Nihon Seiji* (Japanese Politics within World Politics). Tokyo: Yuhikaku, 1983.

3. T. J. Pempel, "Japanese Foreign Economic Policy: The Domestic Bases for International Behavior," in *Between Power and Plenty*, edited by Peter Katzenstein (Madison, WI: University of Wisconsin Press, 1978), pp. 139–90.

4. Interviews, Ministry of Foreign Affairs.

5. Japan's reliance on the majors was a serious problem in public policy following the oil shock, primarily because most of them were U.S. or British companies, and Japanese officials felt they shortchanged Japan in favor of North America or Europe in providing suddenly scarce oil resources. Since 1973 Japan has begun to move toward increased reliance on government-to-government sales and away from purchases from the majors.

6. Valerie Yorki, "Oil, the Middle East and Japan's Search for Security," in *Japan's Economic Security*, edited by Nobuyoshi Akao (New York: St. Martins, 1983), pp. 45–70.

7. Yoshi Tsurumi, "Japan," *Daedalus*, 104 (Fall 1975): 124.

8. In April 1984 President Mubarak visited Japan, thus becoming the first Egyptian head of state to visit the country. *Look Japan*, June 10, 1980, p. 15.

9. Japan Economic Institute, *Report* no. 7, February 20, 1981, p. 3.

10. Pempel, "Japanese Foreign Economic Policy," p. 164.

11. *Nihon Kokusei Zue, 1984* (Statistical Sketch of Japan, 1984). Tokyo: Yano Hisahiro Kinenkai, 1984, p. 113.

12. Chalmers Johnson, *MITI and the Japanese Miracle* (Stanford, CA: Stanford University Press, 1982), *passim*, but especially Chapters 1 and 9.

13. This viewpoint was first articulated in the May 1971 report of the Industrial Structure Council's interim study on "Trade and Industrial Policy for the 1970s," and further advanced in the Council's much more expanded final report, "Japan's Industrial Structure— A Long-Range View" (Tokyo: Ministry of Finance, 1974).

14. Ibid., Preface, Part II, paragraph 2.

15. Johnson, *MITI*.

16. Ibid., p. 230.

17. K. Bieda, *The Structure and Operation of the Japanese Economy* (New York: Wiley, 1970), pp. 116–18.

18. Yoshikazu Miyazaki, "Excessive Competition and the Formation of *Keiretsu*," in *Industry and Business in Japan*, edited by Kazuo Sato (White Plains, NY: M. E. Sharpe, 1980), pp. 53–73.

19. Inter-Bank Research Organization, *Banking Systems Abroad* (London: IBRO, n.d.), Chapter 8; Uoshio Suzuki, *Money and Banking in Contemporary Japan* (New Haven, CT: Yale University Press, 1980); Henry Wallich and Mable Wallich, "Banking and Finance," in *Asia's New Giant*, edited by Hugh Patrick and Henry Rosovsky (Washington, D.C.: Brookings, 1976), p. 294.

20. Ibid.; also Pempel, "Japanese Foreign Economic Policy," pp. 152–53.

21. Terutomo Ozawa, *Multinationalism, Japanese Style* (Princeton, NJ: Princeton University Press, 1979); Kozo Yamamura, "General Trading Companies in Japan—Their Origins and Growth," in *Japanese Industrialization and Its Social Consequences*, edited by Hugh Patrick (Berkeley, CA: University of California Press, 1976); Yoshi Tsurumi, *The Sogosoha* (Montreal: IRPP, 1980).

22. Ibid. See also, M. Y. Yoshino, *Japan's Multinational Enterprises* (Cambridge, MA: Harvard University Press, 1976).

23. Data provided by the Japanese Ministry of Finance.

24. *Business Week*, June 16, 1980, p. 97.

25. Based on interviews in Ministry of Foreign Affairs and Ministry of Finance.

26. Data provided by Ministry of Foreign Affairs; comparable data for earlier periods

is available in Gaimusho, *Gaimusho Hakusho* (Tokyo: Okurasho Insatsukyoku, annual).

27. Martha Caldwell, "The Dilemmas of Japan's Oil Dependency," in *The Politics of Japan's Energy Strategy*, edited by Ronald A. Morse (Berkeley, CA: Institute of East Asian Studies, University of California, 1981), pp. 71-82.

28. *MEED*, December 1982, p. 23.

29. *Business Week*, June 16, 1980, p. 96.

30. Yet, in March 1982, Kawasaki sold ten helicopters to Saudi Arabia. These were allegedly for civilian purposes, but could be readily adapted to military use. In 1984 Japan sold all-weather vehicles to the same country under similar circumstances.

31. See Morse, *Japan's Energy Strategy*, expecially Chapter 8.

32. Martin Roth, "Japan Seeks a Way Out of Middle East Oil Dependence," *MEED*, July 20, 1984, p. 3.

33. *MEED*, December 1982.

34. *MEED*, December 1984, p. 21.

35. Nihon Yushutsunyu Ginko, *Sonokino to Katsudo* (The Export Import Bank: Its Functions and Activities). Tokyo: NYG, n.d.

36. Ibid., pp. 5-7. See also Yukio Noguchi, "The Government-Business Relationship in Japan: The Changing Role of Fiscal Resources," in *Policy and Trade Issues of the Japanese Economy*, edited by Kozo Yamamura (Seattle, WA: University of Washington, Press, 1982).

37. Nihon Yushutsunyu Ginko, *Gyomu Hokokusho*, (Administrative Report) FY 1981, pp. 10, 17, 20.

38. Interviews, OECF.

39. See Japan International Cooperation Agency, *Organization and Functions* (Tokyo: JICA, 1982).

40. *Nihon Kokusei Zue, 1983*, pp. 424-25.

41. Interviews at Ministry of Foreign Affairs.

42. Kokusai Kyoryoku Jigyodan, *Chukinto ni tai suru JICA Kyoryoku Jigyo no Gaiyo* (Outline of the Cooperative Activities of JICA in the Middle East). Tokyo: JICA, 1982, p. 3.

43. Ministry of Foreign Affairs, *The Developing Countries and Japan: Japan's Economic Cooperation* (Tokyo: MFA, 1979), p. 20.

44. Hiroshi Irisawa, "Technical Cooperation Toward Middle East Countries," *Digest of Japanese Industry and Technology*, no. 175 (1982): 12.

Chapter 7: The European Community and the Euro–Arab Dialogue

1. Quoted in European Communities, "The European Community and the Arab World," DE 38, 1982.

2. Another consequence of this convergence of Arab and European interests has been growing tension between the United States and Europe over Middle East policy. As Adam M. Garfinkle put it, "To Washington's consternation, Europe's political fragmentation, military weakness and economic vulnerability have rendered it both solicitous of Arab favor and reluctant to contribute directly to the strategic defense of the region." See his "America and Europe in the Middle East: A New Coordination?" *ORBIS* 25, no. 3 (Fall 1981): 633. See also John P. Richardson, "Europe in the Middle East: Shaping a Political Role, *SAIS Review* (Winter 1981-1982): 197-217; Dominique Moisi, "Europe and the Middle East," in *The Middle East and the Western Alliance*, edited by Steven L. Spiegel (London: Allen & Unwin, 1982) pp. 18-31; Udo Steinbach, "Western Europe and EEC Policies Towards Mediterranean and Middle Eastern Countries," in *Middle East Contemporary Survey*, vol. 12, 1977-

1978, edited by Colin Legum (New York: Holmes and Meier, 1979), pp. 40–48; Stephen J. Artner, "The Middle East: A Chance for Europe?" *International Affairs* (London) 56 (Summer 1980): 440–42.

3. For an excellent study of Saudi and Iranian industrialization in refining and petrochemicals and its impact on European markets for these goods, see Louis Turner and James Bedore, *Middle East Industrialization* (London: Saxon House, 1979).

4. "The European Community and the Arab World," p. 5.

5. Interview at the European Commission, Brussels, January 1982.

6. See H. A. H. Gadel Hak, *The Mediterranean Policy of the European Community.* Doctoral dissertation, University of Amsterdam, 1978. See also Samy Afify Hatem, *The Possibilities of Economic Cooperation and Integration between the European Community and the Arab League* (Munich: Florentz, 1981).

7. Quoted in Alan R. Taylor, "The Euro-Arab Dialogue: Quest for an Interregional Partnership," *Middle East Journal* 32 (Autumn 1978): 429–43.

8. The agreement with Iran lasted until 1973, when the Shah asked for a new agreement that would not only include traditional exports but also the products of Iranian industrialization. Negotiations for such an agreement were unsuccessful. Curiously, Iran sent a delegation to Brussels to re-open talks in August 1979, and discussions were going well until the seizure of the American hostages. Interview at the European Commission, Brussels, January 1983.

9. All of these agreements take the same form and have been published by the European Commission. They are titled EEC-Algeria Cooperation Agreement, EEC-Lebanon Cooperation Agreement, and so on, and were published by the Directorate-General for Information between 1980 and 1982.

10. Interviews at the European Commission, Brussels, January 1983.

11. For a breakdown of EIB loans, see European Investment Bank, *Annual Report 1981,* pp. 82–83, 85. See also European Investment Bank, "Financing Outside the Community: Mediterranean Countries" (October 1978).

12. European Commission, "EEC-Tunisia Cooperation Agreement" (February 1982), pp. 13–19.

13. For treatment of the EAD, see Taylor, "The Euro-Arab Dialogue"; D. J. Allen, "The Euro-Arab Dialgoue," *Journal of Common Market Studies* 16 (June 1978): 323–42; Harold B. Malmgren, "The Euro-Arab Dialogue," *World Trade Outlook* (August 1980): 1–5, R. K. Ramazani, "The European Community and the Middle East," in *Middle East Contemporary Survey,* vol. 1, edited by Colin Legum (New York: Holmes and Meier, 1978) pp. 48–57; "The European Community and the Arab World." For the Arab view of the EAD, see Nijmeddin Dajani, "The Euro-Arab Dialogue: The Arab Viewpoint," in *Euro-Arab Cooperation,* edited by E. Volker (Leydon, Netherlands: A. W. Sijthoff, 1976), Chapter 12; Dieler Bielenstein, *Europe's Future in the Arab View: Dimensions of a New Political Cooperation in the Mediterranean Region* (Saarbraüken, Germany: Verlag Greitenbach, 1981).

14. On this point, see Moisi, "Europe and the Middle East," pp. 24–26.

15. See "Henry Wants the Arabs All to Himself," *The Economist,* June 8, 1974, p. 47; Richardson, "Europe in the Middle East," pp. 109–10.

16. "The European Community and the Arab World," p. 29.

17. Ibid.

18. Richardson, "Europe in the Middle East," pp. 111–14.

19. Interviews at the European Commission, Brussels, January 1983.

20. For treatment of the work of the EAD over the first five years, see Allen, "The Euro-Arab Dialogue," and "Arabs and Europe: The Great Divide," *The Middle East* (June 1977): 25–32.

21. See, for example, "Euro-Arab Dialogue on Ice," *The Middle East* (July 1979): 88–89.

22. Interviews at the European Commission, Brussels, January 1983.

23. Richardson, "Europe in the Middle East," p. 112–14.

24. See Garfinkle, "America and Europe."

25. Interviews at the European Commission, Brussels, January 1983.

26. Ibid.

27. For a slightly more positive view of the EAD and its future prospects, see Allen, "The Euro-Arab Dialogue," p. 341.

28. See Turner and Bedore, *Middle East Industrialization*, Chapter 6.

29. Interview at European Commision, Brussels, January 1983.

30. Interview at CEFIC, Brussels, January 1983.

SELECT BIBLIOGRAPHY

TECHNOLOGY TRANSFER AND TRADE

Belassa, Bela. *The Changing International Division of Labour in Manufactured Goods,* World Bank: mimeo, May 1979.

Brandt, Willy. *North/South: A Program for Survival,* Cambridge, Mass: MIT Press, 1980.

Cortes, Mariluz, and Peter Bocock. *North–South Technology Transfer: A Case Study of Petrochemicals in Latin America,* Baltimore: Johns Hopkins University Press, 1984.

Ellul, Jacques. *The Technology Society,* New York: Knopf, 1964.

Frobel, Folker, Jhurgen Heinrichs, and Otto Kreye. *The New International Division of Labour,* New York: Cambridge University Press, 1980.

Granger, John V. *Technology and International Relations,* San Francisco: W. H. Freeman, 1979.

Landes, David. *The Unbound Prometheus,* Cambridge: Cambridge University Press, 1969.

Myrdal, Gunnar. "The Transfer of Technology to Underdeveloped Countries." *Scientific American* (September 1974), pp. 172–178.

Organization for Economic Cooperation and Development (OECD). *The Case for Positive Adjustment Policies,* Paris: OECD, 1979.

———. *North–South Technology Transfer: The Adjustments Ahead,* Paris: OECD, 1981.

Office of Technology Assessment (OTA). *Technology Trade and Transfer to the Middle East.* Washington, D.C.: OTA, 1984.

Root, F. R. "The Role of International Business in the Diffusion of Technology Innovation," 20, no. 4. *Economics and Business Bulletin* (Summer 1968), pp. 17–25.

Ruggie, John. *The Antinomies of Interdependence.* New York: Columbia University Press, 1983.

Servan-Schreiber, Jean-Jacques. *The American Challenge,* New York: Atheneum, 1968.

United Nations Conference on Trade and Development (UNCTAD). *Transfer of Technology: Technological Dependence, Its Nature, Consequences and Policy Implications.* Report by the UNCTAD Secretariat, June 1974.

Vernon, Raymond. "International Investment and International Trade in the Product Cycle," *Quarterly Journal of Economics,* 80 (May 1966), pp. 190–204.

Vernon, Raymond, ed. *The Technology Factor in International Trade.* New York: Columbia University Press, 1970.

Yoffie, David. *Power and Protectionism.* New York: Columbia University Press, 1983.

BRITAIN

Abadi, Jacob. *Britain's Withdrawal from the Middle East, 1947–1971*. Princeton, NJ: Kingston Press, 1982.

Anthony, Vivian. *Banks and Markets*. London: Heineman, 1979.

Blank, Stephen. *Industry and Government in Britain: The Federation of British Industries in Politics, 1945–1965*. Lexington, Mass.: Lexington Books, 1973.

Brittain, Samuel. *Steering the Economy: The Role of the Treasury*. London: Secker and Warburg, 1969.

Bullard, Sir Reader. *Britain and the Middle East*, London: Hutchinson Unity Library, 1964.

Calleo, David. *Britain's Future*. New York: Horizon Press, 1968.

Frankel, Joseph. *British Foreign Policy, 1945–1973*. London: Oxford University Press, 1975.

Hayward, Jack, and Michael Watson. *Politics, Planning and Public Policy*. Cambridge: Cambridge University Press, 1975.

Katzenstein, Peter. *Between Power and Plenty: Foreign Economic Politics of Advanced Industrialized States*. Madison, WI: University of Wisconsin Press, 1977.

Monroe, Elizabeth. *Britain's Moment in the Middle East*. Baltimore: Johns Hopkins University Press, 1981.

Nasir, Sari J. *The Arabs and the English*. 2nd ed. London: Longman, 1979.

OECD. *The Export Credit Financing Systems in OECD Member Countries*. Paris: OECD, 1982.

Rosecrance, Richard. *Defense of the Realm: British Strategy in the Nuclear Epoch*. New York: Columbia University Press, 1968.

Royal Institute of International Affairs. *British Interests in the Mediterranean and the Middle East*. London: Oxford, 1958.

Shanks, Michael. *Planning and Politics: the British Experience. 1960–1976*. London: George Allen and Unwin, 1977.

Shonfield, Andrew. *Modern Capitalism: The Changing Balance of Public and Private Power*. New York: Oxford University Press, 1965.

Spiegel, Steven. *The Middle East and the Western Alliance*. London: Allen and Unwin, 1982.

"UK and the Gulf, 1971–1981." *Middle East Economic Digest* (Special Report). December 1981.

Young, Stephen. *Intervention in the Mixed Economy: The Evolution of British Industrial Policy 1964–1972*. London: Croon Helm, 1974.

Zysman, John. *Governments, Markets and Growth: Financial Systems and the Politics of Industrial Change*. Ithaca, New York: Cornell University Press, 1983.

FRANCE

Andrews, William G. *French Politics and Algeria*. New York: Appleton-Century-Crofts, 1962.

Berthelot, Yves, and Jacques DeBendt. *Impact des relations avec le Tiers Monde sur l'economie française*. Paris: Documentation Française, 1982.

Cameron, Rondo E. *France and the Economic Development of Europe, 1800–1914.* Princeton: Princeton University Press, 1961.

Cohen, Stephen. *Modern Capitalist Planning.* Cambridge: Harvard University Press, 1969.

Cohen, William B. "Legacy of Empire: The Algerian Connection." *Journal of Contemporary History.* 15 (January 1980), pp. 97–123.

"France and the Middle East." *Middle East Economic Digest,* May 1982.

Franko, Lawrence G., and Sherry Stephenson. "French Export Behavior in Third World Markets." In *World Trade Competition: Western Countries in Third World Markets.* New York: Praeger, 1981, pp. 183–229.

Grosser, Alfred. *French Foreign Policy Under De Gaulle.* Boston: Little, Brown, and Co. 1965.

Kindleberger, Charles P. "The Postwar Resurgence of the French Economy." In Stanley Hoffman, *In Search of France.* New York: Harper and Row, 1963, pp. 118–158.

Kolodziej, Edward. "France and the Arms Trade." *International Affairs* (July 1980), pp. 54–72.

———. *French International Policy Under De Gaulle and Pompidou.* Ithaca, New York: Cornell University Press, 1974.

Morse, Edward. *Foreign Policy and Interdependence in Gaullist France.* Princeton: Princeton University Press, 1973.

Seager, Frederick. "New Directions in French Middle East Policy." *Middle East Review* (Spring/Summer 1982), pp. 49–54.

Smith, Tony. *The French Stake in Algeria.* Ithaca, New York: Cornell University Press, 1978.

Smouts, Marie-Claude. "External Policy of François Mitterrand." *International Affairs* 59 (Spring 1983), pp. 155–167.

Suleiman, Ezra N. *Politics, Power and Bureaucracy in France: The Administrative Elite.* Princeton: Princeton University Press, 1974.

Tint, Herbert. *French Foreign Policy Since the Second World War.* New York: St. Martins, 1972.

Vernon, Raymond. *Big Business and the State.* Cambridge: Harvard University Press, 1974.

Willis, F. Roy. *The French Paradox: Understanding Contemporary France.* Stanford, CA: Hoover Institution Press, 1982.

Zysman, John. *Political Strategies for Industrial Order.* Berkeley: University of California Press, 1977.

WEST GERMANY

Feis, Herbert. *Europe: The World's Banker, 1870–1914.* New Haven: Yale University Press, 1930.

Gerschenkron, Alexander. *Bread and Democracy in Germany.* New York: Fertig, 1966.

Hanrieder, Wolfram F. *The Stable Crisis: Two Decades of German Foreign Policy.* New York: Harper and Row, 1970.

Hardach, Karl. *The Political Economy of Germany in the Twentieth Century.* Berkeley: University of California Press, 1976.

Hartrich, Edwin. *The Fourth and Richest Reich.* New York: Macmillan, 1980.

Herszowicz, Lukasz. *The Third Reich and the Middle East.* London: Routledge and Kegan Paul, 1966.

Holbik, Karel, and Henry Myers. *West German Foreign Aid 1956–1966: Its Economic and Political Aspects.* Boston: Boston University Press, 1968.

Kaiser, Karl. *German Foreign Policy in Transition: Bonn Between East and West.* London: Oxford University Press, 1968.

Knusel, Jack L. *West German Aid to Developing Nations.* New York: Praeger, 1968.

Morgan, Roger. "West Germany's Foreign Policy Agenda." *The Washington Papers,* no. 54, Beverly Hills: Sage, 1978.

Spindler, Andrew. *The Politics of International Credit: Private Finance and Foreign Policy in Germany and Japan.* Washington: The Brookings Institution, 1984.

Steinbach, Udo. "German Policy on the Middle East and the Gulf." *Aussenpolitik,* vol. 32, no. 4 (1981), pp. 315–331.

Stern, Fritz. *Gold and Iron: Bismarck, Bleichroder and the Building of the German Empire.* New York: Knopf, 1977.

Wallich, Henry. *Mainsprings of the German Revival.* New Haven: Yale University Press, 1955.

"West Germany and the Middle East," *Middle East Economic Digest.* (February 1982).

JAPAN

Abegglen, James C., and Akio Etori. "Japanese Technology Today." *Scientific American,* November 1983.

Akao, Nobutoshi, ed. *Japan's Economic Security.* New York: St. Martin's, 1983.

Caldwell, Martha. "Petroleum Politics in Japan: State and Industry in a Changing Policy Context." Ph.D. diss. University of Wisconsin, 1981.

Campbell, William R. "Japan and the Middle East." In Robert S. Ozaki and Walter Arnold (eds.), *Japan's Foreign Relations.* Boulder, CO: Westview Press, 1985.

Economic Cooperation of Japan. Tokyo: JETRO, annual.

Irisawa, Hiroshi. "Technical Cooperation Toward Middle East Countries," *Digest of Japanese Industry and Technology,* no. 175, 1982.

Johnson, Chalmers, *MITI and the Japanese Miracle.* Stanford: Stanford University Press, 1982.

Morse, Ronald A ., ed. *The Politics of Japan's Energy.* Berkeley: Institute of East Asian Studies, University of California, Berkeley, 1981.

Nakamura, Takafusa. *The Postwar Japanese Economy: Its Development and Structure.* Tokyo: University of Tokyo Press, 1981.

Okimoto, Daniel I., ed. *Japan's Economy: Coping with Change in the International Environment.* Boulder, Co.: Westview Publishing, 1982.

Ozawa, Terutomo. *Multinationalism, Japanese Style.* Princeton: Princeton University Press, 1979.

Patrick, Hugh, and Henry Rosovsky, eds. *Asia's New Giant: How the Japanese Economy Works*. Washington, D.C.: Brookings Institution, 1976.

Pempel, T.J. "Japanese Foreign Economic Policy: The Domestic Bases for International Behavior." In Peter J. Katzenstein (ed.), *Between Power and Plenty: Foreign Economic Policies of Advanced Industrial States*. Madison: University of Wisconsin Press, 1978.

Pepper, Thomas, Merit E. Jarow, and Jimmy W. Wheeler. *The Competition: Dealing with Japan*. New York: Praeger, 1985.

Shmuelevitz, Aryeh. *The Persian Gulf and Japan*. Tel Aviv: Shiloah Center for Middle Eastern and African Studies, Tel Aviv University, December 1980.

Tsurumi, Yoshi. (Chap. 7). In *The Japanese Are Coming*. Cambridge: Ballinger, 1976.

——. *Japanese Business*. New York: Praeger, 1978.

Vernon, Raymond. *Two Hungry Giants: The United States and Japan in the Quest for Oil and Ores*. Cambridge: Harvard University Press, 1983.

White Paper on International Trade—Japan, Tokyo: JETRO, annual.

Yoshitsu, Michael M. *Caught in the Middle East: Japan's Diplomacy in Transition*. Lexington, Mass: Lexington Press, 1984.

——. "Iran and Afghanistan in Japanese Perspective." *Asian Survey*, May, 1981.

THE EUROPEAN COMMUNITY

Allen, D. J. "The Euro-Arab Dialogue." *Journal of Common Market Studies*, 26, (June 1978), pp. 323–342.

Artner, Stephen J. "The Middle East: A Chance for Europe? *International Affairs* (London), 56 (Summer 1980), pp. 420–442.

Bielenstein, Dieter. *Europe's Future in the Arab View: Dimensions of a New Political Cooperation in the Mediterranean Region*. Saarbracken: Verlag Greitenbach Publishers, 1981.

Garfinkle, Adam. "America and Europe in the Middle East: A New Coordination?" *Orbis*, 25, no. 3 (Fall 1981), 631–648.

Hak, H. A. Gadel. *The Mediterranean Policy of the European Community*. PhD. diss. University of Amsterdam, 1978.

Hatem, Samy Afify. *The Possibilities of Economic Cooperation and Integration between the European Community and the Arab League*. Munich: Florentz, 1981.

Richardson, John P. "Europe in the Middle East: Shaping a Political Role." *SAIS Review* (Winter 1981-1982), pp. 197–217.

Steinbach, Udo. "Western Europe and EEC Policies Toward Mediterranean and Middle Eastern Countries." In Colin Lwegum, *Middle East Contemporary Survey*. vol. 12, 1977–1978, New York: Homes and Meier, 1979.

Taylor, Alan R. "The Euro-Arab Dialogue: Quest for an Interregional Partnership." *Middle East Journal*, 32 (Autumn 1978), pp. 429–443.

Turner, Louis, and James Bedore. *Middle East Industrialization*. London: Saxon House, 1979.

Volker, E. *Euro-Arab Cooperation*. Leydon: A. W. Sijthoff, 1976.

Index

ACP countries, EC trade relations with, 149
active cooperation agreements, 11
advisors, foreign experts as, 48
aerospace, 170
Aerospatiale, 85
agricultural productivity, up-grading, 19
agriculture, feasibility studies in, 154
aircraft, 41
air transportation, improvement of, 154
air transport equipment, 41
Algeria, 13; bilateral strengths in trade, 33; expanding markets, 30; financing technology imports, 23
Andean Pact countries, 13
Anglo-Arab relations: Arab affluence and, 57; after World War II, 56-57
Anglo-Persian Oil Company, 60
Arab-British Chamber of Commerce (ABCC), 65
Arabian Oil Company (AOC), 130
Arab Institute for Water Desalination and Resources, 154
Arab League, 147, 168; creation of, 144
Arab Polytechnic Institute, 154
Arafat, Yasir, 124
arms sales, 41, 45-46; Britain, 56, 64; France, 78, 79; Japan, 134; United States, 45
arms trade, see arms sales
Arrangement on Guidelines for Officially Supported Export Credits, 51
Association for Overseas Technical Scholarship (AOTS), 140)
Aswan Dam (Egypt), 18
Ausführkredit-Gesellschaft (AKA), 116

Baghdad Railway, 97
balance-of-trade surplus; Britain, 57

Bandhar Khoumeni petrochemical plant (Iran), 47, 130
bank guarantees, 66
Bank of Japan, 127, 128
Banque de France, 89, 90, 91
Banque Francaise du Commerce Exterieur (BFCE), 89, 90, 91
BASF, 170
Berne Union, 52
bilateral cooperation agreements, 148-152
bilateral strengths in trade, 33-40
BMZ, see Ministry for Economic Cooperation
Bouygues, 85
Brazil, 13
Brazzaville Conference, 73
Britain: export of nuclear power equipment, 42; historical context, 52-58; petroleum reserves in the North Sea, 55; status as global power, 53; strategy assessment, 69-71; supportive policies for technology transfer, 65-69; technology trade in the postcolonial era, 50-71; trade and investment policy, 58-65
British Council, 67
British Electricity International (BEI), 68
British Overseas Trade Board (BOTB), 62, 64
British Technology Group, 62
British trade in the Middle East, 36-37
broad-based planning, 16
Brussels Declaration, 149, 153

Camp David accords, 77, 148, 155
Canada, 30
capital investments, 19
Carrington, Lord, 63
Centre Nationale de la Recherche Scientifique (CNRS), 87

CFCE, *see* French Center of Foreign Trade

Chambers of Commerce, German (DIHT), 112-113, 167

Chevenenment, Jean-Pierre, 77

Cheysson, Claude, 145

Chiyoda Chemical and Engineering and Construction Company, 131

Christian Democratic Union (CDU), 111

CIT-Alcatel, 85

Cogelex, 85

commercial aircraft exports, 45

Commerzbank, 103

Commissariat al' Energie Atomique (CEA), 87

Committee for Middle East Trade (COMET), 61, 64, 167

Compagnie Francaise d'Assurance pour le Commerce Exterieur (COFACE), 89-92

Company for Technical Cooperation (GTZ), 112, 118-119

comparative policy analysis, 174-175

competition, 162; German complaints, 107; international maintenance of, 21; Japanese economy and, 142; technology transfer, 10; West Germany, 102-103

competitive bidding, 61

computers, 21

Confederation of British Industries (CBI), 64

conglomerates, 128

consultants, technological planning, 17

consulting engineers, 60; French, 83

consulting services, West Germany, 105

Continental Bank of Bahrain, 60

contract construction, Japanese, 132

cooperation agreements, technology transfer, 11-16

Cooperation Council, 151

Copenhagen Declaration, 152, 150

Coordinating Committees (COCOM), 82, 109

cost escalation scheme (CES), 67

Credit National, 90

Creusot-Loire, turnkey transfers, 85

decision-making, industrial, banking influence on, 128

Defense Sales Organization (DSO), 64

DEG, *see* German Development Company

de Gaulle, Charles, 73

desalination plants, 141

d'Estaing, Giscard, 75, 76

Detecon, 105

Deutsche Bank, 103

Deutsche Bundespost (German post office), 105

Deutsche Entwicklungsgesellschaft (DEG), 110, 112, 118, 119

development assistance, 46, 47

Development Assistance Committee (DAC), 47

DIHT, *see* Chambers of Commerce, German

direct foreign investment, *see* foreign direct investment

Direction des Affaires Internationales (DAI), 78

Direction Ministerielle a' la Armement (DMA), 78

Directorate of External Economic Relations (DREE), 86, 87

dirigism, 80

dirt bikes, direct sales, 141

diversification of energy sources, Japan's, 135

division of labor, international, 3, 7, 157, 159

double-edged diplomacy, 77

Dorsch Consult, 106

Dresdner Bank, 103

Dubai International Trade Center, 60

Dublin formula, 152

economic assistance, 18

economic cooperation, Japanese government, 137-141

economic cooperation agreements, 11

Economic Research Institute, 124
Egypt, 30; U.S. sales, 33
El-Nasr Transformers and Electrical Products Manufacturing Company (Elmaco), 118
employment of foreign experts as advisors, 48
energy policy, Japan's, 134-135
energy research programs, EEC assistance in, 151
engineers, training of, 48
Euro-Arab dialogue, 76, 149, 152-157, 172; first deliberative session of, 153; General committee of, 153
European Chemical Trade Association (CEFIC), 157
European Common Market, 55
European Community (EC), 12, 30, 47, 143; Mediterranean policy, 149
European Economic Community (EEC), 3, 55, 80, 147, 149
European Investment Bank (EIB), 151
Europe and Middle East, in historical perspective, 145-147
Evian Accords (1962), 73
experts, foreign, as advisors, 48
export credits, 138
Export Credits Guarantee Department (ECGD), 65, 69
Export Guarantees and Overseas Investment Act, 66
Export-Import Bank, 127, 132
export insurance, Britain, 66
exports, effects of oil decline, 32
exports, Western, to Middle Eastern countries, 30
exchange rate changes, insurance against, 115
extended terms guarantee, 67

feasibility studies, 48
Federal Ministry of Economics, 110
Federal Ministry of Research and Technology (DMFT), 111
Federal Office of Commerce in Frankfurt-Eschborn, 109

Federal Republic of Germany, *see* West Germany
Federation of German Industries (BDI), 113
finance, technology transfer, Japan, 136-137
financing, of overseas projects, 127
financing, technology transfer, Britain, 65-67; France, 89-92; long term, 117; West Germany, 114-116
Fiscal Investment and Loan Program (FILP), 136
flexibility, in energy demand, 135
foreign aid: British program, 68-69; West Germany, 116
Foreign Exchange and Trade Laws, 128
foreign direct investment, 12, 18, 20, 46, 138, 172; Britain, 59-60; France, 82; French tax policy, 88; government policies and, 132; Japanese, 129-130, 141; West Germany, 105
Foreign Office, 63
foreign students, in German universities, 119
Framatome, 85
France: cooperation agreements, 11; exports to Middle East, 35-36; historical context, technology trade, 72-79; petroleum imports, 35; share of regional market, 33; strategy assessment, 94-96; supportive policies for technology transfer, 89-94; technology trade, 72-96
Franco-Arab Chamber of Commerce (FACC), 88
French Center of Foreign Trade (CFCE), 86, 87
Free Democratic Party (FDP), 98
Fudo Construction Company of Japan, 131
Fujitsu, 132

General Agreement on Tariffs and Trade, 80

General Committee, projects funded by, 154
German Consult AG, 106
German Development Company (DEG), 112, 117-118, 119
German economic miracle, 170
German Mechanical Engineering Trade Association (VDMA), 113
German-Orient Society, 98
Germany: cooperation agreements, 11; medical equipment sales, 44. *See also* West Germany
Gesellschaft Für Technische Zusammenarbeit (GTZ), 118-119
Gibb, Sir Alexander, and Partners, 60
grant assistance, Japan, 138
Greater East Asia Co-Prosperity Sphere, 122
Group on Export Credits and Credit Guarantees (ECG), 51
GTZ, *see* Company for Technical Cooperation
Gulf Cooperation Council (GCC), 148, 150

Hallstein Doctrine, 98
Harris, John R., 60
Hawksley, Watson, 60
Health and Social Security, Department of, 63
heavy capital equipment, purchase of, 161
hermes, 114, 116
Hitachi, 132
Hoechst, 170
Hong Kong, 161
Hospitalia International, 107
human capital, 6; expanding base of, 9

imports, effects of oil decline, 32
India, 12; investment in human capital, 9
indicative planning, 80
industrial development, West Germany, 97-121
industrial productivity, upgrading, 19

Industry, Department of, 63
infrastructural construction, 18- 19
infrastructural projects, 161; France, 93; Japanese credits for, 139; West Germany, 106-107
insurance, technology transfer: Britain, 65-67; ceiling for, 115; France, 89-92; Japan, 136; West Germany, 114-116
Interministerial Committee for Export Guarantees, 115
International Aeradio (IAL), 68
international division of labor, shaping of, 7
International Military Services (IMS), 64
Iran, 23, 30, 33; German trade with, 37; as major recipient of Japanese investment money, 130; and technology transfer, 9
Iran-Iraq War, 35, 39, 106, 155, 173
Iran-Japan Petrochemical Company (IJPC), 130, 131
Iraq, 23, 30
Ishikawajima-Harima Heavy Industries, 131
Italian Nuclear Agency, 42
Italy, 30; machinery market, 43; trade in Middle East, 38-39
Itoh, C., 129, 131

jacuzzis, direct sales, 141
Japan, 30; cooperation agreements, 11; export of nuclear power equipment, 42; exports to Middle East, 40; share of regional market, 33
Japan, marketing technology, 122-142; historical context, 122-125; oil imports, 125; pattern of energy consumption, 123; strategy assessment, 141-142; supportive policies for technology trade, 133-141
Japan Cooperation Center for the Middle East, 129
Japan Economic Research Center, 130

Japanese Emigration Service (JEMIS), 137
Japan Export-Import Bank, 136
Japan External Trade Organization (JETRO), 127, 168
Japan International Cooperation Agency (JICA), 137
Japan Palestinian Friendship Committee, 124
jet aircraft, direct sales, 141
JETRO, *see* Japan External Trade Organization
joint ventures, 14, 46, 109, 162, 172; Japanese, 132; limitations, 15; use in Middle East, 15

keiretsu (conglomerates), 128
knowledge capital, 6
Kohl, Helmut, 99
Kraftwerk Union, 107, 170
Kreditanstalt für Wiederaufbau (KFW), 112
Krupp-Koppers GmbH, 107-108
Kuwait, 23, 30, 33

League of Arab States, 148
Lebanon: collapse of political order, 173; EC trade agreement with, 150
les grand contrats, 91, 166
Libya, 30 licensing, 109
Lome Agreement, 149
Lurgi, 170

machinery, 41
machinery and equipment exports, 43
management contract, 14
management agreement, 14
managers, training of, 48
Mannesman Anlagenbau (MAB), 108
manufacturing companies, major, in Japan, 131-132
manufacturing facilities, construction of, 133
market entry guarantee scheme (MEGS), 63
market incentives, Japan, 126

market studies in industrial sectors, initiation of, 154
Marshall Plan, 53
Marubeni, 129, 131
medical equipment sales, 41, 44-45
medical supplies sales, 44-45
Merlin Gerin, 85
Mexico, 12
microprocessors, technology gains in, 171
Middle East: and industrialized world, relationship between, 29; technology trade and transfer in, 23-25; U.S. share of exports, 33
Middle East Association (MEA), 64
military hardware sales, 164, 170
Minister of Foreign Trade, 86
Ministry of Economic Affairs and Finance, 86
Ministry for Economic Cooperation (BMZ), 110, 111-112
Ministry of Finance (MOF), Japan, 127
Ministry of Foreign Affairs, 86
Ministry of International Trade and Industry (MITI), 111, 126-127, 134
Ministry for Research and Technology, 118; merger with Ministry of Industry, 81
Mitsubishi, 128, 129, 130
Mitsui, 128, 129, 131
mixed economy, 58
Mitterrand, Francois, 77
Monroe, Elizabeth, 52
multilateral private organizations, funds from, 138

national banking structure, 128
National Economic Development office (NEDO), 59, 62
National Electric Company (NEC), 132
National Enterprise Board, 62
natural resource development, in Japan, 132
National Resources Development Commission, 62

Near and Middle East Association
(NMV), 113
NEDO, see National Economic Development Office
newly industrializing countries
(NICs), 2, 175
new technology, 29
Nissho Iwai, 129
Nissan Motors, 132
nuclear plants, 41
nuclear power technology, export of,
42-43; France, 93, 164, 170

oceanography, feasibility of projects,
154
Official Development Assistance
(ODA), 138
oil crisis, 146, 148
oil dependence: Britain, 54; Europe,
146; France, 77; Japan, 134-135
oil embargo, 30
oil and gas imports, France, 74
oil prices, 144; influence on technology transfer, 27; quadrupling of,
146
oil trade, West Germany, 100
Oki, 132
on-the-job training, 113
OPEC countries, 27; increase in
French exports to, 82
Organization for Economic Cooperation and Development (OECD), 11,
69
Orient Institute of Hamburg, 113
Overseas Development Administration, 68
Overseas Development Assistance
(ODA), 47
Overseas Development Association
(ODA), 66
Overseas Economic Cooperation
Fund (OECF), 137
Overseas Projects Fund, 63
Overseas Technical Cooperation
Agency (OTCA), 137

Paris Metro, 84, 93
passive agreements, 11

pax Britannica, 58
Persian Gulf, Britain's withdrawal
from, 54
personnel transfers, 46
Philipp Holzmann, 106, 107
physical capital, 6, 8
planning, technological, 16-17
PLO representation, Euro-Arab dialogue, 152-153
political instability, foreign investment and, 47
Pompidou, Georges, 75
private trade associations, Britain, 70
Process of technology transfer, 16-23
product specialization, 40-46
protectionism, 156, 157

quasi-public committees, Britain, 70

radiological protection, feasibility of
projects, 154
realpolitik, 100
research and development: defined,
6; in France, 81, 87; support for local, 151

Sadat, Anwar, 124
Saudi Arabia, 23, 33, 40; Britain's
trading partner, 37; export of nuclear power equipment, 42; rank
in Japan's market, 30; and technology transfer, 9
Science, defined, 6
scientific and technical cooperation,
Britain, 68
scientific and technical cooperation
agreements, 11
scientists, training of, 48
sea transportation, improvement of,
154
Seiko, 132
Selsdon, Lord, 61
semiconductors, 171
service contracts, 48
short-term transfers, 172
Siemens, 107, 170
Sofrerail, 105
Sofretes, 105

solar energy, feasibility of projects, 154
South Korea, 161
specialized technology trade, 21, 167, 168
Suez crisis, 54, 75
Sumitomo, 128, 129

Taiwan, 161
tax credits, 127
technical assistance: French foreign aid and, 92-94; West Germany, 116
technicians, training of, 48
Technip, 85, 105
technology, defined, 6
technology assistance agreement, 14, 19, 20
technology-for-oil deals, 28, 110, 173
technology imports, 7; three kinds of, 8
technology needs, 8-9
technology transfer, 2-5; actors in the process, 9-11; common interest, 22; forms of, 11-16; generic process of, 7-23, 162; major trends, 26-49; process of, 16-23; promotion and regulation of, 10; ramifications of, 2; technology and, 5-7
telecommunications trade, 43-44, 105, 141, 164, 170, 171
textile exports, 141, 150
Thatcher, Margaret, 61, 64
Thomson-CSF, 85
top-down planning, 17
trade, 28-46; bilateral strengths in, 33-40
Trade, Department of (DOT), 63
trade companies (sogo sosha), Japanese, 128-129
trade and investment policy: Britain, 58-65; France, 79; Japan, 125-133; West Germany, 101-114
trade promotion, 63
trade statistics, 29
training: pre-contract, 113; and technology transfer, 9

training, technology transfer: Britain, 67-68; France, 92-94; W. German scientists and engineers, 118; West Germany, 116
tripartite, 59
Tunisia, 109
Tunisian agreement, 151
turnkey projects, 13, 20, 162, 172; Japanese, 132; limitations, 14
turnkey facilities, West Germany, 108

Union des Industries Chimiques (UIC), 88
Union of Independent Consulting Engineers (VUBI), 106, 113
United Nations Educational, Scientific, and Cultural Organization (UNESCO), 12
United States: medical equipment sales, 44; share of regional market, 33

V-Consult, 106
VDMA, see German Mechanical Engineering Trade Association
Verbank der Chemischen Industrie (VCI), 88
Vernon, Raymond, 2
vocational training, expansion of, 151
VUBI, see Union of Independent Consulting Engineers

West Germany, technology trade, 97-121; excellence in scientific and technical education, 118; historical context, 97-101; share of regional market, 33; strategy assessment, 119-121; supportive policies for technology transfer, 114-119; trade with the Middle East, 37
White Paper on World Markets, 127
workers, retraining of, 21
World Bank, and technology transfer, 10

ABOUT THE AUTHORS

THOMAS L. ILGEN is the Jones Foundation Associate Professor of Political Studies at Pitzer College, a member of the Claremont Colleges. He has also taught in the Department of Government at Cornell University and in the Department of Politics at Brandeis University as well as working as a research associate at the Center for International Affairs at Harvard University and as a visiting fellow at the Center of International Studies at Princeton University. He teaches courses on international relations, political economy, and science and technology policy. Professor Ilgen is the author of *Autonomy and Interdependence: United States-West European Monetary and Trade Relations, 1958-1984* and co-author of *Controlling Chemicals: Regulatory Politics in Europe and the United States* and has published articles on international economic affairs and science and technology issues. He holds a B.A. degree from Oberlin College and M.A. and Ph.D. degrees from the University of California, Santa Barbara.

T.J. PEMPEL is Professor of Government and Adjunct Professor in the Johnson School of Management at Cornell University. He teaches courses in comparative politics, the politics of Japan, Japanese business, political economy and comparative public policy. A member of the Cornell faculty since 1972, he was also director of the university's China-Japan Program from 1980 to 1985. Professor Pempel is author of several books, including *Policy and Politics in Japan: Creative Conservatism; Patterns of Japanese Policymaking; Japan: The Dilemmas of Success;* and *Policymaking in Contemporary Japan*, as well as numerous articles in journals and anthologies.

Dr. Pempel received his B.S., M.A. and Ph.D. degrees from Columbia University. He has been active in the administration of the American Political Science Association, The Association for Asian Studies and the Social Science Research Council and has served as a member of the editorial boards of several scholarly journals. He has lived in Japan for several years as a Fulbright Fellow, a Japan Foundation Fellow and as a visiting scholar at Tokyo and Kyoto Universities.